English Pronunciation

in Use

Intermediate

Self-study and classroom use

Second Edition

Mark Hancock

CAMBRIDGE UNIVERSITY PRESS
Cambridge, New York, Melbourne, Madrid, Cape Town,
Singapore, São Paulo, Delhi, Mexico City

Cambridge University Press
The Edinburgh Building, Cambridge CB2 8RU, UK

www.cambridge.org
Information on this title: www.cambridge.org/9780521185127

© Cambridge University Press 2003, 2012

First published 2003
Second edition 2012
Reprinted 2012

Printed and bound in the United Kingdom by the MPG Books Group

A catalogue record for this publication is available from the British Library

ISBN 978-0-521-18512-7 Book with answers
ISBN 978-0-521-18514-1 Book with answers and Audio CDs (4)
ISBN 978-0-521-18513-4 Book with answers and CD-ROM/Audio CDs (4)

Contents

Section A sounds
Letters and sounds

Combining sounds

Section B Stress
Word Stress

Stress patterns

Section C Intonation

Section D Understanding pronunciation in use

Speed

Tone

Accents

Section E Reference

Acknowledgements

I would like to thank Roslyn Henderson for getting me started on this new edition, and Claire Cole for her early, influential suggestions, especially for the new structure of the book. I would also like to thank Andy George, Janet Weller and Frances Reynolds for taking the book through its later stages of development.

Thanks also to Robin Walker for our discussions of the issues surrounding English as a Lingua Franca. However, I take full responsibility for any possible shortcomings in the way it is represented in this book.

The author and publishers are also grateful to the following contributors:

Barbara Bradford, Ian Chitty, Sarn Rich and Wayne Rimmer, for making suggestions which helped shape this new edition; Bridget Richardson for reviewing the first draft of the new edition; Kamae Design for design and page make-up; James Richardson, Martin Goldman, Craig Stevenson and Hart McLeod for audio production.

The author and publishers acknowledge the following sources of copyright material and are grateful for the permissions granted. While every effort has been made, it has not always been possible to identify the sources of all the material used, or to trace all copyright holders. If any omissions are brought to our notice, we will be happy to include the appropriate acknowledgements on reprinting.

The Park, New Forest Community Media for the material on pp.100–101 and pp.118–119.

Harborough FM for the material on pp.102–103

Knowsley Community College, KCCLIVE, for the material on pp.108–109

Glastonbury FM (G-FM) for the material on pp.110–111

Jill Daley, Insight Radio, 2010 for the material on pp.128–129

Photographs

p.10: © Supri Suharjoto/Shutterstock; p.13: © Dmitriy Shironosov/Shutterstock; p.21: Image Source/Alamy; p.29: © Scott Hartop/Alamy; p.31: © Eric Nathan/Alamy; p.37: © George Doyle/Thinkstock; p.43: © Sergei Khakimsullin/Shutterstock; p.45: © Nick White/Thinkstock; p.49: Blend Images/Alamy; p.52: Moodboard/Alamy; p.53: Stockbyte/Thinkstock; p.55: iStockphoto/Thinkstock; p.56: Bananastock/Thinkstock; p.63: Bubbles Photography/Alamy; p64 (T): © Jon Sparks/Alamy; p.64 (B): (c) Angel Terry/Alamy; p.68 © Ann & Steve Toon/Alamy; p.70: Monkey Business Images/Shutterstock; p.72 (T): iStockphoto/Thinkstock; p.72 (B): © Sue Robinson/Shutterstock; p.74: Jupiter Images/Thinkstock; p.77: © Freddie Jones/Alamy; p.78: © Philip Wolmuth/Alamy; p.79: © Paul Doyle/Alamy; p.80: Hemera/Thinkstock (eggs); p.80: Stockbyte/Thinkstock (bread); p.80: iStockphoto/Thinkstock (jam); p.80: BrandX/Thinkstock (grapes); p.80: Artjazz/Shutterstock (juice); p.81: ER_01/Shutterstock (soup); p.81: © Denis Vrublevski/Shutterstock (honey); p.81: Art Directors & Trip/Alamy (biscuits); p.81: © Jiri Hera/Shutterstock (juice); p.81: iStockphoto/Thinkstock (carrots, apples); p.81:Photo Objects.net/Thinkstock (milk); p.81: Rimglow/Fotolia (teapot); p.82: iStockphoto/Thinkstock; p.84: © David Le Lossy/Thinkstock; p.85: Science Photo Library/Alamy; p.86: Big Cheese Photo LLC/Alamy; p.87: Huntstock Inc/Alamy; p.90 (T): Image Source/Alamy; p.90 (B): Digital Vision/Thinkstock; p.91: Culture Creative/Alamy; p.92: Comstock/Thinkstock; p.93: MBI/Alamy; p.95: © Sean Locke/iStockphoto; p.96 (B): © Yanik Chauvin/Shutterstock; p.96 (T): © Yuri Acurs/Shutterstock; p.98: © Galen Rowell/Mountain Light/Alamy; p.99: Corbis Super RF/Alamy; p.100: Image Broker/Alamy; pp.102, 125: Getty Images; p.103: © Ken McKay/ITV/Rex Features; p.104: © Adam Seward/Alamy; p.106: F1online digitale Bildagentur GmbH/Alamy; p.107: © Joe Gough/Shutterstock; p.109: AKP Photos/Alamy; p.111: © Stephen Inglis/Shutterstock; p.113: Digital Vision/Thinkstock; p.114: Jaubert Images/Alamy; p.116: Radius Images/Alamy; p.118: © David Robertson/Alamy; p.121: Datacraft-Sozaijiten/Alamy; p.127 (L): © F.Krause/Shutterstock; p.127: Grynold/Shutterstock; p.127 (B): Monkey Business Images/Shutterstock; p.128: © Alex Segre/Alamy.

Picture research by Alison Prior.

Illustrations by Karen Donnelly, Mark Draisey, Mark Duffin, Dylan Gibson, Julian Mosedale, Peter Richardson, David Shenton, Ian West

To the student

English Pronunciation in Use is a set of materials to help students of English to work on pronunciation, for both speaking and understanding. It is written mainly for students of intermediate level (B1 and B2).

What will I need?

You will need a CD player to listen to the recorded material that goes with this book. It will be useful if you also have equipment to record your own voice, so that you can hear your own progress. This symbol 🔊 A1 indicates the track number for recorded material, in this example, CD A, track 1.

Also, when you are studying individual sounds, it is sometimes useful if you have a mirror. With this, you can compare the shape of your own mouth to the mouth in diagrams like this one from Unit 8.

See page 167 for a labelled diagram of the mouth and throat.

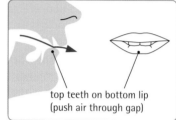

top teeth on bottom lip
(push air through gap)

How is *English Pronunciation in Use* organised?

There are 60 units in the book. Each unit looks at a different point of pronunciation. Each unit has two pages. The page on the left has explanations and examples, and the page on the right has exercises.

The 60 units are divided into four sections:

Section A *Sounds* (Units 1–26): This section is about how to pronounce and spell the sounds of English, and how to make the differences between the sounds clear. There are also some units about how sounds are joined together.

Section B *Stress* (Units 27–36): This section is about which parts of words and sentences are normally stressed and which parts are normally not stressed.

Section C *Intonation* (Units 37–45): This section is about how speech is divided into speech units and how the position of the main stress can change the meaning of a speech unit. There is also a unit on rising and falling tones.

Section D *Understanding pronunciation in use* (Units 46–60): This section is to help improve your listening skills by listening to pronunciation features in radio interviews and natural conversation. The first group of units deals with the pronunciation features of fast speech. The next group of units helps you to understand features of intonation. The last few units deal with aspects of pronunciation which change across different accents of English, both native and non-native.

After the 60 units, there is a fifth section, Section E *Reference*, which contains the following:

- E1 Introduction to phonemic symbols
- E2 Pronunciation test
- E3 Guide for speakers of specific languages
- E4 Sound pairs
- E5 English as a Lingua Franca
- E6 Glossary

At the end of the book there is an Answer key with answers to all the exercises.

What order shall I do the units in?

You could simply use the units in order, 1–60, but it is probably more useful and interesting to vary the order, e.g. do a unit from Section A, then a unit from Section B, followed by a unit from Section C, etc. The material in Section D may be more difficult because the recordings are taken from the radio and natural conversation, so the language level is a little higher.

If you have problems in hearing the difference between individual sounds in Section A of the book, you will be directed to one of the exercises in Section E4 *Sound pairs*.

You may want to focus your work more closely. If so, here are more ideas:

- Do the *Pronunciation test* (E2) in Section E. Each set of test exercises (e.g. A1–A6, etc.) corresponds to one of the main sections of the book (e.g. Section A, etc.) and tests the pronunciation features covered in that section. Count your score for each section. If you did especially well in any one of the sections, then you may want to miss out the units in that section of the book.

- Look at E3 *Guide for speakers of specific languages*. Find your own language (the languages are in alphabetical order). The notes there will tell you which units are less important for speakers of your language and which sound pairs in Section E4 are particularly recommended for practice.

Do I need to know the phonemic symbols?

It is possible to use this book without knowing phonemic symbols. However, it is useful to learn them because they make it easier to analyse the pronunciation of words. Also, many dictionaries use phonemic symbols to show pronunciation. In Section E1 *Introduction to phonemic symbols*, you will find a table of the phonemic symbols, plus a set of puzzles to help you learn them.

Is this book only about pronunciation in speaking?

No, it isn't. All of the pronunciation features in the book are just as important for listening as for speaking, but one section, Section D, focuses particularly on listening. You do not need to produce the features of pronunciation in this section, but it is very useful to be able to understand them.

What accent of English is used in this book?

As a model for you to copy when speaking, we have used only one accent, from the South of England. But when you are listening to people speaking English, you will hear many different accents. If you are not used to these accents, it can be very difficult to understand what is being said. For this reason, you will hear a variety of accents, both native and non-native, in some parts of the listening material for this book. In addition, one group of units in Section D deals specifically with different accents.

What is in E5 *English as a Lingua Franca?*

Today, English is used as an international language or *Lingua Franca*. This means that it is often used for communication outside the countries where it is the native language, such as the USA, Britain, Australia, etc. This section explains which parts of the book are most useful for you if you want to be understood using English as a Lingua Franca.

What is in E6 *Glossary?*

In this book, there are some words which are specific to the subject of pronunciation. You can find an explanation of the meaning of these words in Section E6 *Glossary*.

How should I use the recordings?

When you are working with the recordings on the CDs, you should replay a track as often as you need to. When you are doing an exercise, you may also need to pause the recording after each sentence to give you time to think or to write your answers. When you are instructed to repeat single words there is a space on the recording for you to do so, but if you are repeating whole sentences you will have to pause the recording each time.

To the teacher

Although *English Pronunciation in Use* has been written so that it can be used for self-study, it will work equally well in a class situation. In a classroom context, the learners can get immediate guidance and feedback from the teacher. Also, they can practise some of the dialogues and other exercises in pairs. You can direct students with particular pronunciation difficulties to do specific units on their own.

In order to simplify the jargon in the book, many of the terms you may be familiar with are not used. For example, the term *initial consonant cluster* is not used. The unit on initial consonant clusters is called Unit 21 *Dream, cream, scream: Consonant groups at the beginning of words*.

The following is an explanation of how the main sections of the book are organised.

Section A aims to cover the sounds of English and their main spellings. The units are organised by letters rather than sounds. This was considered to be a more intuitive route into the material for non-specialist users. At the same time, this organisation helps to highlight sound–spelling regularities in English.

The order of the units is more or less alphabetical. The first of the vowel sounds are covered via the five vowel letters of the alphabet, and their 'long' and 'short' pronunciations, e.g. the letter A as in *plane* or *plan*. The remaining vowel sounds are presented as vowels which typically occur before a letter R. The consonant sounds are presented in the alphabetical order of their more common spellings.

Units 1–20 focus on individual letters and sounds. Individual sounds are not necessarily presented as minimal pairs. Vowels are paired according to their spelling, not their potential for being confused with one another. Consonants are paired mainly where they share the same place of articulation. The units are not organised according to minimal pairs for two reasons:

- Any sound can form a minimal pair with a number of other sounds, not just one; organising units according to minimal pairs would therefore lead to a huge number of units and a lot of duplication.

- Many minimal pairs will be redundant for any given learner, so learners need to be selective. Potentially confusing minimal pairs are gathered together in Section E4 *Sound pairs*. Learners are encouraged to select from these according to their own needs.

Units 21–26 focus on sounds in combination: consonant clusters, suffixes and juncture.

Units 27–31 in **Section B** focus on word stress, including some of the most common patterns. Students will also have to learn the stress of new words as they learn them, since many rules are too complicated to be useful, or have too many exceptions. Units 32–36 in Section B focus on stress patterns, or rhythm. The term *stress pattern*, as used here, is <u>not</u> connected with the idea of contrastive stress or nuclear stress. It simply refers to the rule that in the unmarked case, lexical words are accented while function words are not. This results in phrases having typical stress patterns such as ●●●● for questions like *What do you think*?

Section C focuses on intonation. Units 37 and 38 focus on tonality, i.e. the way speech is divided into tone units, or *speech units* as they are labelled here. Units 39–44 focus on tonicity, i.e. the placement of tonic stress, or *main stress* as it is labelled here. These units show how phrases in context may not follow the typical patterns shown in Section B. For example, in the question *What do you think?*, there may be main stress on the word *you* even though it is a function word. This is often called contrastive stress. Unit 45 focuses on tone, with a simple introduction to falling and rising tones. It is not possible or necessary for students to produce complex tone patterns at this level. However, there are more units on tone in Section D, where the focus is on receptive awareness.

Section D focuses on raising students' awareness of the pronunciation features of natural speech. The material is based on excerpts from local radio programmes and natural conversation. Units 46–50 focus on fast speech, including features such as discourse markers (e.g. fillers), linking and assimilation. Units 51–55 focus on tone, demonstrating some of the most common meanings of tone choices. Units 56–58 focus on the most common areas of variation among the various native varieties of English. Units 59 and 60 focus on typical features of non-native accents.

Note that some of the pronunciation points in the book may be irrelevant to some learners. For example, for learners whose aim is mainly to communicate with other non-native speakers of English (using English as a Lingua Franca), accurate production of certain sounds is probably not necessary. Units 59 and 60, and Section E5, explain which pronunciation features are high priority and which are not important for learners aiming to use English mainly as a Lingua Franca with other non-native speakers.

Note: The material in Section E3 *Guide for speakers of specific languages* is based on the pronunciation notes in *Learner English* (Michael Swan and Bernard Smith: 2001)*. Nevertheless, I have had to extrapolate from the information presented there, as many of the minimal pairs presented in this book are not specifically mentioned in the pronunciation notes in that book.

*Swan, M. and B. Smith 2001 *Learner English* (Second Edition). Cambridge: Cambridge University Press.

1 From zero to hero
Playing with the sounds of English

A

It is common for speakers to play with the sounds of the language. Read these sentences from newspapers and magazines. Notice that the blue phrases contain words which sound similar. They contain rhymes: the final vowel or vowel + consonant sounds are the same or similar-sounding, e.g. *sign* and *time*.

Appearance is very important in the fashion business. According to company director Martha Friedl, **'You have to dress for success.'**

Fernando goes from zero to hero after scoring a last-minute goal in the European championship.

'On this island, nothing happens in a hurry,' says Jamie, 'You just have to relax and go with the flow.'

In the age of the text message, it is perhaps a sign of the times that many teenagers can no longer write with a pen.

B

A1 Listen to this poem. Notice the pronunciation of the blue words.

It's very strange, but did you know
Shoe will never rhyme with toe?
And foot will never sound like boot;
Boot's like suit and flute and fruit.
Foot's like put and feet's like seat;
Great's like eight but not like eat.

Work is not pronounced like fork.
Fork's like walk and also talk.
Why is beard not like heard?
Why does bird rhyme with word?
This is what I've sometimes found:
Spelling's often not like sound.

Spelling is not always a good guide to pronunciation. Listen to these groups of words from the poem. Notice that A does *not* rhyme with B even though the spelling of the end of the word is the same. B rhymes with C even though the spelling of the end of the word is different. The phonemic symbols make this clear.

A	B	C
shoe /ʃuː/	toe /təʊ/	know /nəʊ/
foot /fʊt/	boot /buːt/	suit /suːt/
great /greɪt/	seat /siːt/	feet /fiːt/
work /wɜːk/	fork /fɔːk/	walk /wɔːk/
beard /bɪəd/	heard /hɜːd/	bird /bɜːd/

Note: The rhyming words above may not rhyme in all accents. For more on accent variation, see Units 56–60.

Exercises

1.1 Underline the phrases containing rhymes in these sentences from newspapers and magazines.

EXAMPLE We bring you the latest <u>news and views</u> from the sporting world.

1 Fancy flying to the Mediterranean for a weekend of fun in the sun?

2 An extremely low tide has left many boats high and dry on the beach.

3 'You don't get to the top by doing nothing,' says manager Bob Clarke, 'Hard work is the name of the game.'

4 'I'm a man with a plan,' Mitchell tells Democratic Party conference.

5 Back in the 1970s, school classrooms were all chalk and talk. Nowadays, kids expect their lessons to be entertaining.

6 Motorists have been advised to steer clear of Junction 15 during the roadworks.

1.2 🔊 A2 Read the poem below and write the words from the box in the gaps. Listen, check and repeat.

~~do~~   doll   go   goal   hour   magazine   rude   sounds   slower   wood

It's very strange, but did you know

........Do........ will never sound like [1].......................?

Ocean doesn't rhyme with *clean;*

Clean's like *green* and [2].............................. .

[3].............................. will never rhyme with *roll;*

Roll's like *hole* and also [4].............................. .

[5].............................. doesn't rhyme with *flower*

And *four* will never sound like [6].............................. .

Good's like [7].............................. but not like *food,*

Would's like *could* but not like [8].............................. .

You know that *wounds* are not like *pounds*

'Cause letters aren't the same as [9].......................... .

1.3 🔊 A3 Which word does not rhyme with the others? Underline it. The phonemic symbols will help you. Listen and check your answers.

EXAMPLE hair   <u>here</u>   there   where   /heə   hɪə   ðeə   weə/

1 car   star   far   war   /cɑː   stɑː   fɑː   wɔː/
2 slow   cow   go   know   /sləʊ   caʊ   gəʊ   nəʊ/
3 nose   grows   does   goes   /nəʊz   grəʊz   dʌz   gəʊz/
4 clear   near   bear   hear   /klɪə   nɪə   beə   hɪə/
5 really   early   nearly   clearly   /rɪəlɪ   ɜːlɪ   nɪəlɪ   clɪəlɪ/
6 close   choose   lose   shoes   /cləʊz   tʃuːz   luːz   ʃuːz/
7 above   glove   love   move   /əˈbʌv   glʌv   lʌv   muːv/

1.4 Find groups of rhyming words or letter names in these pictures. There are three words or letter names in each group.

EXAMPLE   boot – suit – fruit

....

....

....

....

....

....

....

2 Plane, plan
The vowel sounds /eɪ/ and /æ/

A

When you say the letters of the alphabet, A has the long vowel sound /eɪ/. You hear this sound in the word *plane*. But the letter A is also pronounced as the short vowel sound /æ/, as in the word *plan*.

A4 Listen to the sound /eɪ/ on its own. Look at the mouth diagram to see how to make this long vowel sound.

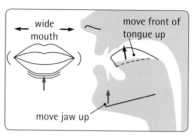

Listen to the target sound /eɪ/ in the words below and compare it with the words on each side.

target /eɪ/

meat	**mate**	met
come	**came**	calm
white	**wait**	wet
buy	**bay**	boy

Listen and repeat these examples of the target sound.

play	played	plate
grey	grade	great
aim	age	eight

longer ←——→ shorter

The plane was delayed so we waited and played.

B

A5 Listen to the sound /æ/. Look at the mouth diagram to see how to make this short vowel sound.

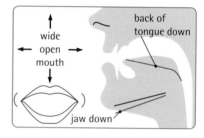

Listen to the target sound /æ/ in the words and compare it with the words on each side.

target /æ/

mud	**mad**	made
sing	**sang**	sung
pen	**pan**	pain
hot	**hat**	heart

Listen and repeat these examples of the target sound.

bank	bag	back
hand	cash	catch
ham	has	hat

longer ←——→ shorter

Accent variation SE / NE : /ɑː/ or /æ/ ⇒ Unit 57.
Accent variation SE / NZ : /æ/ or /e/ ⇒ Unit 57.

A man in a black hat with a bag of cash in his hand

C Spelling

	frequently
/eɪ/	A-E (*mate*), AY (*say*), EY (*grey*), EI (*eight*), AI (*wait*), EA (*great*)
/æ/	A (*hat*)

Exercises

2.1 Write the words for these things in the correct part of the table.

words with /eɪ/	words with /æ/
cake	apple

2.2 [🔊 A6] Look at the blue words or syllables in the dialogue. Do they contain 1 /eɪ/ or 2 /æ/ ? Write 1 or 2 in the gap after each word. Then listen and check your answers.

Kate: What are your plans ..2.. for the holiday, ..1.. Jack? ....

Jack: I'm off to Spain .... with Jane ....

Kate: Sounds great! .... How are you getting there?

Jack: Train .... to Manchester .... and the plane .... to Malaga.
And you? What are you doing?

Kate: No plans .... I'm a bit short of cash .... actually .... , so I'm staying .... here.

Jack: Oh. In that .... case .... , Kate .... , can you do me a favour? ....

Kate: What?

Jack: Can you go to my flat .... and feed the cat .... ?
It's just for a few days ....

Kate: When do you get back .... ?

Jack: I'm back .... on Saturday ....

Kate: Well, okay .... then.

> **Follow-up:** Play the recording again. Pause and repeat after each line.

2.3 [🔊 A6 (cont.)] Listen and underline the word you hear. If you find any of these difficult, go to Section E4 *Sound pairs* for further practice.

1 Man or men?   Did you see the *man / men*?   (⇒ Sound pair 1)
2 Cap or cup?   Have you seen my *cap / cup*?   (⇒ Sound pair 2)
3 Hat or heart?   She put her hand on her *hat / heart*.   (⇒ Sound pair 3)
4 Pain or pen?   I've got a *pain / pen* in my hand.   (⇒ Sound pair 4)
5 Stay or stare?   There's no reason to *stay / stare*.   (⇒ Sound pair 5)

> **Follow-up:** Record yourself saying the sentences in 2.3, choosing one of the two words each time. Make a note of which words you say. Then listen to your recording in about two weeks. Is it clear which words you said?

3 Back, pack
The consonant sounds /b/ and /p/

A7 When you say the alphabet, the letters B and P have the sounds /biː/ and /piː/. In words, they have the consonant sounds /b/ and /p/.

Look at the mouth diagram to see how to make these sounds.

Listen to the sounds /b/ and /p/.

The mouth is in the same position for both sounds, but:

- in /b/ there is voice from the throat, whereas in /p/ there is no voice from the throat
- when /p/ is at the start of a word, there is a small explosion of air when the lips open. With /b/ this does not happen.

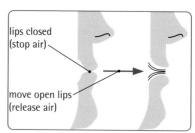

lips closed (stop air)

move open lips (release air)

B

A8 Now listen to the sound /b/ on its own.

Listen to the target sound /b/ in the words below and compare it with the words on each side.

target /b/

pack	**back**	pack
cap	**cab**	cap
very	**berry**	very
covered	**cupboard**	covered

Listen and repeat these examples of the target sound.

bought	bike	broke
rubber	about	able
job	web	tube

The boy bought a blue bike but his new blue bike broke.

C

A9 Listen to the sound /p/ on its own.

Listen to the target sound /p/ in the words below and compare it with the words on each side.

target /p/

bay	**pay**	bay
lab	**lap**	lab
full	**pull**	full
coffee	**copy**	coffee

Listen and repeat these examples of the target sound.

post	park	price
open	happen	spring
shop	help	jump

Penny went to post a parcel and paid a pound to park.

D Spelling

	frequently	notes
/b/	B (*job*), BB (*rubber*)	B is sometimes silent (*comb*).
/p/	P (*open*), PP (*happen*)	PH is pronounced /f/ (*phone*). P is sometimes silent (*psychology*).

Exercises

3.1 🔊 A10 **Listen and read this dialogue. What are the three misunderstandings?**
Complete the table.

Mel: Oh, hello, Stef – back from the shops already? Is it still raining?
Stef: Yeah, it's pouring!
Mel: Boring? If you're bored, get yourself a hobby!
Stef: No, I said pouring, with a P.
Mel: Oh, I see, pouring, right. Was there anything in the post box today?
Stef: Nothing interesting, just some bills.
Mel: Oh? I wonder who put pills in the post box!
    Did you remember to buy a gift for Tom's birthday?
Stef: Yes. Now I just need to wrap it.
Mel: Rabbit? What do you need a rabbit for?

Stef says:	Mel hears:
1 ...pouring.........	...boring.........
2	....
3 .... it	....

Follow-up: Play the recording again.
Pause and repeat after each line.

3.2 🔊 A11 **Read the joke and write the letter *b* or *p* in each gap.**
Listen and check your answers. Then practise saying the joke.

A baboon goes into a pet shop to buy peanuts and ...b..ananas.
'Sorry,' says the sho...p..keeper, 'This is a pet shop – we only sell
food for ......ets.'
'OK,' says the baboon, 'I'd like to ......uy food for my pet rabbit.'
'What does your pet rabbit eat?' asks the shopkeeper.
'......eanuts and bananas,' re......lies the ......aboon.

3.3 🔊 A12 **Listen. In one word in each group, the B or P is not pronounced. Underline the word.**

EXAMPLE   double   <u>doubt</u>   Dublin

1 lamb	label	lab
2 crab	robbed	climb
3 cup	cupboard	copy
4 photo	potato	paper
5 recipe	repeat	receipt
6 possibly	psychology	special
7 Cambridge	combine	combing

3.4 🔊 A13 **Listen and tick (✓) the sentence you hear, A or B. If you find any of these difficult,**
go to Section E4 *Sound pairs* for further practice.

A	**B**	
1 There's a bear in that tree.	There's a pear in that tree.	(⇒ Sound pair 28)
2 He had the beach to himself.	He had the peach to himself.	(⇒ Sound pair 28)
3 They burned it.	They've earned it.	(⇒ Sound pair 29)
4 Say 'boil'.	Save oil.	(⇒ Sound pair 29)
5 This is a nicer pear.	This is a nice affair.	(⇒ Sound pair 30)
6 Would you like a copy?	Would you like a coffee?	(⇒ Sound pair 30)

Follow-up: Record yourself saying the sentences in 3.4, choosing sentence A or B. Make a note
of which sentence you say. Then listen to your recording in about two weeks. Is it clear which
sentences you said?

4 Rice, rise
The consonant sounds /s/ and /z/

A ⏺A14 When you say the alphabet, the letters C and S are pronounced /siː/ and /es/. Notice they both have the consonant sound /s/. But S is also often pronounced as the consonant sound /z/.

Listen to the sounds /s/ and /z/. Look at the mouth diagram to see how to make these consonant sounds. Notice that in the sound /s/, there is no voice from the throat. It sounds like the noise of a snake. In the sound /z/, there is voice from the throat. It sounds like the noise of a bee.

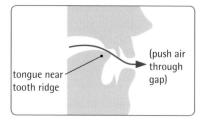

tongue near tooth ridge

(push air through gap)

B ⏺A15 Now listen to the sound /s/ on its own.

Listen to the target sound /s/ in the words below and compare it with the words on each side.

Then listen and repeat the examples of the target sound.

target /s/

zoo	**Sue**	zoo
rise	**rice**	rise
shave	**save**	shave

Examples

sad	city	science	scream
glasses	concert	last	
bus	place	class	six

Lucy sang six or seven sad songs for her last concert.

C ⏺A16 Listen to the sound /z/ on its own.

Listen to the target sound /z/ in the words below and compare it with the words on each side.

Then listen and repeat the examples of the target sound.

target /z/

Sue	**zoo**	Sue
place	**plays**	place
breathe	**breeze**	breathe

Examples

zoo	zero		
dozen	busy	scissors	exact
size	wise	bees	roses

A dozen pretty roses, a thousand busy bees

 Note: The vowel sound is shorter before /s/ than /z/, e.g. in *place* and *plays*. If you have difficulty making the difference, exaggerate the length of the vowel in *plays*. (For the pronunciation of -s endings such as plurals, see Unit 23.)

D ## Spelling

	frequently	sometimes	notes
/s/	S (*sad*), SS (*class*), C (*place*)	SC (*science*)	/ks/ can be written X (*six*). S is not always pronounced /s/ (*sugar*, *rise*, *plays*).
/z/	Z (*zero*), S (*nose*)	ZZ (*buzz*), SS (*scissors*)	/gz/ can be written X (*exact*). -SE at the end of a word is usually pronounced /z/ (*rise*).

E Pronunciation may be connected to grammar: use /juːs/ = noun   use /juːz/ = verb
close /kləʊs/ = adjective   close /kləʊz/ = verb   house /haʊs/ = noun   house /haʊz/ = verb

Exercises

4.1 **🔊A17** Look at the blue words in the story. Do they contain /s/ or /z/? Write *s* or *z* in the gap after each word. Listen and check your answers. Then practise saying the joke.

A woman was ..*z*..taking a zebra ..*z*..along the street .... A police ....
officer stopped .... her and said: 'The street is no place .... for zebras,
Madam. You should take it to the zoo .... !'

'You're right, officer .... ,' said the woman, 'I'll take it straight .... there!'

Later, the officer saw .... the woman with the zebra again. 'I said you
should take that zebra to the zoo!' he said ....

'Yes .... , we went, and it was great,' said the woman, 'Now he wants to
go to the museum ....'

4.2 **🔊A18** Find a route from Start to Finish. You may *not* pass a square if the word contains the sound /z/. You can move horizontally (⟷) or vertically (↕) only. Listen and check the words in the correct route.

START

spots	squares	prize	since	six	sports
streets	wise	sells	sits	exact	escapes
rice	rise	sense	science	lose	lost
loose	desert	smokes	songs	crisps	box
place	face	snacks	seas	voice	boxes
plays	phase	nose	smiles	focus	concert

FINISH

4.3 **🔊A19** Listen to the sentences. Look at the words in blue. Underline the words which contain the sound /s/ and circle the words which contain the sound /z/. Then listen again and repeat.

EXAMPLE   You can have my tent. It's no <u>use</u> to me. I never ⟨use⟩ it.

1 I'm not going to advise you. You never take my advice.
2 Your tooth is loose. You'll lose it if you're not careful.
3 The shop's very close to home, and it doesn't close till late.
4 I can't excuse people who drop litter. There's no excuse for it.

4.4 **🔊A19 (cont.)** Listen and underline the word you hear. If you find any of these difficult, go to Section E *Sound pairs* for further practice.

1 Price or prize? I got a good *price / prize* for that painting.   (⇒ Sound pair 31)
2 He sat or he's at? I don't know where *he sat / he's at*.   (⇒ Sound pair 31)
3 Suit or shoot? They didn't *suit / shoot* him.   (⇒ Sound pair 32)
4 Saved or shaved? I've *saved / shaved* a lot in the past few days.   (⇒ Sound pair 32)
5 Sink or think? We didn't *sink / think*.   (⇒ Sound pairs 33)
6 Closed or clothed? They were *closed / clothed* for the cold weather.   (⇒ Sound pairs 33)

> **Follow-up:** Record yourself saying the sentences in 4.4, choosing one of the two options each time. Make a note of which words you say. Then listen to your recording in about two weeks. Is it clear which words you said?

5 Down town

The consonant sounds /d/ and /t/

A20 Listen to the sounds /d/ and /t/. Look at the mouth diagram to see how to make these consonant sounds. The mouth is in the same position for both sounds, but:

- in /d/ there is voice from the throat, whereas in /t/ there is no voice from the throat

- when /t/ is at the start of a word, there is a small explosion of air when the tongue moves. With /d/, this does not happen.

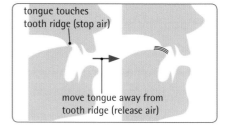

tongue touches
tooth ridge (stop air)

move tongue away from
tooth ridge (release air)

B

A21 Now listen to the sound /d/ on its own.

Listen to the target sound /d/ in the words below and compare it with the words on each side.

target /d/

town	**down**	town
wrote	**road**	wrote
they	**day**	they
page	**paid**	page

Listen and repeat these examples of the target sound.

dance	daughter	dream
sudden	advice	address
dad	food	mind

David's daughter didn't dance, but David's dad did.

 Note: The vowel sound is shorter before /t/ than /d/, for example in *wrote* and *road*. If you have difficulty making the difference, exaggerate the length of the vowel in *road*.

C

A22 Listen to the sound /t/ on its own. Listen to the target sound /t/ in the words below and compare it with the words on each side.

target /t/

die	**tie**	die
hard	**heart**	hard
three	**tree**	three
each	**eat**	each

Listen and repeat these examples of the target sound.

taste	Thomas	train	twelve
butter	until	hated	
fruit	worked	toast	

Grapefruit tastes so bitter; toast and butter's better.

Accent variation SE / Am / C : /t/ or /d/; /t/ or /ʔ/ ⇒ Unit 58.

 Note: In fast speech, many speakers drop the /d/ or /t/ when they come between two other consonant sounds. So *facts* /fækts/ sounds like *fax* /fæks/.

D ## Spelling

	frequently	sometimes	rarely	notes
/d/	D (*dog*), DD (*address*)			
/t/	T (*tie*), TT (*butter*)	(E)D past tense ending	TH (*Thomas*)	T can be silent (*listen*).

Exercises

5.1 [A23] Complete the rhymes with words from the box. Then listen and check. The second time you listen, pause after each line and repeat it.

> rude   said   ~~late~~   head   fight   polite   food   wait

There was a young lady called Kate,
Who always got out of bed ......*late*...... .
The first thing she ....
When she lifted her ....
Was: 'I thought it was better to ....'

There was a young waiter called Dwight,
Who didn't like being ....
If you asked him for .... ,
He was terribly ....
And invited you out for a ....

5.2 [A24] Listen and underline the word you hear in each pair.

1 build   <u>built</u>
2 wide   white
3 weighed   weight
4 heard   hurt
5 down   town
6 dry   try
7 send   sent

5.3 [A25] Put the words from 5.2 into the sentences below. Then listen and repeat the sentences.

EXAMPLE   Last year, Tom ..*weighed*.. more than Sam, but now they both have the same ...*weight*.... .

1 It wasn't .... in a day; it takes ages to .... a cathedral like that.
2 When you're out in the mountains, you have to .... to stay ....
3 He .... it to the wrong address, so he had to .... another copy.
4 It .... my ears when I .... that noise.
5 The .... sofa is too .... to go through that door.
6 We went .... the hill and into the ....

5.4 [A26] Listen and underline the word you hear. If you find any of these difficult, go to Section E4 *Sound pairs* for further practice.

1 Wider or whiter?   Choose Dentocream for a *wider / whiter* smile!   (⇒ Sound pair 34)
2 Dry or try?   You have to *dry / try* it out.   (⇒ Sound pair 34)
3 Breeding or breathing?   These animals aren't *breeding / breathing*!   (⇒ Sound pairs 35)
4 Thought or taught?   She *thought / taught* for a long time.   (⇒ Sound pairs 35)
5 Aid or age?   For us, *aid / age* is not important.   (⇒ Sound pairs 36)
6 What or watch?   *What / Watch* a game!   (⇒ Sound pairs 36)

> **Follow-up:** Record yourself saying the sentences in 5.4, choosing one of the two words each time. Make a note of which words you say. Then listen to your recording in about two weeks. Is it clear which words you said?

6 Meet, met
The vowel sounds /iː/ and /e/

A

When you say the letters of the alphabet, E has the long vowel sound /iː/. You hear this sound in the word *meet*. But the letter E can also be pronounced as the short vowel sound /e/, as in the word *met*.

A27 Listen to the sound /iː/. Look at the mouth diagram to see how to make this long vowel sound.

Listen to the target sound /iː/ in the words below and compare it with the words on each side.

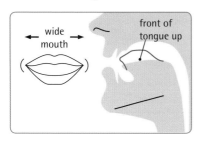

target /iː/

met	**meet**	mate
list	**least**	last
pay	**pea**	pier
bit	**beat**	bet

Listen and repeat these examples of the target sound.

key	keys	keeps
pea	peas	piece
scene	seas	seat

longer ←——→ shorter

Steve keeps the keys beneath the seat.

⚠ **Note:** When there is an /iː/ sound before the letter R at the end of a word, speakers of Silent R accents add the vowel /ə/ and do not pronounce the /r/. Compare the vowels in these words: *knee – near, pea – pier, he – hear*. Many dictionaries show this vowel before R as /ɪə/. For more on Silent R accents, see Unit 56.

B

A28 Listen to the sound /e/. Look at the mouth diagram to see how to make this short vowel sound.

Listen to the target sound /e/ in the words below and compare it with the words on each side.

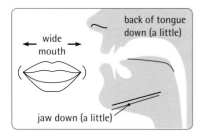

target /e/

man	**men**	mean
heard	**head**	had
mate	**met**	meat
sit	**set**	sat

Listen and repeat these examples of the target sound.

vet	death	rest
friend	said	many
check	shelf	leg

'It's best to rest,' said the vet to the pet.

C Spelling

	frequently	sometimes	notes
/iː/	EE (*feet*), EA (*eat*) E-E (*scene*)	E (*me*), IE (*piece*)	Many other vowel sounds are spelt EA, though /iː/ is the most common.
/e/	E (*men*)	EA (*death*), IE (*friend*), A (*many*), AI (*said*)	If E is followed by R, the vowel is not /e/, but /ɜː(r)/ for example in *serve*. (See Unit 19.)

Exercises

6.1 Write the words for the things in the correct part of the table.

words with /iː/	words with /e/
green	pen

6.2 🔊A29 Complete the table with the correct forms of the verbs. Then listen, check and repeat. What is interesting about the verb *read*?

present tense (vowel = /iː/)	sleep	meet	....	....	leave	dream
past tense (vowel = /e/)	slept	....	felt	read	....	....

6.3 🔊A30 Put the words from 6.2 into the conversation below. Then listen again and pause and repeat after each sentence.

Tony: How was the meal last night?
Did you ......meet...... anybody interesting?
Sara: Yes, I ¹.................... some nice people, but I ².................... tired so I left early.
Tony: When did you ³.................... ?
Sara: I ⁴.................... at ten and went home to bed.
Tony: ⁵.................... well?
Sara: Not really. I ⁶.................... for a bit but I had a terrible ⁷.................... and woke up.
Tony: Oh. Can you remember what you ⁸.................... about?
Sara: No, but I couldn't get back to sleep so I ⁹.................... .
Tony: What did you ¹⁰.................... ?
Sara: Oh, just a magazine.
Tony: So how do you ¹¹.................... this morning?
Sara: Dreadful!

6.4 🔊A30 (cont.) Listen and underline the word you hear. If you find any of these difficult, go to Section E4 *Sound pairs* for further practice.

1 Men or man? Did you see the *men / man*?   (⇒ Sound pair 1)
2 Pen or pain? I've got a *pen / pain* in my hand.   (⇒ Sound pair 4)
3 Pear or pier? That's a very small *pear / pier*.   (⇒ Sound pair 8)
4 Live or leave? I want to *live / leave*.   (⇒ Sound pair 10)
5 Bed or bird? Did you see the *bed / bird*?   (⇒ Sound pair 12)
6 Left or lift? You should take the *left / lift*.   (⇒ Sound pair 13)

Follow-up: Record yourself saying the sentences in 6.4, choosing one of the two words. Make a note of which words you say. Then listen to your recording in about two weeks. Is it clear which words you said?

7 Carrot, cabbage

Unstressed vowels /ə/ and /ɪ/

A **A31** In words with two or more syllables, at least one syllable is weak (does not have stress).

Listen to these words which have two syllables, and the second syllable is weak.

  carrot   cabbage

In weak syllables, native speakers of English very often use the weak vowel sounds /ə/ and /ɪ/.

Listen again to the two words above: the O in *carrot* is pronounced /ə/ and the A in *cabbage* is pronounced /ɪ/.

B **A32** Look at the mouth diagram to see how to make the sound /ə/.

Listen to these examples and repeat them. The weak vowels in the unstressed syllables in blue are pronounced /ə/.

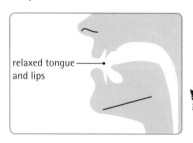
relaxed tongue and lips

weak A:	away	banana	woman	sugar
weak E:	garden	paper	under	
weak O:	police	doctor	correct	
weak U:	support	figure	colour	

I ate an apple and a banana in a cinema in Canada.

Notice that:

- In words like *paper*, *sugar*, *colour*, the final R is not pronounced in the model accent in this book, so *vista* /ˈvɪstə/ rhymes with *sister* /ˈsɪstə/, for example. See Unit 56 for more on this.

- Many proficient non-native speakers of English do not change vowels in weak syllables to /ə/. See Unit 60 for more on this.

C **A33** Look at the mouth diagram to see how to make the sound /ɪ/.

Listen to these examples and repeat them. The weak vowels in the unstressed syllables in blue are pronounced /ɪ/.

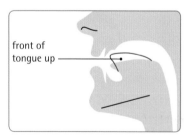
front of tongue up

weak A:	orange	cabbage		
weak E:	dances	wanted	begin	women
weak I:	music	walking		
weak U:	lettuce	minute		

Alex's lettuces tasted like cabbages.

D Spelling

Notice in the examples above that nearly any vowel spelling may be pronounced as a weak vowel.

 Note: Often, whole words are pronounced as weak syllables, with a weak vowel. For example: half an hour, going to work, Jim was late. See Units 32–36.

Exercises

7.1 🔊**A34** Listen to the poem. Underline the words which rhyme.

Mr Porter loves his pasta.
No one else can eat it faster.
Mr Porter's sister Rita
Buys the pasta by the metre.
Mr Porter's older daughter
Boils it all in tubs of water.

7.2 🔊**A35** Listen. In each sentence or phrase there are two vowels which are not /ə/. Underline them.

EXAMPLE   an <u>a</u>pple and a ban<u>a</u>na

1 from Canada to China
2 The parrot was asleep.
3 The cinema was open.
4 the photographer's assistant
5 a question and an answer
6 a woman and her husband
7 a pasta salad

7.3 🔊**A36** Write the words in the correct part of the table. Then listen and check.

~~orange~~ ~~woman~~ return collect market begin visit asleep
salad teaches teacher needed letter sofa peaches quarter women

vowel in weak syllable = /ə/	vowel in weak syllable = /ɪ/
woman	orange

7.4 🔊**A37** Read the phonemic symbols on this shopping list and write the words. Then listen and check.

EXAMPLE   /ˈkæbɪdʒɪz/ = ..cabbages..

1 /ˈletɪsɪz/ ....
2 /bəˈnɑːnəz/ ....
3 /ˈkærəts/ ....
4 /ˈsɒsɪdʒɪz/ ....
5 /ˈɒrɪndʒɪz/ ....
6 /ˈʃʊgə/ ....
7 /ˈpepəz/ ....
8 /ˈpɪːtʃɪz/ ....

7.5 🔊**A38** Listen and underline the word you hear.

1 Dress or address?   Where's Kate's *dress / address*?
2 Away or way?   Take that *away / way*.
3 Teacher's (er = /ə/) or teaches (e = /ɪ/)?   The German *teacher's / teaches* English.
4 Driver or drive?   What a nice *driver / drive*!
5 Officer's (er = /ə/) or office's (e = /ɪ/)?   The *officer's / office's* here.
6 Woman /ˈwʊmən/ or women /ˈwɪmɪn/?   What time did the *woman / women* arrive?
7 Sleep or asleep?   The *drivers sleep / driver's asleep* in the van.

Follow-up: Record yourself saying the sentences in 7.5, choosing one of the two options. Make a note of which words you say. Then listen to your recording in about two weeks. Is it clear which words you said?

8 Few, view

The consonant sounds /f/ and /v/

A   **A39** Listen to the two sounds /f/ and /v/. Look at the mouth diagram to see how to make these consonant sounds. Notice that in the sound /f/, there is no voice from the throat, and when you say this sound, you can feel the air on your hand when you put it in front of your mouth. In /v/, there is voice from the throat.

top teeth on bottom lip
(push air through gap)

B   **A40** Now listen to the sound /f/ on its own.

Listen to the target sound /f/ in the words below and compare it with the words on each side.

target /f/

view	**few**	view
leave	**leaf**	leave
pound	**found**	pound
copy	**coffee**	copy

Freda found four frogs laughing on the floor.

Listen and repeat these examples of the target sound.

photo	four	floor	frog
offer	safer	selfish	gift
knife	stuff	laugh	

⚠️ **Note:** The vowel sound is shorter before /f/ than /v/, for example in *leaf* and *leave*. If you have difficulty making the difference, exaggerate the length of the vowel in *leave*.

C   **A41** Listen to the sound /v/ on its own.

Listen to the target sound /v/ in the words below and compare it with the words on each side.

target /v/

ferry	**very**	ferry
safe	**save**	safe
wet	**vet**	wet
ban	**van**	ban

Listen and repeat these examples of the target sound.

visa	vote	Venice
clever	wives	loved
drove	twelve	of

Clever Trevor drove a van to Venice.

D Spelling

	frequently	sometimes
/f/	F (*fell*), FF (*offer*), PH (*photo*), GH (*laugh*)	
/v/	V (*never*)	F (*of*)

Exercises

8.1 How many /f/ and /v/ sounds are there when you say these numbers? Write the number of sounds.

EXAMPLE   55   .....4.....

1 512 ....   **2** 745 ....   **3** 5½ ....   **4** 11.75 ....   **5** 7,474 ....

8.2   🔊A42 Write *f* or *v* in each gap in this joke. Then listen and check your answers and practise saying the joke.

A giraffe goes into a ca...f..é and asks for a coffee. The girl who is ser......ing fetches the coffee and lea......es the bill on the table. The giraffe ......inishes the coffee and looks at the bill – ......ery expensi......e, at ......our pounds se......enty-five.

He gi......es the girl a fiver to cover the bill and turns to lea......e. The girl says, 'You know, it's strange, but I'......e ne......er seen a giraffe in here be......ore.'

'That's not so strange,' says the giraffe, 'if you charge nearly ......ive pounds for a coffee!'

fiver = five pounds

8.3   🔊A43 Listen and underline the word you hear. Practise saying the words, making the difference clear.

singular + 's (contains /f/)	1 leaf's	2 knife's	3 thief's	4 half's	5 wife's	6 life's	7 loaf's
plural (contains /v/)	1 <u>leaves</u>	2 knives	3 thieves	4 halves	5 wives	6 lives	7 loaves

8.4   🔊A44 You will hear the sentence beginnings below. Listen and complete the words. Then underline the correct option in the sentence endings. Practise saying the full sentences. Pronounce the /f/ and /v/ sounds carefully.

sentence beginnings	sentence endings
EXAMPLE The kni..*ves*.....	*not / <u>aren't</u>* sharp enough.
1 The last loa............	*been / have been* sold already.
2 The footballer's wi............	*– / are* in the VIP seating area.
3 It's autumn and the first lea............	*already / have already* fallen.
4 Be careful, your li............	*– / are* in danger!
5 In most matches, the second hal............	*usually / are usually* more exciting.

8.5   🔊A44 (cont.) Listen and underline the word you hear. If you find any of these difficult, go to Section E4 *Sound pairs* for further practice.

1 Thief's or thieves'?   These are the *thief's / thieves'* fingerprints.   (⇒ Sound pair 37)
2 Few or view?   She's painted a *few / view*.   (⇒ Sound pair 37)
3 Copy or coffee?   Do you want a *copy / coffee*?   (⇒ Sound pair 30)
4 Boat or vote?   What are you going to do with your *boat / vote*?   (⇒ Sound pair 29)
5 Worse or verse?   I don't know which is *worse / verse*.   (⇒ Sound pair 38)
6 Free or three?   We got *free / three* tickets!   (⇒ Sound pairs 39)

Follow-up: Record yourself saying the sentences in 8.5, choosing one of the two words. Make a note of which words you say. Then listen to your recording in about two weeks. Is it clear which words you said?

9 Gate, Kate
The consonant sounds /g/ and /k/

A 🔊A45 Listen to the two sounds /g/ and /k/. Look at the mouth diagram to see how to make these sounds. Notice that the mouth is in the same position for both sounds, but:

- in /g/ there is voice from the throat, whereas in /k/ there is no voice from the throat
- when /k/ is at the start of a word, there is a small explosion of air when the lips open. With /g/, this does not happen.

back of tongue touches top of mouth (stop air)

move back of tongue away from top of mouth (release air)

B 🔊A46 Now listen to the sound /g/ on its own.

Listen to the target sound /g/ in the words below and compare it with the words on each side.

target /g/

Kate	**gate**	Kate
back	**bag**	back
leak	**league**	leak

Listen and repeat these examples of the target sound.

gave	ghost	guest	grandma
bigger	ago	angry	
leg	egg	frog	

Grandma gave the guests eggs and frog's legs.

⚠ **Note:** The vowel sound is shorter before /k/ than /g/, for example in *leak* and *league*. If you have difficulty making the difference, exaggerate the length of the vowel in *league*.

C 🔊A47 Listen to the sound /k/ on its own.

Listen to the target sound /k/ in the words below and compare it with the words on each side.

target /k/

gap	**cap**	gap
glasses	**classes**	glasses
blog	**block**	blog

Listen and repeat these examples of the target sound.

king	cut	queen	
cooking	school	soccer	taxi
cake	milk	comic	ache

The king cooked the carrots and the queen cut the cake.

D Spelling

	frequently	sometimes	notes
/g/	G (*go*), GG (*bigger*)	GH (*ghost*), GU (*guest*)	G can be silent (*sign*, *foreign*).

	beginning	middle	end	notes
/k/	C (*can*), K (*king*)	CC (*soccer*), CK (*locker*)	K (*milk*), CK (*black*), C (*comic*), CH (*ache*)	/k+w/ may be spelt QU e.g. *quick*. /k+s/ may be spelt X e.g. *six*. K is silent in words beginning KN (*know*, *knife*).

Exercises

9.1 🔊A48 Read the rhyme and write the letter *k, c, g* or *q* in each gap. Then listen, check your answers and practise saying the rhyme.

Douglas met a ..*g*..irl he knew,
Standing ....uietly in the queue.
In her ba........ , she had some eggs,
A box of figs and chicken le........s,

A pack of bur........ers, tuna stea........s,
Party snacks and cho........olate ....akes,
Pink ice ....ream, a box of dates,
Cans of drin........ and plasti........ plates.

Douglas looked. 'Oh,' said he,
'You're having ....uests tonight, I see!'
The ....irl said: 'Yes, that's ....uite true.'
And then invited Douglas too.

9.2 🔊A49 Listen and read this dialogue. What are the three misunderstandings? Complete the table.

Stef: Oh no – I think I left my glasses at college …
Mel: Your classes?
Stef: No, glasses – with a G. They're not in the bag.
Mel: In the back of what?
Stef: Not back – bag!
Oh, here they are – they were in the pocket of my coat.
Mel: In the pocket of your *goat*!?
Stef: Coat, not goat!
Mel: Okay, okay, calm down – no need to get angry!

Stef says:	Mel hears:
1 glasses	classes
2	....
3	....

Follow-up: Play the recording again. Pause and repeat after each line.

9.3 🔊A50 Listen and underline the word you hear. If you find any of these difficult, go to Section E4 *Sound pairs* for further practice.

1	Ghost or coast?	Did you see the *ghost* / *coast*?	(⇒ Sound pair 40)
2	Glasses or classes?	I don't need *glasses* / *classes*.	(⇒ Sound pair 40)
3	Bag or back?	My *bag's* / *back's* wet.	(⇒ Sound pair 40)
4	Goat or coat?	She's lost her *goat* / *coat*.	(⇒ Sound pair 40)
5	Blog or block?	Why does nobody visit my *blog* / *block*?	(⇒ Sound pair 40)

Follow-up: Record yourself saying the sentences in 9.3, choosing one of the two words. Make a note of which words you say. Then listen to your recording in about two weeks. Is it clear which words you said?

10

He, we, you
The sounds /h/, /w/ and /j/

A

The sounds /h/, /w/ and /j/ only happen before a vowel sound.

🔊A51 Listen to the sound /h/. Look at the mouth diagram to see how to make this sound.

Listen to the target sound /h/ in the words below and compare it with the words on each side.

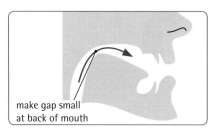

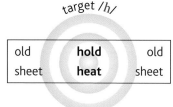

target /h/

| old | **hold** | old |
| sheet | **heat** | sheet |

Listen and repeat the examples of the target sound.

he	hair
head	heart
hurry	who
ahead	perhaps
behave	

Accent variation: /h/ is cut in some accents; see Unit 58.

B

🔊A52 Listen to the sound /w/. Look at the mouth diagram to see how to make this sound.

Listen to the target sound /w/ in the words below and compare it with the words on each side.

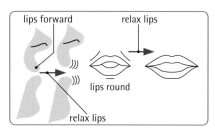

target /w/

| verse | **worse** | verse |
| good | **would** | good |

Listen and repeat the examples of the target sound.

we	wage
water	one
what	why
sandwich	language
quick	square

C

🔊A53 Listen to the sound /j/. Look at the mouth diagram to see how to make this sound.

Listen to the target sound /j/ in the words below and compare it with the words on each side.

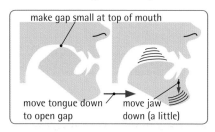

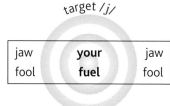

target /j/

| jaw | **your** | jaw |
| fool | **fuel** | fool |

Listen and repeat the examples of the target sound.

you	year
yellow	used
university	euro
few	news
cure	tube
view	

 Note: in American accents, /j/ is cut in some words, e.g. *news*.

D ## Spelling

	frequently	other	note
/h/	H (*hill*)	WH (*who*)	H may be silent (*hour*, *honest*).
/w/	W (*will*), WH (*when*)	O (*one*, *once*)	/k+w/ may be spelt QU (*quite*). W may be silent (*write*).
/j/	Y (*you*), I (*view*), E (*few*), U (*cure*)		

Exercises

10.1 Each of these sentences contains several examples of the sound shown at the end.
Underline the examples of the sound and write the number.

EXAMPLE <u>Wh</u>ich lang<u>u</u>age <u>w</u>ould you like to <u>w</u>ork in? /w/ = ..4...

1 Your uniform used to be yellow. /j/ = ...
2 Haley's horse hurried ahead. /h/ = ...
3 This is a quiz with twenty quick questions. /w/ = ...
4 We went to work at quarter to twelve. /w/ = ...
5 New York University student's union /j/ = ...

10.2 A54 Listen to this dialogue. Most of the words begin with /h/, /w/ or /j/. Underline the
ten words which **do not**. The first word is given as an example.

Wendy: Hi, Ewan*! How's your wife?
  Ewan: Hello, Wendy! Yolanda's well.
    How's your husband? Well, I hope?
Wendy: Yes, Harry's well.
    We heard you had a holiday?
  Ewan: Yes, one whole week without worrying about work!
Wendy: Where were you?
  Ewan: We went walking in Wales.
Wendy: How was the weather? Wet? Windy?
  Ewan: We had wonderful weather.
    What about you? What have you been doing?
Wendy: Surfing.
  Ewan: Wow! Where?
Wendy: The world wide web!

*pronounced /juːən/

Follow-up: Play the recording again. Pause and repeat
after each line.

10.3 In these groups of words, three words begin with the same consonant sound and one word begins
with a different sound. Underline the one with the different sound. You can use a dictionary.

EXAMPLE <u>hour</u> half home high

1 union   used   under   university
2 water   whale   whole   window
3 when   who   where   which
4 year   euro   uniform   untie
5 how   honest   healthy   happy
6 one   write   world   waste

10.4 A54 (cont.) Listen and underline the word you hear. If you find any of these difficult, go to
Section E4 *Sound pairs* for further practice.

1 Art or heart?   This is the *art / heart* of the country.   (⇒ Sound pair 41)
2 Hearing or earring?   She's lost her *hearing / earring*.   (⇒ Sound pair 41)
3 West or vest?   The *west / vest* is very warm.   (⇒ Sound pair 38)
4 Aware or of air?   They weren't made *aware / of air*.   (⇒ Sound pair 38)
5 Use or juice?   What's the *use / juice*?   (⇒ Sound pair 42)
6 Heat or sheet?   I can't sleep in this *heat / sheet*.   (⇒ Sound pairs 43)

Follow-up: Record yourself saying the sentences in 10.4, choosing one of the two options. Make
a note of which words you say. Then listen to your recording in about two weeks. Is it clear which
words you said?

11 Kite, kit
The vowel sounds /aɪ/ and /ɪ/

A

When you say the letters of the alphabet, I has the long vowel sound /aɪ/. You hear this sound in the word *kite*. But the letter I is also pronounced as the short vowel sound /ɪ/, as in the word *kit*.

A55 Listen to the sound /aɪ/. Look at the mouth diagram to see how to make this long vowel sound.

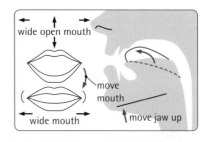

Listen to the target sound /aɪ/ in the words below and compare it with the words on each side.

target /aɪ/

mate	**might**	meet
bay	**buy**	boy
tip	**type**	tape
quit	**quite**	quiet

Listen and repeat these examples of the target sound.

why	wide	wife
buy	buys	bike
lie	lies	light

longer ←——→ shorter

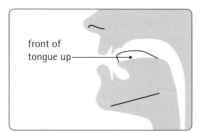

Mike's wife buys Mike's bike lights.

B

A56 Listen to the sound /ɪ/. Look at the mouth diagram to see how to make this short vowel sound.

Listen to the target sound /ɪ/ in the words below and compare it with the words on each side.

target /ɪ/

peak	**pick**	pack
wheel	**will**	while
set	**sit**	sat
feet	**fit**	fat

Listen and repeat these examples of the target sound.

king	kid	kit
hill	hid	hit
film	fish	fit

longer ←——→ shorter

Sid's kids knew where Sid hid the biscuit tin.

C Spelling

	frequently	sometimes	notes
/aɪ/	I-E (*smile*), IE (*die*), Y (*cry*)	IGH (*high*), UY (*buy*)	These spellings are not always pronounced /aɪ/ (*fridge*, *city*, *friend*).
/ɪ/	I (*win*)	Y (*gym*)	The sound /ɪ/ is also a weak vowel (see Unit 7), and can be spelt many ways in an unstressed syllable (*needed*, *cities*, *village*, *lettuce*).

Exercises

11.1 🔊A57 Listen to the sentences. Each sentence contains a word with /aɪ/ and a related word with /ɪ/. Write the related words in the table.

EXAMPLE I lit a match to light the fire.

word with /aɪ/	related word with /ɪ/
light	*lit*
1 child	....
2 bite	....
3 drive	....
4 hide	....
5 crime	....
6 write	....
7 ride	....

11.2 Join the beginnings to the correct endings to make words, then write the words in the correct part of the table. Use each ending / beginning more than once.

beginnings: wi   li   mi   ni   fi   ti   si   qui
endings: ght   fe   t   ce   ne   me   le   de   ll   sh   te   n

words with /aɪ/	words with /ɪ/
wife	*will*

11.3 🔊A58 Read the story and fill the gaps with the words given in phonemic symbols. Listen and check. Practise saying the story.

The spider and the fly

Bill and Jim, were /sɪtɪŋ/ ...*sitting*... in their prison cell one [1]/naɪt/ .... They were watching a [2]/flaɪ/ .... trying to escape from a spider's web. 'That isn't a [3]/naɪs/ .... way to [4]/daɪ/ ....,' said Jim, and he helped the fly. To Jim's surprise, the fly spoke. 'I'm a magic fly,' it said. 'You saved my [5]/laɪf/ .... Now I will give you one [6]/wɪʃ/ ....'

Jim didn't need much [7]/taɪm/ .... to think about this. 'I wish I was out of here,' he replied. There was a bright [8]/laɪt/ .... and Jim disappeared.

Bill was lying there in silence when a spider [9]/əraɪvd/ .... Thanks to Jim, it had no [10]/dɪnə/ .... To Bill's surprise, it spoke. 'I'm a magic spider,' it said, 'and I will [11]/gɪv/ .... you one wish.'

Bill, who didn't [12]/laɪk/ .... being alone, replied, 'I wish my friend Jim was back in here with me!'

11.4 🔊A59 Listen and underline the word you hear. If you find any of these difficult, go to Section E4 *Sound pairs* for further practice.

1 Live or leave?	I don't want to *live* / *leave* here.	(⇒ Sound pair 10)
2 Fill or feel?	Can you *fill* / *feel* it?	(⇒ Sound pair 10)
3 Litter or letter?	Who dropped the *litter* / *letter*?	(⇒ Sound pair 13)
4 Lift or left?	You should take the *lift* / *left*.	(⇒ Sound pair 13)

Follow-up: Record yourself saying the sentences in 11.4, choosing one of the two words. Make a note of which words you say. Then listen to your recording in about two weeks. Is it clear which words you said?

12 Sheep, jeep, cheap
The consonant sounds /ʃ/, /dʒ/ and /tʃ/

A   **A60** Listen to the sound /ʃ/. Look at the mouth diagram to see how to make this consonant sound. Notice that there is no voice from the throat, and you can feel the air on your hand when you put it in front of your mouth. If you add voice from the throat, you get the sound /ʒ/, as in *television*, but this sound is not common in English.

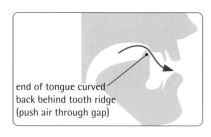

end of tongue curved back behind tooth ridge (push air through gap)

Listen to the target sound /ʃ/ in the words below and compare it with the words on each side.

target /ʃ/

sort	**short**	sort
suit	**shoot**	suit
catch	**cash**	catch
choose	**shoes**	choose

Listen and repeat these examples of the target sound.

should	shirt	sugar
fashion	nation	ocean
wish	push	English

B   **A61** Listen to the sounds /dʒ/ and /tʃ/. Look at the mouth diagram to see how to make these consonant sounds. With /tʃ/ there is no voice from the throat, with /dʒ/ there is. Notice that you can make the sound /ʃ/ into a continuous sound, but you cannot do this with /tʃ/ and /dʒ/.

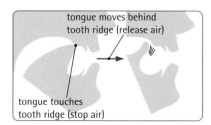

tongue moves behind tooth ridge (release air)

tongue touches tooth ridge (stop air)

C   **A62** Now listen to the sound /dʒ/ on its own.

Listen to the target sound /dʒ/ in the words below and compare it with the words on each side.

target /dʒ/

chose	**Joe's**	chose
tune	**June**	tune
use	**juice**	use
draw	**jaw**	draw

Listen and repeat these examples of the target sound.

job	general	July
danger	agent	object
edge	age	village

D   **A63** Listen to the sound /tʃ/ on its own.

Listen to the target sound /tʃ/ in the words below and compare it with the words on each side.

target /tʃ/

Jane	**chain**	Jane
share	**chair**	share
trips	**chips**	trips
what's	**watch**	what's

Listen and repeat these examples of the target sound.

chair	cheese	chicken
kitchen	future	question
rich	which	March

E   ## Spelling

	beginning	middle	end
/ʃ/	SH (*shoe*), S (*sugar*)	SH (*fashion*), SS (*Russia*), TI (*nation*), C (*ocean*)	SH (*finish*)
/dʒ/	J (*jaw*), G (*general*)	G (*page*), J (*major*)	GE (*rage*), DGE (*ledge*)
/tʃ/	CH (*chair*)	CH (*teacher*), T (*future*)	TCH (*watch*)

Exercises

12.1 Write these nationality words in the correct columns.

Belgian Welsh Dutch Russian Chinese German
Japanese Polish French Chilean Turkish

contains /dʒ/	contains /ʃ/	contains /tʃ/
Belgian		

12.2 [A64] Make word chains from the words. The last sound in each word should be the same as the first sound in the next word. Listen, check and repeat.

EXAMPLE

judge charge match teach gym church

teach – church–charge–judge–gym–match

2 child dish shirt push jump teach

jump – ....

1 brush change job much page shape

much – ....

3 cash cheek fridge juice sugar switch

fridge – ....

12.3 [A65] Listen and read this dialogue. What are the four misunderstandings? Complete the table.

Stef: You should wash those sheets!
Mel: Watch those cheats? Who's cheating?
Stef: No, wash the sheets. And put away those shoes.
Mel: Choose what?
Stef: Not choose, shoes. Take care of them – shoes aren't cheap, you know.
Mel: I know they're not sheep! What are you talking about?!

Stef says:	Mel hears:
1 wash	watch
2	
3	
4	

Follow-up: Play the recording again. Pause and repeat after each line.

12.4 [A65 (cont.)] Listen and underline the word you hear. If you find any of these difficult, go to Section E4 *Sound pairs* for further practice.

1 Watch or wash? You'll have to *watch / wash* the baby. (⇒ Sound pair 44)
2 Jane or chain? Spar is a supermarket (*Jane / chain*) (⇒ Sound pair 45)
3 Save or shave? He didn't *save / shave* at all last year. (⇒ Sound pair 32)
4 Use or juice? What's the *use / juice*? (⇒ Sound pair 42)
5 What's or watch? *What's / Watch* the time*! / ?* (⇒ Sound pairs 46)
6 Trees or cheese? I saw something in the *trees / cheese*! (⇒ Sound pairs 47)

Follow-up: Record yourself saying the sentences in 12.4, choosing one of the two options. Make a note of which words you say. Then listen to your recording in about two weeks. Is it clear which words you said?

13

Lent, rent
The consonant sounds /l/ and /r/

A

🔊 A66 Listen to the sound /l/. Look at the mouth diagram to see how to make this sound. Notice that you can make it into a long continuous sound, and there is voice from the throat.

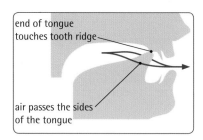

end of tongue touches tooth ridge

air passes the sides of the tongue

Listen to the target sound /l/ in the words below and compare it with the words on each side.

target /l/

rent	**lent**	rent
correct	**collect**	correct
fries	**flies**	fries
code	**cold**	code

Listen and repeat these examples of the target sound.

leave	lots	little
caller	help	slow
fill	final	mobile

Lola leaves lots of silly little messages on Alan's mobile.

B

🔊 A67 Listen to the sound /r/. Look at the mouth diagram to see how to make this sound. Notice that you can make it into a long continuous sound, and there is voice from the throat. But when you finish the sound, the jaw opens a little and the tongue goes straight again.

end of tongue curved back

move tongue to relaxed position   move jaw down a little

Listen to the target sound /r/ in the words below and compare it with the words on each side.

target /r/

late	**rate**	late
play	**pray**	play
chain	**train**	chain
jaw	**draw**	jaw

Listen and repeat these examples of the target sound.

rude	wrote	rhyme
very	sorry	address

Terry wrote a rude email to the wrong address and was very sorry.

⚠️ **Note:** In many accents, including the model accent in this book, R is not pronounced unless it is followed by a vowel sound. For more on this, see Unit 56. L may also be silent in some words.

C

Spelling

	frequently	sometimes	notes
/l/	L (*leave*), LL (*call*)		L can be silent, e.g. *half*, *calm*, *talk*, *could*.
/r/	R (*rude*), RR (*sorry*)	WR (*wrong*), RH (*rhyme*)	

Exercises

13.1 ▶A68 You will hear a rhyme with a lot of /l/ and /r/ sounds. Before you listen, write the letters *l* or *r* in each gap. Then listen, check your answers and practise saying the rhyme.

Lilly ..l.ost her ....ast umb....ella.

....eft it on the t....ain.

Fee...ing ....eally silly,

She ran home in the ....ain.

Rory fe...t so ....ucky,

Walking in the ....ain.

He'd found a ....arge umb....ella

...ying on the t....ain.

13.2 ▶A69 Someone has dictated this story into a computer but hasn't made the difference between the sounds /l/ and /r/ clear enough. The blue words are wrong. Correct them.

> *late*
> I worked ~~rate~~ that day and I didn't ~~alive~~ home until 10
> o'clock. I was very wet because of the lane. Then, to
> my supplies, my key didn't fit in the rock. So I looked
> closely at my keys and saw that they were the long
> ones. I had left my house keys at work. So I got back
> on my motorbike and load back to the office to correct
> them. I got home really tired, so I went to bed, led for
> half an hour, switched off the right and went to sleep.

arrive

Follow-up: Listen to the correct text. Then read it out yourself, making sure that you pronounce the corrected words clearly. Record yourself if you can.

13.3 Underline the word in which the letters L or R are silent in an accent from the South of England.

EXAMPLE   cold   <u>calm</u>   collect   film

1 court	correct	curry	dairy
2 follow	fold	folk	file
3 hurry	ferry	hungry	hair
4 shoulder	should	sailor	slow
5 artist	arrow	arrive	around

13.4 ▶A70 Listen and underline the word you hear. If you find any of these difficult, go to Section E4 *Sound pairs* for further practice.

1 Surprise or supplies?   The *surprise / supplies* came later.   (⇒ Sound pair 50)
2 Collect or correct?   I'll *correct / collect* it tomorrow.   (⇒ Sound pair 50)
3 Flight or fright?   We had a great *flight / fright*.   (⇒ Sound pair 50)
4 Trees or cheese?   I saw something in the *trees / cheese*!   (⇒ Sound pairs 47)
5 Jaw or drawer?   She broke her lower *jaw / drawer*.   (⇒ Sound pairs 47)

Follow-up: Record yourself saying the sentences in 13.4, choosing one of the two words. Make a note of which words you say. Then listen to your recording in about two weeks. Is it clear which words you said?

14 Car, care
The vowel sounds /ɑː(r)/ and /eə(r)/

A71 In many accents in England, the letter R is not pronounced after a vowel. In other places, the R *is* pronounced, for example in most parts of North America. But in both cases, the letter R makes the vowel before it sound different. If the vowel is A, we usually get the vowel sounds in *car* /ɑː/ or *care* /eə/.

Listen to the sound /ɑː/. Look at the mouth diagram to see how to make this long vowel sound.

Listen to the target sound /ɑː/ in the words below and compare it with the words on each side.

Then listen and repeat the examples of the target sound.

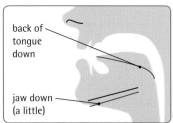
back of tongue down

jaw down (a little)

target /ɑː/

fur	**far**	four
bore	**bar**	bear
hurt	**heart**	hate
much	**march**	match

Examples

calm	card	cart
car	stars	park
harm	hard	half

longer ←——→ shorter

It's hard to park a car in a dark car park.

 Note: Sometimes we get the sound /ɑː/ before L too (e.g. *calm*).

Accent variation [SE] / [Am] : R after a vowel ⇒ Unit 56.
Accent variation [SE] / [NE] : /ɑː/ /æ/ ⇒ Unit 57.

A72 Listen to the sound /eə/. Look at the mouth diagram to see how to make this sound.

Listen to the target sound /eə/ in the words below and compare it with the words on each side.

Then listen and repeat the examples of the target sound.

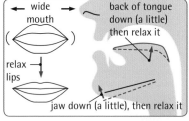
wide mouth

back of tongue down (a little) then relax it

relax lips

jaw down (a little), then relax it

target /eə/

far	**fair**	fear
why	**wear**	wore
dead	**dared**	died
stars	**stairs**	stays

Examples

share	shared
fair hair	fair-haired
pear	pears
where	where's

longer ←——→ shorter

Sarah and Mary share their pears fairly.

C Spelling

	frequently	other
/ɑː/	AR (*car*), AL (*half*)	EAR (*heart*) A (*ask*, *path*, *aunt*): Southern English accent
/eə/	ARE (*care*), AIR (*fair*), EAR (*bear*), ERE (*where*)	EIR (*their*)

Exercises

14.1 Make words by joining these beginnings to the correct endings, then write them in the correct part of the table. You may use the beginnings / endings more than once.

beginnings: ba   fa   ra   da   sta   squa   ca   ha   cha
endings: r   re   lf   ir   rd   rt   lm

words with /ɑː/	words with /eə/
bar	bare

14.2 The words in phonemic symbols below are some of the answers from 14.1, as pronounced by a speaker from the South of England. Write the words.

EXAMPLE   /kɑːm/ ....*calm*............

1 /tʃeə/ ....
2 /stɑː/ ....
3 /keə/ ....
4 /tʃɑːt/ ....

5 /skweə/ ....
6 /fɑː/ ....
7 /steə/ ....
8 /hɑːf/ ....

14.3 **A73** Look at the blue syllables in the dialogue. Do they contain 1 /ɑː/ or 2 /eə/? Write 1 or 2 in the gap after each word. Then listen and check your answers.

Martin: I've got a job interview tomorrow.
Claire: Oh. Where? ..2..
Martin: A company called Car ...1... Care. ....
Claire: What do they make?
Martin: Alarms .... and spare .... parts .... for cars. ....
Claire: So it's a factory job?
Martin: No, it's in the marketing .... department. ....
I'm starting .... to panic!
Claire: Stay calm .... Now, you'll have to look fairly .... smart ....
Martin: What shall I wear ....?
Claire: Wear .... a dark .... suit if you've got one.
Martin: And what about my hair ....?
I haven't got time to go to the barber's ....
Claire: I'll cut it for you.
Martin: Are you sure?
Claire: Yes, I used to work at a hairdresser's ....
Sit there .... in that chair .... and we'll get started ....

Follow-up: Play the recording again. Pause and repeat after each line.

14.4 **A73 (cont.)** Listen and underline the word you hear. If you find any of these difficult, go to Section E4 *Sound pairs* for further practice.

1 Heart or hat?   She put her hand on her *heart / hat*.   (⇒ Sound pair 3)
2 Nowhere or no way?   There's *nowhere / no way* to go.   (⇒ Sound pair 5)
3 Fair or far?   It isn't *fair / far*.   (⇒ Sound pair 6)
4 Part or port?   This is the main *part / port* of Athens.   (⇒ Sound pair 7)
5 Pear or pier?   That's a very small *pear / pier*.   (⇒ Sound pair 8)
6 Come or calm?   She told me to *come / calm* down.   (⇒ Sound pair 9)

Follow-up: Record yourself saying the sentences in 14.4, choosing one of the two options. Make a note of which words you say. Then listen to your recording in about two weeks. Is it clear which words you said?

15 Some, sun, sung
The consonant sounds /m/, /n/ and /ŋ/

A

🔊 A74 The consonant sounds /m/, /n/ and /ŋ/ are made by stopping the flow of air out of the mouth so that it goes through the nose instead. The three sounds are different because the air is stopped by different parts of the mouth. You can feel this when you say the words *some, sun, sung*.

Listen to the sound /m/. Look at the mouth diagram to see how to make this sound.

 Note: Always close your lips for /m/, even at the end of a word.

Listen to the target sound /m/ in the words below and compare it with the words on each side.

Then listen and repeat the examples of the target sound.

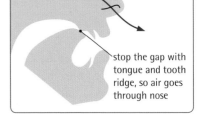

stop the gap with the lips, so air goes through nose

target /m/

nice	**mice**	nice
sun	**some**	sun
swing	**swim**	swing

Examples

miss	more	make
smoke	jump	harmed
comb	autumn	film

B

🔊 A75 Listen to the sound /n/. Look at the mouth diagram to see how to make this sound.

Listen to the target sound /n/ in the words below and compare it with the words on each side.

Then listen and repeat the examples of the target sound.

stop the gap with tongue and tooth ridge, so air goes through nose

target /n/

might	**night**	might
warm	**warn**	warm
rang	**ran**	rang

Examples

now	new	know
snow	dinner	against
gone	open	listen

C

🔊 A76 Listen to the sound /ŋ/. Look at the mouth diagram to see how to make this sound.

Listen to the target sound /ŋ/ in the words below and compare it with the words on each side.

Then listen and repeat the examples of the target sound.

stop the gap with back of tongue and top of mouth, so air goes through nose

target /ŋ/

some	**sung**	some
ham	**hang**	ham
thin	**thing**	thin

Examples

sing	singer	sink
bang	bank	banks
thing	think	finger

D Spelling

There may be a silent B or N after /m/ (*comb, autumn*). There may be a silent K before /n/ (*knife*). N is usually pronounced /ŋ/ when the next sound after it is /k/ or /g/; the N in *thin* is /n/, but the N in *think* is /ŋ/.

Exercises

15.1 🔊A77 Listen and read this dialogue. What are the three misunderstandings? Complete the table.

Stef: Your mum rang this morning.
Mel: Ran where?
Stef: No, rang – on the phone.
Mel: Oh. Something wrong?
Stef: No. She wants to know if you're going home for half-term.
Mel: Half turn? What does she mean?
Stef: No, term – with an M! After the exam.
Mel: Oh, right.
Stef: She said she'd ring back about nine.
Mel: Your what?
Stef: Sorry?
Mel: You said 'about mine' …
Stef: No, I said nine. Nine o'clock!

Stef says:	Mel hears:
1 rang	ran
2	
3	

> **Follow-up:** Play the recording again. Pause and repeat after each line.

15.2 🔊A78 Read the rhymes and write the letters *m*, *n* or *ng* in each gap. Listen and check your answers. Then practise saying the rhymes.

I knew a you..ng.. woma....... called June
Whose mu....... used to sing 'Blue Moon'.
Her voice was stro.......
But the ....otes were all wro.......
And she sa....... the whole so....... out of tu.......e.

A slim you....... ma....... called Tim
Spent all his ti.......e in the gy....... .
He worked out for lo.......er;
Got stro.......er and stronger.
.......ow Tim is no lo.......er so sli....... .

15.3 Underline the word which does not contain the consonant sound shown.

EXAMPLE /n/ knife <u>autumn</u> winter snow

1 /n/	nose	knee	finger	hand
2 /ŋ/	signs	sings	pink	angry
3 /m/	comb	summer	climb	kind
4 /n/	column	window	knock	knew
5 /n/	king	queen	prince	knit
6 /ŋ/	swing	strange	single	English

15.4 🔊A79 Listen and underline the word you hear. If you find any of these difficult, go to Section E4 *Sound pairs* for further practice.

1 Robin or robbing?   My friend likes *Robin Banks / robbing banks*.   (⇒ Sound pair 48)
2 Ran or rang?   Tom *ran / rang* yesterday.   (⇒ Sound pair 48)
3 Swing or swim?   She had a *swing / swim* in the garden.   (⇒ Sound pairs 49)
4 Warned or warmed?   The *son warned / sun warmed* me.   (⇒ Sound pairs 49)
5 Singing or sinking?   The people were *singing / sinking* fast.   (⇒ Sound pair 48)

> **Follow-up:** Record yourself saying the sentences in 15.4, choosing one of the two options. Make a note of which words you say. Then listen to your recording in about two weeks. Is it clear which words you said?

16 Note, not
The vowel sounds /əʊ/ and /ɒ/

A

🔊A80 When you say the letters of the alphabet, O has the long vowel sound /əʊ/. You hear this sound in the word *note*. But the letter O is also pronounced as the short vowel sound /ɒ/, as in the word *not*.

Listen to the sound /əʊ/. Look at the mouth diagram to see how to make this long vowel sound.

Listen to the target sound /əʊ/ in the words below and compare it with the words on each side.

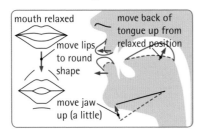

target /əʊ/

bought	**boat**	boot
blouse	**blows**	blues
cost	**coast**	cast
ball	**bowl**	bull

Listen and repeat these examples of the target sound.

toe	toes	toast
comb	code	coat
roll	rose	rope

longer ← → shorter

Rose knows Joe phones Sophie, but Sophie and Joe don't know Rose knows.

B

🔊A81 Listen to the sound /ɒ/. Look at the mouth diagram to see how to make this short vowel sound.

Listen to the target sound /ɒ/ in the words below and compare it with the words on each side.

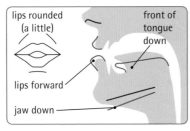

target /ɒ/

won't	**want**	went
luck	**lock**	lack
get	**got**	goat
fund	**fond**	phoned

Listen and repeat these examples of the target sound.

wrong	rob	rock
want	wash	watch
doll	dog	dot

Accent variation SE / Am : /ɒ/ or /ɑː/ ⇒ Unit 57.

Ron dropped a rock on his watch.

C Spelling

	frequently	sometimes	notes
/əʊ/	O (*old*), O-E (*stone*), OW (*show*), OA (*coat*), OE (*toe*)		If there is an R after the letter O (and the R does not have a vowel after it), O has a different pronunciation (see Unit 19).
/ɒ/	O (*dog*)	A (*wash*), OU (*cough*)	

Exercises

16.1 Write the words for the things in the correct part of the table.

words with /əʊ/	words with /ɒ/
bone	lock

16.2 🔊A82 Read the dialogue and fill the gaps with the words given in phonemic symbols. Listen and check. Practise saying the dialogue.

Doctor: Hello. Come in and sit down.

John: Hello, /ˈdɒktə/ .... doctor ....

Doctor: What's ¹/rɒŋ/ .... ?

John: I ²/wəʊk/ .... up with a bad throat and a ³/kɒf/ ....

Doctor: Oh. And have you ⁴/gɒt/ .... a blocked ⁵/nəʊz/ .... ?

John: Yes. And my ⁶/ˈbɒdɪ/ .... feels ... I don't ⁷/nəʊ/ ....

Doctor: Hot and ⁸/kəʊld/ .... at the same time?

John: Yes, exactly! How did you know?

Doctor: Hmm ... You've got a broken ⁹/bəʊn/ .... , I'm afraid.

John: ¹⁰/ˈsɒrɪ/ .... ? A broken bone?!

Doctor: No, just ¹¹/ˈdʒəʊkɪŋ/ .... ! You've got a cold. Go ¹²/həʊm/ .... and rest.

16.3 Read the words and underline the one with the different vowel sound.

EXAMPLE   soap   hope   sold   <u>soup</u>

1 come	gone	long	want
2 what	hot	most	watch
3 drove	love	woke	hole
4 snow	low	cow	show
5 both	cloth	clothes	road
6 word	wash	boss	cost
7 post	lost	coast	rose

16.4 🔊A82 (cont.) Listen and underline the word you hear. If you find any of these difficult, go to Section E4 *Sound pairs* for further practice.

1 Cost or coast?	What's the *cost / coast* like?	(⇒ Sound pair 14)
2 Shot or shut?	They *shot / shut* the door.	(⇒ Sound pair 15)
3 Boat or boot?	There's water in my *boat / boot*.	(⇒ Sound pair 16)
4 Woke or walk?	I *woke / walk* the dog.	(⇒ Sound pair 17)
5 Phoned or found?	Tim *phoned / found* her.	(⇒ Sound pair 18)

Follow-up: Record yourself saying the sentences in 16.4, choosing one of the two words. Make a note of which words you say. Then listen to your recording in about two weeks. Is it clear which words you said?

17 Thick, they
The consonant sounds /θ/ and /ð/

A 🔊 A83 Listen to the two sounds /θ/ and /ð/. Notice that in /θ/, there is no voice from the throat. Instead, you can feel the air from your mouth on your hand. In the sound /ð/ there is voice from the throat. It is possible to make both sounds long. Look at the mouth diagram to see how to make these consonant sounds.

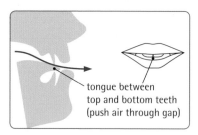

tongue between top and bottom teeth (push air through gap)

B 🔊 A84 Now listen to the sound /θ/ on its own.

Listen to the target sound /θ/ in the words below and compare it with the words on each side.

target /θ/

sick	**thick**	sick
boat	**both**	boat
free	**three**	free

Listen and repeat these examples of the target sound.

thank	third	thought
birthday	maths	healthy
earth	month	length

Martha and Thelma both have birthdays on the third of the month.

C 🔊 A85 Listen to the sound /ð/ on its own.

Listen to the target sound /ð/ in the words below and compare it with the words on each side.

target /ð/

day	**they**	day
breeze	**breathe**	breeze
van	**than**	van

Listen and repeat these examples of the target sound.

these	though	they
other	weather	clothes
breathe	with	sunbathe

Accent variation: in some accents TH is pronounced /t/ or /f/ instead of /θ/ and /d/ instead of /ð/ ⇒ Unit 58.

These clothes are perfect for sunbathing, but this weather isn't!

D ## Spelling

	always	notes
/θ/	TH (*three*)	In a few names of places and people, TH is pronounced as /t/ (*Thailand*, *Thomas*).
/ð/	TH (*then*)	

Exercises

17.1 🔊A86 Find a route from Start to Finish. You may pass a square only if the word in it has the sound /θ/. You can move horizontally (◄──►) or vertically (↕) only. Listen and check the words in the correct route. Repeat the words.

START

south	bath	bathing	thought	breath	youth
southern	third	their	through	though	thumb
path	cloth	mouth	fifth	with	worth
month	clothes	thousand	brother	that	teeth

FINISH

17.2 🔊A87 Complete this rhyme using the words from the box. Listen, check and repeat.

Earth   Heather   ~~brother~~   neither   mothers   brothers   ~~another~~   together   birth   either

Arthur had a ....*brother*..........
And he didn't want ....*another*.......... .
And of the brothers, ...
Wanted sisters, ...
The last thing on this ....
They wanted was a ....
So Arthur's mother ....
Got them both .... ,
And told them all good ....
Should learn to share their ....

Follow-up: Listen to the poem again. Pause the recording after each line and repeat it.

17.3 One word in each sentence is written wrongly, as if said by a person who doesn't pronounce /θ/ or /ð/ in their accent. Underline the incorrect word and write the correct one.

EXAMPLE   It's <u>free</u> o'clock. ....*three*...........

1 A bat is more relaxing than a shower. ....
2 The train went true the tunnel. ....
3 Don't walk on the ice; it's very fin. ....
4 You need a sick coat in winter. ....
5 I don't know; I haven't fought about it. ....
6 It's a matter of life and deaf. ....

17.4 🔊A88 Listen and underline the word you hear. If you find any of these difficult, go to Section E4 *Sound pairs* for further practice.

1 Youth or use?	There's no *youth / use* talking about that.	(⇒ Sound pairs 33)
2 Thought or taught?	I don't know what she *thought / taught*.	(⇒ Sound pairs 35)
3 Free or three?	*Free / Three* batteries in each packet!	(⇒ Sound pairs 39)
4 Closed or clothed?	They weren't fully *closed / clothed*.	(⇒ Sound pairs 33)
5 Breeding or breathing?	They've stopped *breeding / breathing*.	(⇒ Sound pairs 35)
6 These are or visa?	*These are / Visa* problems we can deal with later.	(⇒ Sound pairs 39)

Follow-up: Record yourself saying the sentences in 17.4, choosing one of the two options. Make a note of which words you say. Then listen to your recording in about two weeks. Is it clear which words you said?

18 Shut, pull, rude
The vowel sounds /ʌ/, /ʊ/ and /uː/

A ⏵A89 When you say the letters of the alphabet, U has the long vowel sound /uː/ (we say it with the consonant /j/ in front of it). You hear the /uː/ sound in the word *rude*. But the letter U is also pronounced as the short vowel sounds /ʌ/ or /ʊ/, as in the words *shut* and *pull*.

Listen to the sound /ʌ/. Look at the mouth diagram to see how to make this short vowel sound.

Listen to the target sound /ʌ/ in the words below and compare it with the words on each side.

Then listen and repeat the examples of the target sound.

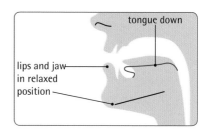

target /ʌ/

shoot	**shut**	shirt
match	**much**	March
look	**luck**	lock

Examples

come   blood   cut
young   does   must

longer ◄──────► shorter

B ⏵A90 Listen to the sound /ʊ/. Look at the mouth diagram to see how to make this short vowel sound.

Listen to the target sound /ʊ/ in the words below and compare it with the words on each side.

Then listen and repeat the examples of the target sound.

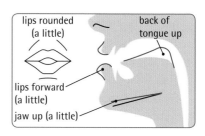

target /ʊ/

luck	**look**	Luke
pool	**pull**	Paul

Examples

full   good   foot
wolf   would   put

longer ◄──────► shorter

C ⏵A91 Listen to the sound /uː/. Look at the mouth diagram to see how to make this long vowel sound.

Listen to the target sound /uː/ in the words below and compare it with the words on each side.

Then listen and repeat the examples of the target sound.

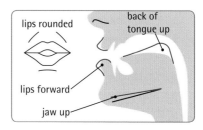

target /uː/

full	**fool**	fall
road	**rude**	road
but	**boot**	boat

Examples

shoe   shoes   shoot
new   lose   soup

longer ◄──────► shorter

D Spelling

If there is an R after the letter U (and the R does not have a vowel after it), U has a different pronunciation (see Unit 19).

Exercises

18.1 🔊A92 Look at the blue syllables in the text and decide if they contain 1 /ʌ/ or 2 /uː/. Write 1 or 2 in the gap after each word. Then listen and check your answers.

I studied ..1.. English at a school ..2.. in London .... last summer .... I was there for two .... months .... : May and June .... England is famous for bad food and weather, but I thought the food .... was good. The pub .... lunches .... were very nice. But it's true .... about the weather. Too .... much .... rain for me!

Follow-up: Listen again and pause after each sentence to repeat it.

18.2 🔊A93 Complete the sentences with the words from the box. The vowel sound is given. Listen, check and repeat.

> brother   wood   moon   juice   won   month   June
> would   full   ~~boot~~   Cup   ~~put~~   son   good

EXAMPLE   Two things you can .....put..... /ʊ/ on a foot are a shoe and a .....boot..... /uː/.

1 The .... /ʌ/ after .... /uː/ is July.

2 My mother's other .... /ʌ/ is my .... /ʌ/.

3 Brazil .... /ʌ/ the World .... /ʌ/ in 2002.

4 Fruit .... /uː/ is .... /ʊ/ for you.

5 There is a .... /ʊ/ .... /uː/ once a month.

6 You pronounce .... /ʊ/ exactly the same as .... /ʊ/.

18.3 Underline the word with the different vowel sound. You can use a dictionary if you are not sure.

EXAMPLE   foot   look   <u>blood</u>   push

1 soon   book   boot   room
2 rude   luck   run   but
3 shoes   does   true   blue
4 pull   full   put   rule
5 good   could   would   shoulder
6 done   move   love   son
7 south   young   couple   won

18.4 🔊A94 Listen and underline the word you hear. If you find any of these difficult, go to Section E4 *Sound pairs* for further practice.

1 Cut or cat?   There's a *cut / cat* on the arm of the sofa.   (⇒ Sound pair 2)
2 Come or calm?   You should try to *come / calm* down.   (⇒ Sound pair 9)
3 Gun or gone?   He's taken his dog and *gun / gone*.   (⇒ Sound pair 15)
4 Shoes or shows?   I've never seen her *shoes / shows* on TV.   (⇒ Sound pair 16)
5 Pool or pull?   It said *'Pool' / 'Pull'* on the door.   (⇒ Sound pair 19)
6 Luck or look?   It's just her *luck / look*!   (⇒ Sound pair 20)
7 Shirt or shut?   The hairdresser's *shirt / shut*.   (⇒ Sound pair 21)
8 A gun or again?   He shot *a gun / again*.   (⇒ Sound pair 22)

Follow-up: Record yourself saying the sentences in 18.4, choosing one of the two options. Make a note of which words you say. Then listen to your recording in about two weeks. Is it clear which words you said?

19 Shirts, shorts

The vowel sounds /ɜː(r)/ and /ɔː(r)/

🔊 A95 In many accents in England, the letter R is not pronounced after a vowel. In other places, the R *is* pronounced, for example in North America. But in both cases, the letter R changes the vowel sound before it. If the vowel letter is E, I, O or U, we often get the vowel sounds in *shirt* or *short*.

Listen to the sound /ɜː/. Look at the mouth diagram to see how to make this long vowel sound.

Listen to the target sound /ɜː/ in the words below and compare it with the words on each side.

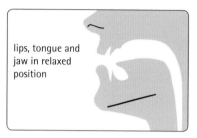

target /ɜː/

short	**shirt**	shut
fair	**fur**	fear
born	**burn**	bone
hard	**heard**	head

Listen and repeat these examples of the target sound.

worm	word	work
burn	bird	birth
sir	serve	surf

longer ◄——► shorter

The first word the girl heard was 'bird'.

B   🔊 A96 Listen to the sound /ɔː/. Look at the mouth diagram to see how to make this long vowel sound.

Listen to the target sound /ɔː/ in the words below and compare it with the words on each side.

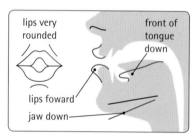

target /ɔː/

shot	**short**	shirt
work	**walk**	woke
far	**four**	fair
boil	**ball**	bowl

Listen and repeat these examples of the target sound.

bore	bored	bought
call	cause	caught
war	wall	walk

longer ◄——► shorter

Accent variation Silent R and R accents ⇒ Unit 56.

Laura thought she saw her daughter falling in the water.

C   Spelling

	spellings with R	other spellings
/ɜː/	IR (*girl*), ER (*serve*), UR (*surf*), OR (*word*), EAR (*heard*)	
/ɔː/	OR (*bore*), AR (*warm*), OUR (*four*), OOR (*door*)	A (*call*), AU (*cause*), AW (*saw*), AL (*walk*), AUGH (*taught*), OUGH (*thought*)

Exercises

19.1 🔊**A97** Listen and read this dialogue. What are the three misunderstandings? Complete the table.

Mel: Where are you going?
Stef: Walking in the park.
Mel: Working in the park?
Stef: No, walking – I need some exercise. Have you seen my shorts anywhere?
Mel: Which shirts? Your wardrobe's full of shirts!
Stef: No, not shirts, shorts – with an O. Oh, here they are.
  You've been playing that for hours. Aren't you bored?
Mel: Bird? What do you mean?
Stef: Oh, never mind!

Stef says:	Mel hears:
1 walking	working
2	
3	

Follow-up: Play the recording again. Pause and repeat after each line.

19.2 🔊**A98** Read the story and fill the gaps with the words given in phonemic symbols. Listen and check your answers.

Not working for free!

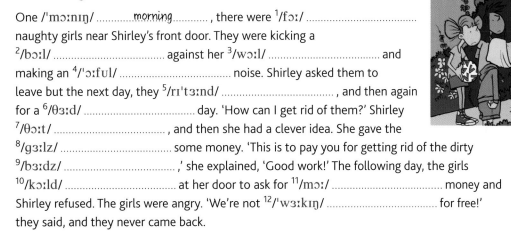

One /'mɔːnɪŋ/ ......morning......, there were [1]/fɔː/ ....
naughty girls near Shirley's front door. They were kicking a
[2]/bɔːl/ .... against her [3]/wɔːl/ .... and
making an [4]/'ɔːful/ .... noise. Shirley asked them to
leave but the next day, they [5]/rɪ'tɜːnd/ .... , and then again
for a [6]/θɜːd/ .... day. 'How can I get rid of them?' Shirley
[7]/θɔːt/ .... , and then she had a clever idea. She gave the
[8]/gɜːlz/ .... some money. 'This is to pay you for getting rid of the dirty
[9]/bɜːdz/ .... ,' she explained, 'Good work!' The following day, the girls
[10]/kɔːld/ .... at her door to ask for [11]/mɔː/ .... money and
Shirley refused. The girls were angry. 'We're not [12]/'wɜːkɪŋ/ .... for free!'
they said, and they never came back.

19.3 🔊**A99** Listen and circle the word you hear. If you find any of these difficult, go to Section E4 *Sound pairs* for further practice.

1 Four or far?	It isn't *four / far*.	(⇒ Sound pair 7)
2 Worst or west?	It's on the *worst / west* coast.	(⇒ Sound pair 12)
3 Walk or woke?	I *walk / woke* the dog.	(⇒ Sound pair 17)
4 Shut or shirt?	The butcher's *shut / shirt*.	(⇒ Sound pair 21)
5 Port or pot?	There's coffee in the *port / pot*.	(⇒ Sound pair 23)
6 Bird or beard?	He has a black *bird / beard*.	(⇒ Sound pair 24)
7 Her or hair?	Is that *her / hair*?	(⇒ Sound pair 25)
8 Worked or walked?	We *worked / walked* all day.	(⇒ Sound pair 26)

Follow-up: Record yourself saying the sentences in 19.3, choosing one of the two words. Make a note of which words you say. Then listen to your recording in about two weeks. Is it clear which words you said?

20 Toy, town
The vowel sounds /ɔɪ/ and /aʊ/

A 🔊 **B1** Listen to the sound /ɔɪ/. Look at the mouth diagram to see how to make this long vowel sound.

Listen to the target sound /ɔɪ/ in the words below and compare it with the words on each side.

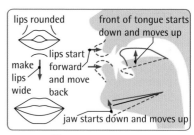

target /ɔɪ/

buy	**boy**	bay
pint	**point**	paint
all	**oil**	I'll

Listen and repeat these examples of the target sound.

toy	noise	voice
boil	coin	choice
employ		enjoyed

longer ◄────► shorter

Roy enjoys noisy toys.

⚠ **Note:** When the vowel sound /ɔɪ/ is before L, e.g. *oil*, *boil*, *soil*, many speakers put the vowel /ə/ between them. You may find it easier to say it this way.

B 🔊 **B2** Listen to the sound /aʊ/. Look at the mouth diagram to see how to make this long vowel sound.

Listen to the target sound /aʊ/ in the words below and compare it with the words on each side.

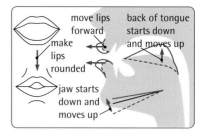

target /aʊ/

fond	**found**	phoned
know	**now**	new
car	**cow**	care

Listen and repeat these examples of the target sound.

how	houses	house
now	sound	south
cow	count	couch

longer ◄────► shorter

⚠ **Note:** When the vowel sound /aʊ/ is before R or L, many speakers put the vowel /ə/ between them, so *hour* rhymes with *shower*, and *foul* rhymes with *towel*.

Mrs Brown counted the cows coming down the mountain.

C ## Spelling

	frequently	notes
/ɔɪ/	OY (*boy*), OI (*coin*)	
/aʊ/	OW (*cow*), OU (*loud*)	Several different vowel sounds are spelt OW or OU.

Exercises

20.1 Put one of the letters *y*, *i*, *u* or *w* in each gap to make a word. The word must contain the sound /ɔɪ/ or /aʊ/. Write /ɔɪ/ or /aʊ/ after each word.

EXAMPLE   to..w..n ..../aʊ/.........

1 bo......s ....
2 no......se ....
3 fo......nd ....

4 po......nt ....
5 ho............................
6 bo......l ....

7 ho......r ....
8 flo......er ....
9 enjo......................

20.2 🔊 B3 Complete the rhymes with the words from the box. Then listen and check. The second time you listen to the rhymes, pause after each line and repeat it.

> south   noise   mouth   loud   crowd   boys   ~~avoid~~   annoyed

I had an old teacher called Lloyd /lɔɪd/
Who everyone tried to ....avoid......... .
If ever the ....
Made any .... ,
Lloyd was always ....

I knew a young boy named McLeod /məˈklaʊd/
Whose voice was amazingly ....
From north to ....
You could hear his ....
As loud as the sound of a ....

20.3 🔊 B4 Listen to this text. Find the words which have an /ɔɪ/ or /aʊ/ sound and write them in the correct part of the table.

> I enjoy living down town. Well, it's very noisy, of course. The traffic is loud, and the young people often shout when they come out of the clubs. But there are lots of good points too. There's a big choice of shops, and it's easy to get around.

words with /ɔɪ/	words with /aʊ/
enjoy	down

Follow-up: Listen again and repeat, sentence by sentence.

20.4 🔊 B4 (cont.) Listen and circle the words you hear.

1 Tie or toy?   He got a *tie / toy* for his birthday.
2 Goodbye or Good boy?   *'Goodbye!' / 'Good boy!'* she said.
3 Phoned or found?   She *phoned / found* a friend.
4 Tone or town?   What an ugly *tone / town*!

Follow-up: Record yourself saying the sentences in 20.4, choosing one of the two options. Make a note of which words you say. Then listen to your recording in about two weeks. Is it clear which words you said?

21 Dream, cream, scream
Consonant groups at the beginning of words

A

🔊 B5 Many consonant pairs consist of these combinations:

- B, C (/k/), F, G, P before L or R
- D, T before R.

	b	c /k/	d	f	g	p	t
+ l	blue	cloud	–	fly	glass	play	–
+ r	brown	crowd	drink	fry	grass	pray	try

Listen and compare similar-sounding words, one beginning with a single consonant sound and the other beginning with a consonant pair.

b: lock – block; low – blow; rain – brain; red – bread; ring – bring
c: loud – cloud; lose – clues; lean – clean; ride – cried
d: ride – dried; rest – dressed; raw – draw
f: light – flight; law – floor; lie – fly; read – freed; ride – fried
g: love – glove; low – glow; rate – great; rain – grain
p: late – plate; lane – plane; rice – price; rise – prize
t: ride – tried; rain – train

B

🔊 B6 The consonant /s/ is the first letter / sound in a great number of different consonant pairs; /s/ may also be the first consonant sound in a group of three consonant sounds, in blue below.

	/k/ (c, k, q)	l	m	n	p	t	w
pair	score ski	slow sleep	small smoke	snow snack	space sport	stay start	sweet swam
group	square /skweə/	–	–	–	spring /sprɪŋ/	straight /streɪt/	–

Listen and compare similar-sounding words. The second word in each pair has the consonant /s/ added to the beginning.

/k/: key – ski; care – scare; cool – school; cream – scream
l: low – slow; lip – slip
m: mile – smile; mall – small
n: know – snow; nail – snail
p: pear – spare; pain – Spain; peak – speak; port – sport; pray – spray
t: take – steak; tart – start; top – stop; tough – stuff; treat – street
w: wear – swear; wet – sweat

MEN SWEAR

No, it's menswear not men swear!

C

🔊 B7 When there are consonant pairs or groups at the beginning of words, many learners add a vowel sound before the consonant group or in the middle of it. Be careful: you may get a different word!

Listen to the difference.

If you say a vowel sound before the A words, they will sound like the B words:

A	B
sleep	asleep
dress	address
street	a street

If you say a vowel sound after the /s/ in the A words, they will sound like the B words:

A	B
sport	support
that ski	That's a key.
that smile	That's a mile.
What snake?	What's an ache?

Exercises

21.1 Look at the pictures and find words beginning with consonant pairs that start with these letters: *b, c, d, f, g, p, t.* There are two words for each letter.

EXAMPLE   *b* = ..bridge,..bread............................

c ....

d ....

f ....

g ....

p ....

t ....

21.2 🔊 **B8** Complete the rhymes with the words above each verse. Listen, check, pause after each line and repeat. Be careful pronouncing the consonant pairs in blue.

queue crowd blue cloud

The brightest ..blue............

The greyest ....

The slowest ....

The greatest ....

grain brain glass grass

The greenest ....

The smallest ....

The cleanest ....

The quickest ....

fruit suit trees breeze

The freshest ....

The sweetest ....

The tallest ....

The smartest ....

21.3 🔊 **B9** Add the letters in the box to the blue words in the text so that it makes sense. Listen and check your answers.

c f g p s t

A journey by air

I was once on a short ...f... light from France to ....pain. It was only a ....mall ....lane and I was by the window. I could see the ....now on the ....round below. Just when we were ....lying through a ....loud, we heard one of the engines ....top. I was really ....cared, but a few moments later, we heard it ....tart again. Everything was fine, but I decided to return to France on the ....rain, even though it was much ....lower!

> **Follow-up:** Play the recording again. Pause after each line and repeat.

21.4 🔊 **B9 (cont.)** Listen and tick the sentence or phrase you hear, A or B.

	A	B
1	that slow bus	That's a low bus.
2	an ice cream	a nicer cream
3	that spot	That's a pot.
4	that street	That's a treat.
5	She loves the States.	She loves the estates.
6	small stream	a smaller stream
7	slow speech	a slower speech
8	straight street	a straighter street

> **Follow-up:** Record yourself saying the phrases and sentences in 21.4, choosing A or B each time. Make a note of which sentence or phrase you say. Then listen to your recording in about two weeks. Is it clear which you said?

22 Left, lunch, last
Consonant groups at the end of words

A 🔊 B10 Listen to this dialogue. Consonant pairs or groups at the end of words are shown in blue.

A: Can you recommen**d** a place for lunc**h**?
B: Well, there's a Frenc**h** restauran**t** in We**st** Street. Wal**k** along the pavemen**t** in fron**t** of the station and turn lef**t** at the po**st** box and it's nex**t** to the ban**k**. If you get lo**st**, ju**st** a**sk** for hel**p** – it's called the Chat Noir. It migh**t** be quite busy though.
A: Oh, we don'**t** min**d** waiting – we can ju**st** stan**d** at the bar. Is it expensive?
B: Not if you get the twel**ve**-poun**d** lunc**h** menu. You get a fir**st** and secon**d** course plus a drink.
A: Soun**ds** good. Than**k** you. Do you wan**t** to join us?
B: No, I mu**st** finish this repor**t**. Enjoy it!

Notice that:

- Many words which end with two consonant letters do not end with two consonant sounds, e.g. *walk* = /wɔːk/; *along* = /əˈlɒŋ/; *turn* = /tɜːn/. (In many accents, the R is pronounced in words like this (see Unit 56).)

- Sometimes a consonant pair may be spelt with only one consonant letter, e.g. *box* = /bɒks/.

- There may be more than two consonant sounds at the end of a word, e.g. *next* = /nekst/.

B Often, consonant groups at the end of words relate to the grammatical function of the word. These often result in groups of two, three or sometimes four consonant sounds (in blue below).

/s/ and /z/ endings (present simple; possessives; plurals; 's contractions) (See Unit 23.)	wants /wɒnts/; stands /stændz/; texts /teksts/
/d/ and /t/ endings (past simple; adjectives) (See Unit 24.)	changed /tʃeɪndʒd/; helped /helpt/
/nt/ endings (negative contractions)	isn't /ɪzᵊnt/; didn't /dɪdᵊnt/
/st/ endings (superlatives, jobs)	coldest /kəʊldɪst/; dentist /dentɪst/
/θ/ endings (ordinal numbers)	sixth /sɪksθ/; twelfth /twelfθ/

Note: Many speakers simplify big consonant groups by cutting one of the consonants, e.g. *stands* /stæn̶dz/; *sixth* /sɪks̶θ/.

C 🔊 B11 You should be sure to pronounce the *final* consonant in a consonant group because this may change the meaning. Listen to these examples.

	With final consonant cut, sounds like:
Your gues**t** was late.	Your guess was late.
There's no win**d**.	There's no win.
Thin**k** about it.	Thing about it.
The shop'**s** closed.	The shop closed.
I walke**d** home.	I walk home.
She *isn't* American.	She *is* an American.

D 🔊 B12 Some learners of English add a vowel after a consonant pair to make it easier to say. But be careful – this may change the meaning.

Listen to these examples.

help   helper   sent   centre   cook   cooker   mix   mixer   past   pasta

Exercises

22.1 🔊 B13 Read the conversation and underline the words which end with a consonant pair or group. Then listen and practise reading the conversation aloud. Pronounce the underlined words carefully.

A: OK, <u>first</u> question: <u>what's</u> the <u>eighth</u> <u>month</u> in the year?
B: It's August.
A: Correct! Second question: what's the highest mountain on Earth?
B: Mount Everest.
A: Correct again! Mount Everest! Next question: which of these cities is furthest east in Europe: Athens, Brussels or Budapest?
B: Is it Budapest, or perhaps Brussels?
A: No, wrong, sorry. It's Athens. OK, last question: what's the biggest land animal in the world?
B: The elephant.
A: Very good! Three out of four correct, that's 75 percent!

22.2 🔊 B14 In this conversation, the speakers have cut the final consonants from the blue words. What did they mean? Write the correct words at the end of each sentence.

A: What did you do last night?
B: I watch a fill by Woody Allen. .....*watched* / *film*.....
A: Oh, I miss that. ....
What time did it star? ....
B: I thing it was about half pass sick. ..../.................../...................
What did you do?
A: My sister ask me to babysit for her. ....
B: Oh. How old her baby? ....
A: Tom isn't really a baby.
It his seven birthday necks week. ..../.................../...................
B: So what did you do?
A: We play card till about nine. ..../...................
Then Tom when upstairs to bed and I watch a DVD. ..../...................
B: Was it good?
B: No, it was the worse film I've ever seen. ....
I switch it off after an hour. ....

> **Follow-up:** Listen to the conversation with all the final consonant groups pronounced carefully. Pause after each line and repeat.

22.3 🔊 B15 Listen and underline the word you hear.

1 They took their *cook / cooker* with them.
2 She was a great *help / helper*!
3 He *did an / didn't* exercise.
4 They *learn / learnt* quickly.
5 Is that your *guess / guest*?
6 They *burn / burnt* the food.
7 It's all in the *past / pasta* now.
8 That *mix / mixer* wasn't very good.

> **Follow-up:** Record yourself saying the sentences in 22.3, choosing one of the two options. Make a note of which words you say. Then listen to your recording in about two weeks. Is it clear which words you said?

23 Wins, weeks, wages
Words with -s endings

A 🔊 B16 Listen to these examples of words with -s endings. Notice that there are three different ways of pronouncing the ending: /s/, /z/ or /ɪz/.

plurals	weeks /wiːks/; eggs /egz/; wages /ˈweɪdʒɪz/
present simple	drinks /drɪŋks/; wins /wɪnz/; watches /ˈwɒtʃɪz/
possessive	Mark's /mɑːks/; Tom's /tɒmz/; Rose's /ˈrəʊzɪz/
is / *has* contractions	it's /ɪts/; he's /hiːz/

B 🔊 B17 We pronounce -s endings as /ɪz/ when the original word ends with one of the sounds below. Listen to the phrases.

/s/ Chris's kisses
/ʃ/ Trish's wishes
/z/ Rose's roses
/tʃ/ The witch's watches
/dʒ/ George's fridges

Notice that when we add /ɪz/ to a word, it is an extra syllable. For example, the name *Chris* has one syllable, but the possessive *Chris's* has two syllables.

C 🔊 B18 All other -s endings are pronounced /s/ or /z/. If the original word ends with one of the consonant sounds /f, k, p, t, θ/, the -s ending is pronounced /s/. Otherwise, it is pronounced /z/. Listen to the examples in the box below.

/s/	/z/
shops /ʃɒps/	bags /bægz/
photographs /ˈfəʊtəgrɑːfs/	grocer's /ˈgrəʊsəz/
parks /pɑːks/	optician's /ɒpˈtɪʃənz/
chemist's /ˈkemɪsts/	credit cards /ˈkredɪt kɑːdz/
months /mʌnθs/	clothes /kləʊðz/

Notice that when we add /s/ or /z/ to a word, it is <u>not</u> an extra syllable. For example, the word *shop* has one syllable and the plural *shops* also has only one syllable.

D 🔊 B19 Make sure you pronounce the -s ending. It is very important to the meaning. Listen to the examples and notice how the -s ending changes the meaning.

noun	**verb**
Jane's nose	Jane knows
Nick's weights	Nick waits

singular	**plural**
My friend spends a lot.	My friends spend a lot.
Our guest came late.	Our guests came late.

Exercises

23.1 ● B20 Write the -s ending form of each verb from the box in the correct part of the table below. Listen, check and repeat.

watch sing go get dance kiss come wash see close push pull

-s = /ɪz/	watches
-s = /s/ or /z/	sings

23.2 ● B21 Listen to the text below and decide if the blue -s endings are pronounced /s/ or /z/. Write the correct phonemic symbol in the gap after each ending. Then listen again. Pause after each sentence and repeat.

There's /..z../ no life on the town's /......./ streets /......./ any more. Nobody goes /......./ there. Nobody stops /......./ and talks /......./ while they're shopping – the shops /......./ have all closed. There used to be a butcher's, /......./ a greengrocer's, /......./ a chemist's, /......./ a newsagent's, /......./ clothes /......./ shops, /......./ lots /......./ of small cafés /......./ – all gone. Now, everybody drives /......./ to the big shopping centres /......./ outside town.

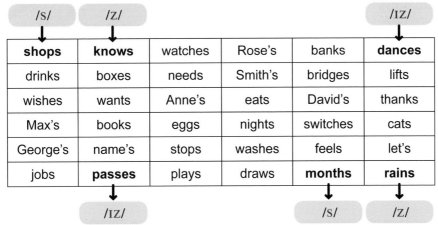

23.3 ● B21 (cont.) Find a route from the top /s/ to the bottom /s/. You may pass a square only if the -s ending in it is pronounced /s/. You can make horizontal (←→), vertical (↕) or diagonal (↗ ↘) moves. Then do the same for /z/ and /ɪz/. Then listen to the correct order of words for each route and check your answers.

	/s/	/z/				/ɪz/
	shops	**knows**	watches	Rose's	banks	**dances**
	drinks	boxes	needs	Smith's	bridges	lifts
	wishes	wants	Anne's	eats	David's	thanks
	Max's	books	eggs	nights	switches	cats
	George's	name's	stops	washes	feels	let's
	jobs	**passes**	plays	draws	**months**	**rains**
	/ɪz/				/s/	/z/

Follow-up: Play the recording again, repeating each of the words and pronouncing the -s endings correctly.

23.4 ● B22 Listen and underline the word you hear.

1 I saw the *bird / birds* fly away.
2 What time did the *guest / guests* leave?
3 He broke his *arm / arms* in the accident.
4 She sang the *song / songs* her father wrote.
5 Where does she park her *car / cars* at night?

6 I read the *book / books* very quickly.
7 The *bag / bags* fell on the floor.
8 The *shop / shops* will be closed.
9 When will the *class / classes* begin?
10 The *box / boxes* won't be big enough.

Follow-up: Record yourself saying the sentences in 23.4, choosing singular or plural. Make a note of which one you said. Then listen to your recording in about two weeks. Is it clear which words you said?

24 Rested, played, watched
Words with -ed endings

A The past tense ending -*ed* is pronounced in three different ways.

/ɪd/	/d/	/t/
rested /ˈrestɪd/	played /pleɪd/	watched /wɒtʃt/

B ▶B23 Listen to the sentences below, first in the present and then in the past tense. Notice how the -*ed* ending is an extra syllable.

I wait(ed) and count(ed) to ten.
The games start(ed) early and end(ed) late.
They heat(ed) the coffee and add(ed) milk.
We want(ed) to pay but we need(ed) more money.

Notice that we pronounce -*ed* endings as /ɪd/ when the original verb ends with /d/ or /t/. When we add /ɪd/ to a verb like this, it is an extra syllable. So, for example, *wait* has the stress pattern ● and *waited* has the stress pattern ●●.

C ▶B24 Listen to the past tense verbs in the rhyme below. Notice how the words in blue rhyme, even though the endings are spelt quite differently. This is clear if you look at the phonemic spellings.

He looked round first, /fɜːst/
And then reversed. /rɪˈvɜːst/
The car that passed /pɑːst/
Was going fast. /fɑːst/
It hit the side, /saɪd/
The driver cried. /kraɪd/
He never guessed /gest/
He'd pass the test. /test/

All other -*ed* endings, other than those mentioned in B above, are pronounced /d/ or /t/. If the original word ends with one of the consonant sounds /f, k, p, s, ʃ, tʃ, θ/, the -*ed* ending is pronounced /t/. Otherwise, it is pronounced /d/. When -*ed* is pronounced /d/ or /t/, it is not an extra syllable. For example, *guess* /ges/ has one syllable and the past tense *guessed* /gest/ also has only one syllable; the letter E is silent. So *guessed* rhymes with *test*.

D ▶B25 Make sure you pronounce the -*ed* ending. It is important to the meaning because it shows that the action is in the past. Listen to the differences in these pairs of sentences.

Present	Past
You never cook a meal.	You never cooked a meal.
I sometimes watch a movie.	I sometimes watched a movie.
We often phone our parents.	We often phoned our parents.

 Note: If it is difficult to say the -*ed* ending in words like *cooked*, imagine that the -*ed* is joined to the word after it. For example, say *cooked all the food* like this: *cook tall the food*.

 Note: If the word after the past tense verb begins with a consonant, you may not hear the -*ed*, e.g. *cooked dinner*, *walked through*.

Exercises

24.1 **B26** Write the past tense of the verbs from the box in the correct part of the table. Then listen, check and repeat.

~~hate~~   ~~walk~~   need   wash   wait   waste   help   taste   phone   dance   end   ask

1 syllable ●	walked
-ed = extra syllable ●●	hated

24.2 **B26 (cont.)** Complete each sentence with the past tense of a verb from the box. In each sentence, the first sound of the verb is the same as the first sound in the person's name.

~~play~~   watch   add   phone   count   mix   cook   start   shout   ~~paint~~

●●●	●●●●● (-ed = extra syllable)
Paul .... played .... games.	Peter .... painted .... pictures.
Ken .... lunch.	Karen .... money.
Fred .... friends.	Stella .... singing.
Marge .... drinks.	Alice .... sugar.
Will .... films.	Sheila .... loudly.

Now listen, check and repeat. Notice the syllable patterns shown with ● and ●●; each word in the first column has one syllable, each word in the second column has two syllables.

24.3 **B27** Match the beginnings and endings of these rhymes. Then listen, check, pause after each sentence and repeat.

1 The people queued
2 The thing you missed
3 The man controlled
4 She saw the child
5 The boat that crossed
6 The man who drowned
7 The snow we rolled
8 Her voice was soft
9 The points we scored
10 We never planned

a was never found.
b are on the board.
c and then she smiled.
d to build on sand.
e was on the list.
f until she coughed.
g the nation's gold.
h to buy the food.
i was nearly lost.
j was hard and cold.

24.4 **B28** Listen and underline the verb form you hear: past or present.

1 I always *walk / walked* away from fights.
2 I think they *want / wanted* to talk.
3 Me and my friends *laugh / laughed* a lot.
4 On Saturdays, we *dance / danced* all night.
5 I always *hate / hated* Sundays.
6 You never *help / helped* Alice.
7 They *enjoy / enjoyed* eating out.
8 They *save / saved* about twenty pounds.

Follow-up: Record yourself saying the sentences in 24.4, choosing the present or past tense. Make a note of which tense you say. Then listen to your recording in about two weeks. Is it clear which tense you said?

25 Pets enter, pet centre
Consonant sounds at word boundaries

A

[B29] In speech, words often join together. Sometimes it is difficult to know where one word finishes and the next word begins. For example, *pets enter* sounds the same as *pet centre* because the consonant /s/ could be at the end of the first word or at the start of the second word.

Listen to the examples. The phrases on the left sound the same as the phrases on the right.

pets enter	pet centre
stopped aching	stop taking
ice cream	I scream
known aim	no name
called Annie	call Danny
clocks tops	clock stops
missed a night	Mr Knight

 Note: The /h/ is often dropped from the beginning of pronouns, so that *thanked him* sounds like *thank Tim*.

B

[B30] When one word ends with a consonant and the next word begins with a vowel, it sounds like the consonant is at the beginning of the next word. For example, say the first line of the chant below as if the words were divided like this:

go tu pa teight /ɡɒ tʌ pə teɪt/

Listen to the chant and repeat. The rhythm of each line is the same. The symbol ‿ shows where the consonant sound joins to the vowel sound of the next word.

Got‿up‿at‿eight,
Got‿on‿a bus,
Went‿into work,
Worked‿until two,
Went‿out for lunch,
Worked‿until six,
Back‿on the bus,
Switched‿on the box,
Slept‿in‿a chair.

box = television

C

[B31] When one word ends with a consonant sound and the next word begins with a similar consonant sound, speakers may cut one of them in fast speech. For example, *Asked Tom* may sound like *Ask Tom*.

Listen to the differences in these phrases.

consonant – vowel	**consonant – consonant**
I asked Alice.	I asked Tom.
The shop's open.	The shop's shut.
I called Andy.	I called David.
Six* eggs.	Six spoons.
He walked away.	He walked towards me.

* The letter X is two separate sounds: /k/ and /s/, so *six* = /sɪks/.

Exercises

25.1 In each sentence, one phrase does not make sense. Replace it with a phrase which sounds the same from the box.

> phoned your   joined us   felt rain   no news is   stopped using
> ships take   ~~'s no good~~   heard you lie

EXAMPLE   It ~~snow good~~; I can't fix it. ....'s no good.......

1 Known uses good news, as they say. ....
2 Have you phone jaw parents this week? ....
3 I've never her July before. ....
4 I think I fell train; let's go inside. ....
5 These ship steak cars across the river. ....
6 They join does for dinner. ....
7 We stop choosing the typewriter when we got the computer. ....

25.2 **⏺ B32** Show where you can join a word ending with a consonant sound to a word starting with a vowel sound using this symbol: ‿ (there are nine in total). Then listen and practise saying the poem.

There was‿an old man called Greg,

Who tried to break open an egg.

He kicked it around,

But fell on the ground,

And found that he'd broken a leg.

25.3 **⏺ B32 (cont.)** In each pair of highlighted words, look at the final consonant in the first word. Is it cut or is it joined to the next word? If it is cut, cross it out. If it joins the next word, draw this symbol: ‿

EXAMPLE   Walter walke̶d towards the waiter; Walter's waiter walked‿away.
             /wɔːkt̶ təˈwɔːdz/   /wɔːkt‿əˈweɪ/

1 Tim and Heather worked together ; Heather never worked alone.

2 Susan ate six sweets at six o'clock and was sick.

3 Lenny talked a lot but he never talked to Lottie.

4 Simon's shop sells only socks; Sara's shop sells skirts and tops

> **Follow-up:** Listen to the sentences and practise saying them.

26 War and peace
Vowel sounds at word boundaries

A

[B33] Many words which end with consonant letters in fact end with a vowel sound. The letters Y and W are pronounced as vowels at the end of a word, and the letter R is silent at the end of a word in the accent from the South of England. (In other accents such as American or Scottish, it is pronounced; see Unit 56.)

So, for example, the words below end with consonant letters (in blue) but with vowel sounds. This is clear from the phonemic spelling.

play /pleɪ/
how /haʊ/
war /wɔː/

However, if the following word begins with a vowel sound, you hear the consonant letter pronounced slightly, in order to separate the vowel sound at the end of the first word from the vowel sound at the start of the next word.

play a game /pleɪj‿ə geɪm/
how about /haʊw‿ə'baʊt/
war and peace /wɔːr‿ən piːs/

Listen to the examples.

/j/	/w/	/r/
play‿a game	how‿about	war‿and peace
try‿again	know‿a place	far‿away
fly‿away	a few‿ideas	more‿or less

B

[B34] You may hear the sounds /j/, /w/ and /r/ pronounced even if the first word *doesn't* end with those letters in the spelling.

free and easy /friːj‿n iːzɪ/
do a job /duːw‿ə dʒɒb/
draw a picture /drɔːr‿ə 'pɪktʃə/

Listen to the examples.

/j/	/w/	/r/
free‿and easy	do‿a job	draw‿a picture
high‿and low	go‿and see	my idea‿of fun
tea‿or coffee	it's too‿easy	law‿and order

C

[B35] Many letters of the alphabet are pronounced with vowel sounds at the beginning or end, so you hear the sounds /j/, /w/ or /r/ put between letters when spelling aloud.

Listen to these three letters pronounced continuously, one after the other:
R-O-A-R-O-A-R-O-A-R-O-A-R-O-A

Notice that:

• R and O are separated by /r/.

• O and A are separated by /w/.

• A and R are separated by /j/.

Now listen to someone spelling out these names:

RORY   PILAR   IAN   CAROL   ERNEST

Exercises

26.1 In each line of this text, there are places where one word ends with a vowel sound and the next word begins with a vowel sound. Put a ‿ symbol to show these places. The sounds which are used to separate the vowels are shown at the end of each line.

It's four‿o'clock, more‿or less. /r/ /r/
The sky above is grey and there's snow on the ground. /j/ /j/ /w/
Where am I? No idea. /r/ /w/
I'll find somewhere dry and try and make a fire. /j/ /j/
Oh – there's an old house. Is the door open? /r/
'Hello, is there anybody in there?' Can't hear anything. /r/ /j/ /r/
There's a chair and a few old books – and a fire in the fireplace. /r/ /w/ /r/
The owner can't be far away … /j/ /r/

> **Follow-up:** Now practise saying the story, joining the words together.

26.2 🔊 B36 Listen to the phrases and put them in the correct column of the table according to the consonant sound between the first and second word. There should be three phrases in each column. Then repeat the phrases.

> ~~blue and green~~   me and you   saw a film   true or false   draw a line
> tie a knot   no idea   law against   three or four

/ j /	/ w /	/ r /
	blue and green	

26.3 🔊 B37 Listen to these short dialogues. What consonant sound do you hear where you see the ‿ symbol? Write /j/, /w/ or /r/ at the end of each line.

EXAMPLE   **A:** I went to‿a museum yesterday. /w/
                B: Oh. Did you see‿anything interesting? /j/

1 A: You don't look well – are you‿all right? / /
   B: No, I think I've got flu‿again. / /

2 A: I saw‿a good film on Friday called *Titanic* / /
   B: Oh, that's so‿old! / /

3 A: Would you like a cup of tea‿or something? / /
   B: No thanks. I'm about to go‿out. / /

4 A: Can you tell me‿a quick way to get to the beach? / /
   B: Sure – I'll draw‿a map for you. / /

26.4 🔊 B37 (cont.) Spell out these names. Record yourself, if possible. Then listen to the CD recording and compare it with yours.

1 TOM   **2** BEN   **3** ERIN   **4** TANIA   **5** ROSIE

27 Saturday September 13th
Introducing word stress

A

We can divide a word into syllables. A syllable is a vowel sound (shown in blue below) and the consonant sounds that go with it. So, for example, if a word has three vowel sounds, it has three syllables.

day /deɪ/ = one syllable
Friday /ˈfraɪdeɪ/ = two syllables
Saturday /ˈsætədeɪ/ = three syllables

If a word has more than one syllable, you give stress to one of the syllables. To give it stress, do one or more of these to the syllable:

• Make it longer: **Sat**urday

• Make it louder: **Sat** urday

• Make it higher: **Sat**urday

We can show stress with circles: each circle is a syllable and the bigger circle shows which syllable has the stress. For example, *Saturday* is ●●●. In phonemic spelling, the stress is shown by the symbol ' at the start of the stressed syllable: /ˈsætədeɪ/.

B

B38 Different words have different stress patterns (patterns of stressed and unstressed syllables).

Listen to these two- and three-syllable words.

●● April, **thir**ty, **mor**ning, **Sun**day	●●● Sep**tem**ber, to**mor**row, e**lev**enth
●● Ju**ly**, mid**day**, thir**teen**, to**day**, thir**teenth**	●●● after**noon**, seven**teen**, twenty-**one**
●●● **Sat**urday, **thir**tieth, **yes**terday, **hol**iday, **sev**enty	

 Note: The stress pattern of numbers with -*teen* is sometimes different when the word is in a sentence. For example, the normal stress pattern of *nineteen* is ●●, but when it is followed by a noun, e.g. *the nineteen nineties*, *nineteen people*, the pattern is ●●.

 Note: *January* and *February* may be pronounced with the stress patterns ●●● or ●●●●.

C

B39 Stress patterns can help you to hear the difference between similar words, e.g. numbers ending in -*teen* or -*ty*.

Listen to these examples.

●●	●●
thir**teen**	**thir**ty
four**teen**	**for**ty
six**teen**	**six**ty
eigh**teen**	**eigh**ty
nine**teen**	**nine**ty

Exercises

27.1 Write the full versions of these words in the correct column, according to their stress pattern.

M̶o̶n̶ Tues Thu Sat today tomorrow Apr Jul Aug Sept Oct
Nov holiday 2nd 11th 13 30 13th 30th 17 70 afternoon

●●	●●	●●●	●●●	●●●
Monday				

27.2 Write one word from 27.1 in the gap in each sentence below. The word must have the stress pattern shown in brackets. Then say the sentences.

1 I'm going to have a party on .... (●●●).
2 My grandfather is .... (●●●) years old.
3 I often sleep for an hour in the .... (●●●).
4 My birthday is on the .... (●●●) of March.
5 In Europe, the weather is warm in .... (●●).
6 I left school when I was .... (●●●).
7 Goodnight. See you .... (●●●).
8 How long is your summer .... (●●●)?

27.3 [B40] Write the stress patterns under each of the blue words in the dialogue. Then listen and check.

A: When do you begin your holiday?
　　　　　　　 ●●　　　●●●

B: On the thirtieth of August.

A: That's next Saturday!

B: We're leaving in the afternoon.

A: And when are you coming back?

B: Saturday September the thirteenth.

A: Thirtieth?

B: No, thirteenth!

Follow-up: Play the recording again. Pause after each line and repeat it.

27.4 [B40 (cont.)] Listen and underline the number you hear.

1 100 dollars! It only cost *17 / 70* last year!
2 He was the *14th / 40th* president of my country.
3 The maximum number of people is *15 / 50*.
4 She was born in *1916 / 1960*.
5 He was *13 / 30* on his last birthday.
6 She'll be *18 / 80* in March.

Follow-up: Record yourself saying the sentences in 27.4, choosing one of the two words. Make a note of which words you say. Then listen to your recording in about two weeks. Is it clear which words you said?

28 Forest, forget
Stress in two-syllable words

A

B41 Listen to this description of a village in the north of England. All the blue nouns and adjectives have two syllables. Notice how they are pronounced.

Cartmel's a **love**ly **litt**le **vill**age in Cumbria. It's by a **riv**er and the **build**ings are all made of stone. There are lots of **gard**ens with **flow**ers, and the **peo**ple are really **friend**ly. It's in a **vall**ey with **for**ests and you can see the **moun**tains in the **dist**ance. It's **fam**ous for its old church, the horse races in **summ**er, and the su**perb** fishing.

Notice that:

- Most two-syllable nouns and adjectives have the pattern ●• (the stress is on the first syllable).

- There are some exceptions. For example, the adjective *superb* in the text has the pattern •● (the stress is on the second syllable). Other examples with the pattern •●: *asleep*, *mistake*, *machine*, *alone*.

B

B42 Listen to this advice for a visitor to Rio de Janeiro, Brazil. All the blue verbs have two syllables. Notice how they are pronounced.

If you de**cide** to go to Niteroi, take the ferry. It's the best way to **trav**el. You can just re**lax** and en**joy** the view, and you be**gin** the day feeling re**freshed**. Don't for**get** to **vis**it Fort Santa Cruz if you can – ask someone to ex**plain** where the bus goes from. But make sure you ar**rive** back at the ferry port before the last boat re**turns** to Rio!

Notice that:

- The most common pattern for two-syllable verbs is •● (the stress is on the second syllable).

- There are plenty of exceptions. For example, the verbs *travel* and *visit* in the text have the pattern ●• (the stress is on the first syllable). Here are more examples with the pattern ●•: *cancel*, *copy*, *answer*, *enter*, *offer*, *listen*, *happen*, *open*.

- Words which come directly from a verb usually keep the same stress pattern as the verb. For example, the adjective *refreshed* in the text comes from the verb *refresh* and has the same stress pattern: •●.

C

B43 Some words are both nouns and verbs. For example, *record* is a noun if you put stress on the first syllable, and a verb if you put stress on the second syllable. Listen to these examples. You will hear each word twice, first as a noun and then as a verb:

record   contrast   desert   export   object   present   produce   protest   rebel

 Note: There is not always a change of stress in words that are both nouns and verbs. For example, *answer*, *picture*, *promise*, *reply*, *travel*, *visit* have stress on the same syllable whether they are verbs or nouns.

 Note: The stress stays in the same place when we make longer words from these two-syllable nouns, adjectives and verbs. For example, in both *happy* (●•) and *unhappy* (•●•), the stress is on the syllable *happ*, and in both *depart* (•●) and *departure* (•●•), the stress is on the syllable *part*.

Exercises

28.1 `B44` Underline all the examples of nouns and adjectives with the pattern ●● in this text. There are 19 in total. Then listen and check.

This is a picture of a kitchen. There's a basket with apples, lemons and an orange. There are a few onions and carrots, and there's a cupboard with some sugar and coffee. There are yellow curtains with a flower pattern in the window. Outside, there's a garden and the weather is sunny.

> **Follow-up:** Practise saying the text. Be careful to pronounce the underlined words with the pattern ●●.

28.2 `B45` Look at the verbs in these sentences and underline the syllable which is stressed. Most of the verbs have the pattern ●● but some have the pattern ●●. Listen and check. Then listen again, pause after each sentence and repeat.

Did you	forget to cancel agree to delay expect to repeat begin to enjoy offer to explain decide to return	the visit?

I	listened and answered received and copied arrived and entered relaxed and enjoyed tidied and repaired unlocked and opened	the questions. the document. the building. the film. the car. the door.

28.3 `B46` Listen and underline the word with a different stress pattern from the others.

EXAMPLE money **machine** mountain message

1	answer	agree	allow	attract
2	middle	minute	mission	mistake
3	compare	correct	copy	collect
4	garden	granny	guitar	grammar
5	complete	common	careful	crazy
6	pronounce	provide	promise	prefer
7	shampoo	shoulder	shower	shopping
8	reason	remove	receive	review

28.4 `B47` Read the sentences and write in the correct stress pattern for the words in blue. Then listen, check and repeat.

EXAMPLE   I got my first record as a present when I was eleven.
record = ●●   present = ●●

1 You've progressed well this year, but I'd like to see even more progress.
progressed = ... progress = ...

2 We import too much petrol and the country's export figures are going down.
import = ... export = ...

3 It started as a student protest, but now the army has rebelled against the government.
protest = ... rebelled = ...

4 In the desert, there is a big contrast between temperatures in the day and at night.
desert = ... contrast = ...

5 These companies produce household objects such as fridges and washing machines.
produce = ... objects = ...

29

Second-hand bookshop
Stress in compound words

A Compound words are made from two smaller words put together, e.g. *book + shop* = *bookshop*. (They may be written as two words, separate or joined with a hyphen, e.g. *shoe shop, half-price*.) In most compound words, the stress is on the first part. For example, the word *bookshop* has two syllables and the stress is on the first syllable.

Listen to these examples.

●•   **book**shop, **bus** stop, **foot**path, **air**port, **shoe** shop, **road** sign, **car** park, **bed**room
●••   **traf**fic light, **bus** station, **sun**glasses, **board**ing card, **win**dow seat, **check**-in desk
●•••   **tra**vel agent, **art** gallery, **su**permarket, **tape** recorder, **pho**tocopy

 Note: If the first part of the compound word is an adjective, there may be stress on the second part too, e.g. ●•● *double room*.

 Note: There may be stress on the second part of a compound noun when:

- the object in the second part is made out of the material in the first part, e.g. ●● *glass jar*

- the first part tells us what type the second part is, e.g. ●● *car door*.

B If the compound word is *not* a noun, we often put stress on the second part too.

Listen to these examples.

●●   **first class, half-price, handmade**
●●•   **bad-temp**ered, **old-fash**ioned, **short-sight**ed
●•●   **over**night, **sec**ond-**hand**

C Sometimes a compound word looks the same as:

- a normal adjective and noun

- a normal noun and verb

but the pronunciation is different. Compare:

●• compound word	●● adjective and noun
We keep these plants in a **green**house during the winter months.	Mr Olsen lives in a small, **green house** next to the river.
●• compound word	●● noun and verb
I saw her **bus** pass.	I saw her **bus pass**.

1

2

Exercises

29.1 🔊 B50 Listen. Write the blue words from the text in the correct columns.

> There's a good shopping centre. You can find almost anything there. There
> are bookshops, shoe shops, a travel agent's, a post office, a hairdresser's,
> a supermarket, everything … and there are a few snack bars if you want
> a hamburger or something. Oh, and there's a sports centre too, with a
> swimming pool and a playground for the kids. But be careful with your
> handbag; I had my credit card stolen there once!

●•	●••	●•••
bookshops	anything	shopping centre

Follow-up: Record yourself saying the text. Make sure you put
the stress in the correct place.

29.2 🔊 B51 Listen. In each sentence, one of the compound words (in blue) has stress on the first
part (●•) and the other has stress on both parts (●●). Underline the word with stress on
both parts (●●). Now listen again and repeat.

EXAMPLE   They did the photocopies <u>overnight</u>.

1 I got this motorbike second-hand.
2 Using a typewriter is so old-fashioned.
3 These earrings were handmade.

4 I'm short-sighted, like my grandmother.
5 All the sunglasses are half-price.
6 The waiting room is for first class only.

29.3 🔊 B51 (cont.) Listen. Which thing is the speaker asking about? Put a tick (✓) next to the
correct picture and write *Yes, I have* or *No, I haven't!* Give a true answer!

EXAMPLE

 a ☐   b ✓   Have you ever seen a ski jump? …

.... No, I haven't! ....

1 a ☐   b ☐   ....

3 a ☐   b ☐   ....

2 a ☐   b ☐   ....

4 a ☐   b ☐   ....

A We can build longer words by adding parts to the beginning or end of shorter words. Usually, this does not change the stress; it stays on the same syllable as in the original word. Look at this example.

	for	**get**		
	for	**get**	ful	
	for	**get**	ful	ness
	for	**gett**	a	ble
un	for	**gett**	a	ble

It was an unforgettable holiday.

Here is a list of beginnings and endings which do not change the stress of the shorter word:

-able (**drink**able)	-hood (**child**hood)	-ish (**child**ish)	-ness (**happ**iness)
-al (**mus**ical)	in- / im- (im**poss**ible)	-less (**child**less)	-ship (**friend**ship)
-er (**play**er)	-ing (**bor**ing)	-ly (**friend**ly)	un- (un**happ**y)
-ful (**help**ful)	-ise / -ize (**civ**ilise / ize)	-ment (em**ploy**ment)	under- (under**pay**)

B 🔊 B52 Some endings *do* change the stress in the shorter word. Listen and look at how the ending *-ion* changes the stress in the word *educate*.

ed	u	cate	
ed	u	**ca**	tion

When we add the endings *-ion* or *-ian*, the stress always moves to the syllable *before* these endings. Here are some more examples.

e	**lec**	tric	
e	lec	**tri**	cian

dec	o	rate	
dec	o	**ra**	tion

mu	sic	
mu	**si**	cian

co	**mmu**	ni	cate	
co	mmu	ni	**ca**	tion

Note: *-tion* and *-cian* are pronounced /ʃən/.

C 🔊 B53 The ending *-ic* also moves the stress to the syllable before it.

Listen to these examples.

scientist	scien**tif**ic
e**con**omy	eco**nom**ic
atom	a**tom**ic
artist	ar**tist**ic

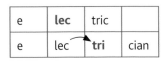 **Note:** When a syllable changes from unstressed to stressed, or stressed to unstressed, the vowel sound often changes. For example, the letter O in *atom* is pronounced /ə/, but in *atomic*, it is pronounced /ɒ/.

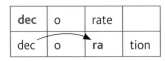 **Note:** The ending *-al* does not change the stress of the word (see Section A above), so, for example, the stress is on the same syllable in these two words: eco**nom**ic, eco**nom**ical.

Exercises

30.1 ⏵B54 Use the beginnings and endings in A on the opposite page to make longer words from the words below. Listen and check. Then listen again and repeat.

EXAMPLE child *childhood, childish, childishness, childless*

1 believe ....

2 enjoy ....

3 care ....

30.2 Write the words from the box in the correct part of the table according to their stress pattern.

population telecommunication nation identification relation communication pronunciation scientific clinic romantic pessimistic investigation public discussion

●●	
●●●	
●●●●	population
●●●●●	
●●●●●●	
●●●●●●●	

30.3 Combine each word below with one of the endings from the box, and write the stress pattern of your new word. You may need to change, add or remove other letters to the first word. Use a dictionary to help you if necessary.

-ion -ic

EXAMPLE inform .... *information* ....   ●●●●

1 introduce ....

2 base ....

3 economy ....

4 describe ....

5 romance ....

6 compete ....

7 optimist ....

8 celebrate ....

9 diplomat ....

10 operate ....

11 explain ....

12 decide ....

31 Public, publicity
Stress in longer words 2

A

B55 There are many longer word endings where the last letter is *-y*. In words with these endings, the stress is placed on the syllable which is two from the end. Listen to these examples, and notice that the stress is on a different syllable in the related words.

pub	lic			
pub	**lic**	i	ty	

na	tion	al		
na	tio	**nal**	i	ty

pho	to	graph		
pho	**tog**	raph	y	

de	mo	crat		
de	**mo**	cra	cy	

per	son			
per	son	**al**	i	ty

tech	nic	al		
tech	**no**	lo	gy	

 Note: If we add the ending *-ic* to a word, the stress goes on the syllable before *-ic*. (See Unit 30.) Notice the change of stress, e.g. pho**tog**raphy, photo**graph**ic.

 Note: In words for an expert in a subject, e.g. *photographer,* the stress stays on the same syllable as in the word ending in *-y*: pho**tog**raphy, pho**tog**rapher.

B

B56 Many words for school and university subjects have either one of the *-y* endings listed above or the ending *-ics*.

Listen to the names of subjects in this text.

> At school, I hated science subjects like physics, chemistry and biology, you know, and … erm … I wasn't very good at mathematics and things. I really liked subjects like history and geography. Anyway, when I went to university, I wanted to do economics, but I couldn't 'cause I was no good at maths, so in the end I did philosophy!

 Note: Many English speakers do not pronounce the second syllable in *history*, so that it sounds like this: /'hɪstri/ ●•. The first part of the word *geography* may be pronounced as one or two syllables: /'dʒɒgrəfi/ ●•• or /dʒiˈɒgrəfi / •●••. Many speakers do not pronounce the second syllable in *mathematics*, so it sounds like this: /mæθˈmætɪks/ •●•.

C

B57 If we combine the various endings in this unit and Unit 30, we can get 'families' of words with moving stress patterns.

Listen to these examples.

photograph	e**con**omy	**dem**ocrat	**na**tion
pho**tog**raphy	eco**nom**ics	de**moc**racy	**na**tional
photo**graph**ic	eco**nom**ical	demo**crat**ic	natio**nal**ity

Exercises

31.1 Make a word ending in *-ity* from each of the words below, and write the stress pattern. Use a dictionary to help you if necessary.

EXAMPLE author <u>authority</u> ....●●●●.....

1 person ....

2 universe ....

3 public ....

4 major ....

5 nation ....

6 real ....

7 able ....

8 electric ....

31.2 Write the words from the box in the correct column according to their stress pattern.

> ~~economics~~ economy physics chemistry geography /ˈdʒɒɡrəfi/
> mathematics /ˌmæθəˈmætɪks/ technology history /ˈhɪstri/ geology
> photography nation nationality

●●	●●●	●●●●	●●●●●	●●●●●
				economics

31.3 ▣B58 Fill each gap with a word from the box which has the stress pattern given. Then listen and check.

> biology mathematics history geography technology ~~chemistry~~

My favourite subjects at school were sciences, especially
●●● ......<u>chemistry</u>...... and ●●●● .... I've always been
good with numbers, so I was good at ●●●● ....
I didn't really like the social science subjects like ●●● ....
and ●● .... When I went to university, I did computer
●●●● ....

31.4 ▣B58 (cont.) Write the word which is missing from each family. The stress pattern will help you. Then listen, check and repeat.

EXAMPLE science, scientist, ...<u>scientific</u>............ (●●●●)

1 electric, electrical, ... (●●●●●)

2 .... (●●●●), biologist, biological

3 real, realise, ... (●●●●)

4 create, creative, ... (●●●●●)

5 act, active, ... (●●●●)

32 Tea for two
Introducing stress patterns

A

🔊 B59 Many words in English are unstressed when they are in sentences. For example, when you say the words *to* or *for* on their own, they sound like the numbers *two* and *four*. However, normally when they are in the middle of sentences, *to* and *for* <u>don't</u> sound like numbers because they are unstressed.

Listen and compare the different stress patterns.

● = stressed word; ● = unstressed word.

● ● ●   ● ● ●
121   One to one.
123   One to three.
T42   Tea for two.
Wait four hours.   Wait for hours.

B

Words which are usually unstressed in the middle of a sentence are called *function words*. Words which are stressed are called *content words*. Here's a list:

function words (unstressed)	content words (stressed)
prepositions (e.g. *to*, *for*)	nouns (e.g. *hour*, *tea*)
the verb *be* (e.g. *is*, *are*, *was*)	main verbs (e.g. *play*, *wait*)
auxiliary verbs (e.g. *can*, *does*)	adjectives and adverbs (e.g. *good*, *quickly*)
articles (e.g. *the*, *an*)	question words (e.g. *who*, *what*)
conjunctions (e.g. *and*, *or*)	contractions with *not* (e.g. *can't*, *isn't*)
personal pronouns (e.g. *you*, *her*)	

The symbol ● represents unstressed syllables. These may be whole words or syllables of a longer word. For example, the phrase *middle of the night* has the stress pattern ●●●●. The three ●●● in this pattern are the second syllable of *middle* and the unstressed words *of* and *the*.

⚠️ **Note:**

- Speakers may choose to stress function words to create a special meaning. For example, the normal pattern for *What do you want?* is ●●●●. However, you can choose to stress the pronoun *you* if you want to contrast it with another pronoun:

  (*I know what he wants, but*) *what do YOU want?* (See Units 40–44.)

- In this book, we only use the ● and ● symbols for normal patterns, not for special meanings.

- If you stress function words by mistake, it may cause a misunderstanding because your listener may look for a special meaning.

- Function words are sometimes stressed at the end of a sentence. For example, the sentence *Yes, I do* has the pattern ●●●.

C

🔊 B60 When you hear sentences in English, you can hear the combination of stressed and unstressed words and syllables as a stress pattern. If this pattern is regular, you can hear it as a regular rhythm.

Listen to the poem below, which has a rhythm of four stressed syllables in each line, each one separated by two unstressed syllables: (●)●●●●●●●●●●●

Leaves on the **trees** and the **sun** in the **sky**;
The **breeze** is so **fresh** and the **grass** is so **high**.
Gone is the **autumn** of **yell**ow and **gold**.
Gone are the **nights** of the **winter** so **cold**.
Wake in the **morning** to **black**birds that **sing**.
These are the **things** that I **love** about **spring**.

Exercises

32.1 ▣ B61 Listen and underline the word you hear.

  1 Omar needs *to / two* clean shirts ready for his trip.
  2 Nadia waited *for / four* months to get her visa.
  3 We had *to / two* open doors for visitors.
  4 Caroline worked *for / four* years in a bank.
  5 My son can count one *to / two* three.
  6 You don't want the soil *to / too* dry.

32.2 ▣ B62 Listen and underline the sentence which does *not* have the same stress pattern as the word at the beginning of the line.

  EXAMPLE ●•• cinema   Wasn't it?   Hasn't she?   <u>Don't you?</u>

  1 •●• tomato   Close the door.   He told me.   I like it.
  2 ••● afternoon Does he drive?   Were you cold?   What happened?
  3 •●• December   It's open.   They arrived.   They listened.

32.3 ▣ B63 Write the sentences from the box in the correct columns of the table. Then listen, check and repeat

> ~~The bus was late.~~   Come and look.   Close the window.   What do you want?
> The water's cold.   Give me a call.   What did she say?   Phone and tell me.
> Nice to see you.   Where's the car?   It's cold and wet.   What's the time?

●••●	•●•●	●•●	●•●•
	The bus was late.		

32.4 ▣ B63 (cont.) Read this poem. Underline each stressed word or syllable. Write the stress pattern after each line. Then listen, check, pause after each line and repeat.

  The <u>evening</u> was <u>cold</u> and <u>dark</u>.   •●••●•●........................

  I was walking my dog in the park.   ....

  He chased a cat   ....

  And fancy that!   ....

  It suddenly started to bark.   ....

33

He asked her her name
Pronouns in stress patterns

A

🔊 B64 Listen to this poem. Notice that the pronouns and the possessive determiners (e.g. *his*, *her*), in blue below, are unstressed.

Grace and Paul

He **saw** her, he **liked** her **face**,
He **asked** her her **name**, she **said** it was **Grace**.
She **liked** him, his **name** was **Paul**,
She **gave** him her **numb**er, he **gave** her a **call**.

He **bought** her a **gift**, he **went** to her **flat**.
She **gave** him a **drink**, she **showed** him her **cat**.
He **liked** her, but **hat**ed her **cat**.
He **nev**er re**turn**ed, and **that** was **that**.

Notice that:

- In fast speech, speakers may cut the sound /h/ from *he*, *his*, *him* and *her*.

- The /r/ at the end of *her* is often pronounced if the next word begins with a vowel sound.

B

Here are some typical stress patterns for short sentences containing pronouns and possessive determiners (e.g. *her*, *my*, *our*).

•	●	•
He	saw	her.
I	liked	him.
We	heard	them.

•	●	•	●
He	liked	her	face.
I	lost	my	keys.
You	met	our	son.

•	●	•	•	●
She	showed	him	her	cat.
You	told	me	your	name.
They	lent	us	their	car.

 Note: Pronouns and possessive determiners may be stressed to give a special meaning, e.g., *I lost **my** keys* to contrast with *I didn't lose **your** keys*. See Units 40–44.

C

🔊 B65 Pronouns often join together with *be*, *have* and *will* to form contractions. Listen to these three rhymes. Notice that the pronouns with contractions (in blue) are unstressed.

pronoun + *be*	pronoun + *have*	pronoun + *will*
/æm/ I'm waiting.	/æv/ I've sold it.	/æl/ I'll see them.
/jə/ You're talking.	/jəv/ You've bought it.	/jəl/ You'll choose them.
/hɪz/ He's sitting.	/hɪz/ He's dropped it.	/hɪl/ He'll buy them.
/ʃɪz/ She's walking.	/ʃɪz/ She's caught it.	/ʃɪl/ She'll lose them.
/ðeʳ/ They're speaking.	/ðev/ They've pushed it.	/ðel/ They'll find them.
Complaining	/ɪts/ It's open.	/wɪl/ We'll send them.
/wɪ/ We're watching.	/wɪv/ We've kicked it.	/ɪtᵊl/ It'll help if
/ɪts/ It's raining.	/ɪts/ It's broken.	they mend them.

Notice that all the contractions are pronounced as one unstressed syllable, except *it'll* which is pronounced as two syllables.

 Note: Don't use contractions at the end of a sentence; say *Yes, I am*, not ~~Yes, I'm~~.

Exercises

33.1 ▶B66 Listen and read these phonemic spellings of sentences from the poem *Grace and Paul*. Write the matching sentences from the poem. Practise saying them.

EXAMPLE /iːˈsɔːrə/ .... He saw her ....

1 /iːˈlaɪktəˈfeɪs/ ....

2 /iːˈɑːsktərəˈneɪm/ ....

3 /ʃɪˈɡeɪvɪməˈnʌmbə/ ....

4 /iːˈbɔːtərəˈɡɪft/ ....

5 /ʃɪˈʃəʊdɪməˈkæt/ ....

33.2 ▶B67 Make as many sentences as possible using the words in the boxes. Write the sentences after the appropriate stress patterns. Then listen, check, pause after each sentence and repeat.

EXAMPLE | I, me, my, you, your, saw, lent, car |

•●•   I saw you, You saw me ....

•●•●   I saw your car, I saw my car, You saw my car, You saw your car

•●••●   I lent you my car, You lent me your car ....

1 | we, us, our, they, them, their, thanked, showed, house |

•●•   ....

•●••●   ....

2 | she, her, I, me, my, met, friend |

•●•   ....

•●••●   ....

....

3 | he, him, his, you, your, a, bought, told, asked, drink, name, question |

•●••●   ....

....

....

33.3 ▶B68 Listen and write the words you hear in the gaps.

EXAMPLE   Can you tell ......her...... to call ......me......., please?

1 Can you give .... to .... , please?

2 Did .... meet .... daughter, Catherine?

3 I don't think .... likes ....

4 What did .... say to .... ?

5 Where did .... buy .... guitar?

6 What's .... mother's name?

7 Where are .... parents from?

8 .... bought presents for .... children.

33.4 ▶B69 Rewrite the sentences below, changing the names to pronouns and making the auxiliary verbs (e.g. *be / have / will*) into contractions. Then write the stress patterns. There should be two stressed syllables in each sentence. Listen, check and repeat.

EXAMPLE   Helen has given Robert some money. She's given him some money. •●••●•

1 Robert is buying presents for the children. ....

2 Bonnie and Max are opening their presents. ....

3 Bonnie and Max will thank Robert for the presents. ....

4 Robert will thank Helen for the money. ....

34 The place is clean
The verb *to be* in stress patterns

A 🔊 B70 Listen to the rhymes below. Notice the pronunciation of the verb *to be* in blue.

A happy hotel guest ...	An unhappy hotel guest ...
The **place** is **clean**,	The **place** was **cold**,
The **gard**en's **green**,	The **sheets** were **old**,
The **beds** aren't **old**,	The **walls** weren't **white**,
The **place** isn't **cold**,	The **room** wasn't **light**,
The **sheets** are **new**,	The **bath** wasn't **long**,
The **blank**ets are **blue**,	The **smell** was **strong**,
The **carp**ets are **thick**,	The **doors** were **low**,
The **serv**ice is **quick**,	The **serv**ice was **slow**,
The **rest**aurant's **fine**,	The **staff** weren't **nice**,
Excellent **wine**.	I **think** there were **mice**,
The **place** is **nice**	The **bed** wasn't **right**,
And a **wond**erful **price**!	A **terr**ible **night**!

Notice that:

- The verb *is* is contracted to *'s* except after words ending in the following sounds: /s/, /z/, /ʃ/, /dʒ/ and /tʃ/. Compare *The garden's green* and *The place is clean*.

- The negative contractions *aren't* and *weren't* have one syllable, but *isn't* and *wasn't* have two.

- Many speakers don't pronounce the /r/ in *are* and *were*. However, the /r/ is pronounced if the next word begins with a vowel sound. Compare *were low* and *were old*.

- Speakers often cut the final *-t* in the negative contractions. However, the final *-t* is normally pronounced if the next word begins with a vowel sound. Compare *isn't cold* and *aren't old*.

- After a pronoun, *am*, *is* and *are* are usually written as a contraction (*'m*, *'s*, *'re*). (See Unit 33.)

B The verbs *is*, *are*, *was* and *were* are normally unstressed, but they are stressed in negative contractions and at the end of sentences. Compare the stress patterns:

•	●	•	●
The	**place**	is	**clean.**

•	●	●	●
The	**beds**	aren't	**old.**

•	•	●
Is	it	**clean?**
Are	they	**old?**

●	•	●
Yes,	it	**is.**
No,	they	**aren't.**

 Note: The verbs *is*, *are*, *was* and *were* may be stressed for special meaning. For example, stress may be used to disagree, as in this short dialogue:
   A: The sheets aren't clean.
   B: They **are** clean – I washed them yesterday!
For more on this, see Units 40–44.

C Because they are unstressed, it may be difficult to hear the difference between *is* and *was*, and *are* and *were*. Listen for the /w/; if you hear it, the sentence is in the past. Look at the phonemic spellings of these sentences. Notice that the /w/ is sometimes the only difference.

present	past
The place is clean. /ðə'pleɪsɪz'kliːn/	The place was clean. /ðə'pleɪswəz'kliːn/
The sheets are new. /ðə'ʃiːtsə'njuː/	The sheets were new. /ðə'ʃiːtswə'njuː/

English Pronunciation in Use Intermediate

Exercises

34.1 [🔊B71] Look again at the rhymes about the hotel guests on the opposite page. Find two more examples for each of the stress patterns below and write them in the correct tables. Use the **bold** type to help you decide. Listen, check, pause after each sentence and repeat. You will hear <u>all</u> the examples.

1

•	●	•	●
The	place	is	clean

3

•	●	●•	●
The	place	isn't	cold

2

•	●	●	●
The	beds	aren't	old

4

•	●•	•	●
The	carpets	are	thick

34.2 [🔊B72] Look at the blue sentences in this dialogue. Write the stress patterns.

Alice: I stayed at the best hotel in town.
Ben: Wow! Was it nice? ●●● ....
Alice: Yes, it was. ●●● ....
It was wonderful! ....
Ben: How much was it? ....
Alice: It wasn't cheap. ....
Ben: Was it worth it? ....
Alice: Yes. I think it was. ....
Ben: Were the staff good? ....
Alice: Yes, they were. ....
They were great! ....
Ben: Um, sounds fabulous. Lucky you!

Follow-up: Listen to the recording. Pause and repeat after each line.

34.3 [🔊B73] Listen and underline the verb you hear.

1 People *are / were* angry.
2 Alice *is / was* here.
3 Your face *is / was* dirty.
4 The birds *are / were* singing.
5 The books *are / were* cheap.
6 The fish *are / were* dying.
7 The place *is / was* nice.
8 Paris *is / was* nice.
9 The children *are / were* tired.
10 My friends *are / were* coming.

34.4 [🔊B73 (cont.)] Listen and fill each gap with one word.

EXAMPLE   That ....*was*........ my favourite.

1 His parents .... rich.
2 The birds .... singing.
3 The beach .... crowded.
4 The children .... at home.
5 He .... going out at the weekend.
6 Her dog .... called Kip.
7 This car .... very expensive.
8 The drinks .... free on this flight.
9 The weather .... terrible.
10 The banks .... closed on Saturday.

35

What do you think?
Auxiliary verbs in stress patterns

A

🔊 B74 Listen to the rhyme below. Notice the pronunciation of the auxiliary verbs in blue.

The Spies

Where did they **meet**?	**Who** did he **ring**?	**Where** have they **been**?
What did they **say**?	**What** will they **drink**?	**Where** did they **go**?
What did they **eat**?	**What** will he **bring**?	**What** does it **mean**?
How did they **pay**?	**What** do you **think**?	**What** do you **know**?

Notice that:

- Auxiliary verbs and pronouns are usually unstressed, so Wh-questions often have the stress pattern ●••●:

●	•	•	●
Wh-word	auxiliary verb	pronoun	main verb
What	do	you	**do?**

- Other stress patterns occur when the sentence contains other unstressed syllables, e.g., *Where do you come from* = ●••●•.

- *Do* as a main verb is pronounced /duː/ (rhymes with *two*), but as an unstressed auxiliary verb it is pronounced /də/. So the two examples of *do* in the sentence *What do you do?* are pronounced differently.

B

🔊 B75 Auxiliary verbs *are* stressed in negative contractions and at the end of sentences. Listen to these examples.

Yes, I **do**.
I **don't know**.
Yes, I **will**.
He **won't say**.
Yes, I **have**.
I **haven't done** it.
Yes, I **can**.
I **can't help**.

 Note: Auxiliary verbs can also be stressed for emphasis or contrast, e.g.
A: I don't eat meat, cheese or vegetables.
B: Oh. What <u>**do**</u> you eat?
For more on this, see Unit 40.

C

🔊 B76 In very fast speech, many of these kinds of questions may be pronounced with only three syllables. Listen.

●•●

What do you **want**?	/ˈwɒt dʒə ˈwɒnt/
What does he **do**?	/ˈwɒt siː ˈduː/
Where have you **been**?	/ˈweə vjə ˈbɪn/
Where did he **go**?	/ˈweə diː ˈgəʊ/

Exercises

35.1 ⏺B77 Listen and complete the questions.

EXAMPLE What .... *did he* .... do?

1 Where .... live?
2 What .... say?
3 Where .... work?
4 What .... see?
5 Where .... gone?

6 Who .... meet?
7 Where .... sit?
8 When .... end?
9 Where .... been?
10 Who .... asked?

35.2 ⏺B78 Write the missing questions in this dialogue and give the stress patterns. Then listen, check, pause and repeat the questions.

EXAMPLE **A:** *What do you do* .... ?   ●••●
 B: I'm a doctor.

1 A: .... ?   ....
 B: I live in Kingston, Jamaica.

2 A: .... ?   ....
 B: I work in the University Hospital.

3 A: .... ?   ....
 B: Yes, I'm married. My husband is a teacher.

4 A: .... ?   ....
 B: He teaches History and Geography.

5 A: .... ?   ....
 B: At the Grove Road Secondary School.

6 A: .... ?   ....
 B: I met him when I was on holiday in Florida.

7 A: .... ?   ....
 B: We got married in 1999.

35.3 ⏺B79 Listen and write the sentences. The phonemic symbols will help you.

EXAMPLE /ˈwɒt dʒə ˈmiːn / *What do you mean?* ....

1 /ˈhuː vjə ˈtəʊld/ .... ?
2 /ˈwɒt diː ˈseɪ/ .... ?
3 /ˈwen dʒə ˈstɑːt/ .... ?
4 /ˈweə ziː ˈgɒn/ .... ?
5 /ˈhaʊ dʒə ˈduː/ .... ?

36 Some milk and eggs
Pronouncing short words (*a, of, or*)

B80 Listen to the rhyme below. Notice the pronunciation of the short words in blue.

Shopping list

Some **milk** and **eggs**,
A **tin** of **peas**,
A **snack** for **lunch**:
Some **fruit** and **cheese**.
The **loaf** of **bread**,
A **jar** of **jam**,
Some **tea** to **drink**,
A **piece** of **lamb**.
Some **pears** or **grapes**,
Some **beans** and **rice**,
A **glass** of **juice**
As **cold** as **ice**!

Notice that:

- Every line in the rhyme has the stress pattern ●●●●, e.g.

•	●	•	●
Some	milk	and	eggs

- Short words like articles, conjunctions and prepositions are usually unstressed. These words in the rhyme are: *some, and, a, of, for, the, to, or, as*.

B81 Listen again to the rhyme in A. Notice that the vowels in all the unstressed syllables are pronounced the same. This sound is written as /ə/ in the phonemic alphabet (see Unit 7). Also, in fast speech, the consonant sounds after the vowel in these words may not be pronounced. In this case, *and* sounds like *an*, and *of* sounds like *a*.

Listen to these examples.

and sounds like *an*:
 an apple and an orange and an onion

of sounds like *a*:
 a bit of this and a bit of that

You don't need to copy the fast speech pronunciation. People will understand you if you use careful speech. But you need to be able to understand fast speech.

⚠ **Note:** The consonant sound in *of* is not dropped when the following word begins with a vowel, e.g. *some of each*.

B82 The vowel sound in *to* and *the* is different if the following word begins with a vowel. In this case, *to* changes from /tə/ to /tu/, and *the* changes from /ðə/ to /ðɪ/.

Listen to the difference.

We need water to drink and food to eat.
I'll have the fish, and the apple pie for dessert.

Exercises

36.1 What are the things in the pictures? Write them in the correct column according to the stress pattern (two phrases in each column). Use these words: *bowl, bottle, jar, packet, bag, pot, carton, kilo*. Then say the phrases aloud.

●●●●●	●●●●●●	●●●●●●	●●●●●●●
a bowl of soup			

36.2 **B83** In these sentences, both of the words in blue are possible and they sound similar in fast speech. Listen and underline the word you hear.

1 I had a salad *as / and* a main course.
2 Give her *an / some* egg if she's hungry.
3 She went to look *at / for* the fruit.
4 He gave me a basket *of / for* bread.
5 Get some pasta *and / or* rice.
6 I like *the / to* cook.
7 She ordered *a / the* soup.
8 Have *some / an* orange juice.
9 He invited me *at / for* lunch.
10 He made this jar *for / of* jam himself.

36.3 **B83 (cont.)** Listen and complete with the correct words. Then listen, check and repeat. Make sure you keep the same stress pattern: ●●●●.

EXAMPLE ....*a*.... glass ....*of*.... milk

1 .... time .... lunch
2 .... egg .... chips
3 .... bag .... nuts
4 .... drink .... eat
5 .... cook .... rice
6 .... fast .... that
7 .... meal .... two
8 .... box .... food
9 .... fish .... meat

36.4 Somebody wrote the sentences below incorrectly because they wrote exactly what they heard. Write the correct sentences.

EXAMPLE We had beans an rice. We had beans and rice.

1 We had a nice cup a tea. ....
2 I don't want a go out tonight. ....
3 I need a drinker water. ....
4 We cook to chicken. ....
5 He can't cooker meal. ....
6 Have a nice cream! ....
7 Come in an sit down. ....

Follow-up: Practise saying the rhyme in A on the opposite page. Tap the table or your foot in time as you say it.

37 // CHILDREN // DRIVE SLOWLY //
Dividing messages into speech units

A ▶B84 When we speak, we divide the words into groups. In this book, we call these groups *speech units*. By changing the way we divide a message into speech units, we can change the meaning of the message. For example, look at this sign which is to warn drivers that there are children in the area.

Normally, you would pronounce this message as two speech units as shown below. We use the symbol // to divide the units.

// CHILDREN // DRIVE SLOWLY //

If you pronounce it as one speech unit, it has a different meaning – probably not the meaning you intended!

Listen and compare the two ways of pronouncing the message.

Intended meaning	Other meaning
// CHILDREN // DRIVE SLOWLY // (There are children around here, so you should drive slowly.)	// CHILDREN DRIVE SLOWLY // (When children drive cars, they usually drive slowly.)

B ▶B85 Speech units are often shown by punctuation in writing. Listen to the difference between the pairs of messages below.

a It was cold outside. There was snow on the ground.
b It was cold. Outside, there was snow on the ground.

a Was that the question he asked?
b 'Was that the question?' he asked.

a I got up, quickly got dressed, and went downstairs.
b I got up quickly, got dressed, and went downstairs.

Notice that:

• The meanings of the messages are changed by the way the words are divided into speech units.

• The speech units are shown by punctuation marks.

C ▶B86 Speech units help to divide the message into chunks which the listener can understand easily. For this reason, we often divide long series of letters or numbers into shorter speech units when we are giving our contact details.

Listen to this address and notice that there are pauses where there are line breaks and where there are gaps in the telephone number. Notice also that when the speaker spells her surname and email address, she divides the letters into groups.

Linda Wharton
29 Bolton Road
Wigan
Lancashire
WI16 9FT
England
Tel: 090 827 7365
email: linwar@applegroove.com

Exercises

37.1 `B87` You will hear each message 1–4 twice. Listen and write the order you hear the different meanings, A and B.

1 B, A   2 ....   3 ....   4 ....

	A Intended meaning	B Other meaning
1	// SLOW // MEN AT WORK // (There are men working, so drive slowly.)	// SLOW MEN AT WORK // (There are men working slowly.)
2	// GUARD DOGS // KEEP OUT // (There are guard dogs, so keep out.)	// GUARD DOGS KEEP OUT // (Guard dogs can't come in.)
3	// POLICE // HAVE ID READY // (There is a police control, so have your ID ready.)	// POLICE HAVE ID READY // (If you are a police officer, you must show your ID.)
4	// NO SMOKING // CHILDREN ALLOWED // (Don't smoke. You can bring children in.)	// NO SMOKING CHILDREN ALLOWED // (Children who are smoking can't come in.)

37.2 `B88` Each message below is two sentences. Listen and decide if the full stop is before or after the underlined word or phrase. Use the symbol // to show where the full stop is.

EXAMPLE   // They're leaving // soon it'll be quieter //

1 // There was nothing   inside   it was empty //
2 // We walked carefully   downstairs   it was dark //
3 // I watched him   silently   he opened the drawer //
4 // The rain didn't stop   the next day   it just carried on //
5 // The weather was hot   at the weekend   it was 40 degrees //
6 // I saw her   clearly   she was hungry //
7 // It was cold   last night   the roads were icy //

Follow-up: Do you think there are any commas in the sentences above? Use the symbol // (in a different colour) to show where they are.

37.3 `B89` You will hear two people giving their contact details. Listen to the way the words, letters and numbers are divided into speech units. Underline the version, A or B, you hear in the boxes below.

	A	B
name	ANNA MARIA	ANN AMARIA
street	Windsor Palace Road	Windsor, Palace Road
phone	935 8226	93 58 226
postcode	W116 9FT	W11 69FT

	A	B
name	JON AILTON	JO NAILTON
street	Padgate High Street	Padgate, High Street
phone	710 82 62 65	71 082 6265
postcode	PA15 3HT	PA1 53HT

Follow-up: Say your own name, address and contact details. Record yourself if possible.

38 // His sister // who was clever // won //
Speech units and grammar

A 🔊 B90 Listen to this story.

// There was a young boy who liked games // He liked cards // dice // and all guessing games // One day // he said to his sister // Guess how many coins I've got in my pocket // The boy's sister said // If I get it right // will you give me one of them? // The boy // who was not very bright // replied // If you get it right // I'll give you both of them // His sister // who was clever // won the two coins // of course //

Notice that:

- The speaker divides the text into speech units. The symbol // shows where the units are divided.

- Speech units are very often connected to grammar. For example, in the story above:

whole sentence	// There was a young boy who liked games //
conditional clause	// If I get it right //
relative clause	// who was not very bright // //who was clever //
items in a list	// dice // // and all guessing games //
quoting	// he said to his sister // // The boy's sister said //
adverb phrase	// one day // // of course //

- Places where speech units are divided are very often shown by punctuation in writing.

B 🔊 B91 Sometimes, differences in grammar are reflected in the pronunciation. For example, in the box below, A and B are distinguished by the way the messages are divided into speech units.

Listen and compare the pronunciation.

	A	B
whole sentence	I see. You've finished.	I see you've finished.
relative clause	The boy who was clever won.	The boy, who was clever, won.
items in a list	Lemon tea and chocolate.	Lemon, tea and chocolate.
quoting	'Who?' asked his sister.	Who asked his sister?
adverb phrase	I watched silently. She slept.	I watched. Silently, she slept.

C 🔊 B92 In A, we saw that speech units are very often connected to grammar. However, this is not a rule. Speakers can divide the message into speech units in different ways, if they choose. We may do this in order to give a special meaning.

Listen to the difference.

normal: // I've told you before // I don't like card games! //
special meaning: // I've told you before // I // don't // like // card games! //

Notice that the speaker divides the second message into very short speech units to make sure the listener hears each word clearly. Perhaps the speaker wants to give more emphasis to the sentence because he or she is angry.

Exercises

38.1 🔊 B93 Read this story. Show where you could divide it into speech units using //. Then listen and check. Practise saying the story.

Sheila went to the doctor to complain about pains in her hand // the doctor suggested that she should have an operation Sheila said If I have the operation will I be able to type with all my fingers yes of course replied the doctor great said Sheila I've never been able to do that before

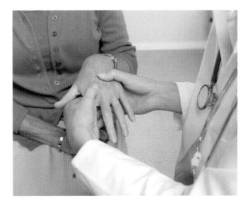

38.2 🔊 B94 Listen and underline the message you hear, A or B.

	A	B
1	You know. The answer's easy.	<u>You know the answer's easy.</u>
2	He told me. You're leaving.	He told me you're leaving.
3	The fire which you started spread fast.	The fire, which you started, spread fast.
4	The driver who was drunk crashed.	The driver, who was drunk, crashed.
5	Cheese salad or omelette?	Cheese, salad or omelette?
6	Fruit juice or coffee?	Fruit, juice or coffee?
7	'Mother!' called the dentist.	Mother called the dentist.
8	'Who?' wrote Rebecca.	Who wrote *Rebecca*?
9	I'm leaving soon. You'll be alone.	I'm leaving. Soon, you'll be alone.
10	I saw her clearly. She was angry.	I saw her. Clearly, she was angry.

38.3 🔊 B95 The speakers below divide these sentences into some very small speech units. Listen and show each speech unit using the // symbol.

EXAMPLE   // It was very expensive // but it was // just // fabulous //

1 // You should visit the waterfall 'cause it is absolutely amazing //
2 // I really cannot understand why people watch this programme //
3 // There's just no way I'm ever going out with him again //
4 // The view was amazing I mean words simply cannot describe it //

39 // Sorry to di<u>sturb</u> you //
Introduction to main stress

A

🔊 B96 Listen to this conversation in an office. The text is divided into speech units using this symbol //. In every speech unit, one syllable has the main stress (shown by underlining).

Mr Clark: // A<u>hem</u> // <u>Mor</u>ning Alan // Sorry to di<u>sturb</u> you //
Alan: // <u>Oh</u> // Mr <u>Clark</u> // I was just making a <u>phone</u> call //
Mr Clark: // A <u>phone</u> call // <u>Oh</u> // I thought you were a<u>sleep</u> or something //
Alan: // I was calling head <u>off</u>ice // and they put me on <u>hold</u> you see //
Mr Clark: // <u>No</u> // I <u>don't</u> see //
Alan: // <u>Well</u> // I was waiting for <u>ages</u> // and the music's so re<u>lax</u>ing //
Mr Clark: // Re<u>lax</u>ing // Is that why you're lying across the <u>desk</u>? //
Alan: // <u>No</u> // that's because of the <u>wind</u> //
Mr Clark: // <u>What</u> wind? //
Alan: // Someone opened a <u>win</u>dow // My papers were blowing all <u>o</u>ver the place // so that's why I'm lying on <u>top</u> of them //
Mr Clark: // <u>Oh</u> // I <u>see</u> // That was very <u>clev</u>er of you //
Alan: // <u>Thank</u> you Mr Clark //
Mr Clark: // <u>Alan</u> // I don't pay you to <u>sleep</u>! // Get back to work im<u>me</u>diately //
Alan: // <u>Yes</u> sir //

B

Normally the main stress is on the last content word in the speech unit, or one of the syllables in it if it is a longer word. This is often the last word, as indicated in the speech units below in blue.

// I was waiting for <u>ages</u> //
// and the music's so re<u>lax</u>ing //
// Is that why you're lying across the <u>desk</u>? //
// that's because of the <u>wind</u> //
// I was just making a <u>phone</u> call //

Notice that in the last example, the main stress is not on the last word because the last two words form a single compound item with stress on the first part.

The main stress is not on the last word or phrase if it is a function word or phrase, as indicated in the speech units below in blue.

// Sorry to di<u>sturb</u> you //
// so that's why I'm lying on <u>top</u> of them //
// That was very <u>clev</u>er of you //

For more information on content words and function words, see Unit 32.

C

Sometimes, the main stress is not on the last content word:

• when the end of the speech unit is a vague word or phrase, not important to the meaning, e.g.
// I thought you were a<u>sleep</u> or something //
// and they put me on <u>hold</u> you see //
// My papers were blowing all <u>o</u>ver the place //

• when the speech unit ends with the name or title of the person being addressed, e.g.
// <u>Mor</u>ning Alan //
// <u>Thank</u> you Mr Clark //
// <u>Yes</u> sir //

• when the last content word is simply repeating something the other person just said, e.g.
A: // I was calling head <u>off</u>ice // and they put me on <u>hold</u> you see //
C: // <u>No</u> // I <u>don't</u> see //

A: // <u>No</u> // that's because of the <u>wind</u> //
C: // <u>What</u> wind? //

⚠️ **Note:** Speakers may put the main stress on any word in the speech unit in order to create special meanings. For more on this, see Units 40–44.

Exercises

39.1 ▶B97 Listen to this conversation. Where is the main stress? Underline one word in each speech unit.

Gill: // <u>Paul</u> // Have you seen a <u>document</u> in here? // I left it on the table this morning//

Paul: // Why? // Was it something important? //

Gill: // Yes // It was a contract // If I've lost it // it will be a disaster //

Paul: // Oh // Do you remember where you left it? //

Gill: // Right here // On this table //

Paul: // Oh // I cleared some papers from here at lunch time // I didn't think they were important //

Gill: // What did you do with them? //

Paul: // I thought they were rubbish //

Gill: // So what did you do with them? //

Paul: // I // I put them in the shredder //

Gill: // I don't believe it! // You've shredded the contract! // And it was the only copy! //

Paul: // Look // I'm sure we can find the pieces // and then we can put it back together //

Gill: // Oh // no //

39.2 ▶B98 Underline the word which you think will have the main stress. Then, listen, check, pause and repeat.

EXAMPLE   // I don't know what to <u>do</u> with it //

1 // I just called to say thank you //
2 // Do you know what time it is? //
3 // I saw her at the coffee machine //
4 // It was very kind of you //

5 // My computer's so slow //
6 // Could you check the spelling for me? //
7 // I think John's in Frankfurt or somewhere //
8 // Good afternoon Mr Smith //

39.3 ▶B99 Underline the syllable with the main stress in each response in blue. Listen and check. Repeat the responses using the same intonation.

	statement / question	response
1	**a** // Can you find the <u>page</u>? //	// <u>Which</u> page? //
	b // Open your <u>books</u> please //	// Which <u>page</u>? //
2	**a** // Try to re<u>mem</u>ber //	// I never forget //
	b // Don't for<u>get</u>! //	// I never forget //
3	**a** // Where did you leave your <u>car</u>? //	// I haven't got a car //
	b // Why don't you <u>drive</u>?//	// I haven't got a car //
4	**a** // Why don't you go to <u>meet</u>ings? //	// I don't like them //
	b // Why do you like <u>meet</u>ings? //	// I don't like them //
5	**a** // You can bring your <u>husb</u>and //	// I'm not married //
	b // When did you get <u>mar</u>ried? //	// I'm not married //

// He <u>will</u> win //

Emphasising a contrasting opinion

A

🔊 C1 Normally, the main stress goes on the last content word in a speech unit. But in conversation, speakers can choose to put the stress anywhere. This is like underlining words in writing; we do this so that the listener will pay attention to the emphasised word.

Listen to this conversation.

A: // He won't win //
B: // <u>Who</u> won't? //
A: // <u>He</u> won't //
B: // He <u>will</u> win //
A: // He <u>won't</u> win //
B: // He <u>will</u>! //
A: // He <u>won't</u>! //
B: // I <u>hope</u> he wins //
A: // <u>I</u> hope he <u>loses</u> //
B: // He <u>won't</u> lose //
A: // He <u>will</u> lose //
B: // <u>You're</u> wrong! //
A: // <u>You're</u> wrong! //
B: // He's <u>won</u>! //
A: // <u>Who's</u> won? //
B: // <u>He's</u> won! //
A: // Oh no! //

Notice that:

- to emphasise a word, each speaker makes it higher, louder or longer

- each speaker is emphasising to show that their opinion is the opposite of the other speaker's.

B

🔊 C2 To say the opposite, we often emphasise the auxiliary verb, e.g. B: // He <u>will</u> win // (The speaker emphasises *will* to contrast with *won't* in the previous line.)

Listen and compare.

normal	emphasised auxiliary
I'm ill.	I <u>am</u> ill!
You're right.	You <u>are</u> right!
She's late.	She <u>is</u> late!
I like you.	I <u>do</u> like you!

normal	emphasised auxiliary
I enjoyed it.	I <u>did</u> enjoy it!
I've finished.	I <u>have</u> finished!
He'll win.	He <u>will</u> win!
I can swim.	I <u>can</u> swim!

Notice that:

- Auxiliary verbs are normally unstressed (see Unit 35), but when we emphasise them, they are stressed.

- Auxiliary verbs are often contracted, e.g. *'ll* instead of *will*. However, when we emphasise them they are not contracted.

- The auxiliary *do* is not normally said in positive statements. However, it may be used to give emphasis, e.g. **A:** You don't like me. **B:** I <u>do</u> like you!

We can also give a different opinion by contrasting the pronoun, e.g. **A:** You're <u>wrong</u>! **B:** <u>You're</u> wrong!

Notice that pronouns are normally unstressed (see Unit 33), but when we emphasise them, they are stressed.

We can also contrast opinions by using a word with the opposite meaning and emphasising it, e.g. **A:** I <u>hope</u> he wins. **B:** I hope he <u>loses</u>.

Exercises

40.1 [● C3] **Read this conversation. Which words in the blue lines do you think the speakers will emphasise? Underline them. Then listen and check.**

A: // I won't pass //
B: // You <u>will</u> pass //
A: // You'll pass //
B: // I don't know //
A: // You won't fail //
B: // I might fail //
A: // I will fail //
B: // The exam's not hard //

A: // It's very hard //
B: // But not too hard //
A: // Too hard for me //
B: // But you're very clever! //
A: // You're the clever one //
B: // Yes // I suppose you're right //

> **Follow-up:** Listen to the conversation again and repeat B's lines. Remember to emphasise the underlined words.

40.2 [● C3 (cont.)] **Listen to sentences from the box in section B opposite. Decide if the sentence you hear is normal or has an emphasised auxiliary.**

1 = <u>emphasised</u>
2 ....
3 ....

4 ....
5 ....
6 ....

7 ....
8 ....

40.3 [● C4] **Write three different ways to disagree with each of A's sentences, and underline the words you would emphasise. Then listen, check and repeat.**

1
  A: I'll win.

B: No, ...<u>I'll win!</u>............ (opposite subject)
B: You ....<u>won't win!</u>... (negative)
B: No, you'll ....<u>lose!</u>.............. (word with opposite meaning)

2
  A: I finished first.

B: No, ... (opposite subject)
B: No, you .... (negative)
B: No, you .... (word with opposite meaning)

3
  A: You're stupid!

B: No, ... (opposite subject)
B: I'm .... (negative)
B: No, I'm .... (word with opposite meaning)

40.4 [● C5] **Look at the responses in blue. Underline the word you think the speaker will emphasise in each. Then listen and check.**

EXAMPLE   **a** Anybody can ride a bike.   <u>I</u> can't!
            b Why don't you go cycling?   I <u>can't</u>!

1 a You can watch the match on TV.   I haven't got a TV!
   b Why didn't you watch the match?   I haven't got a TV!

2 a The maths exam wasn't difficult.   It was difficult!
   b What did you think of the exam?   It was difficult!

3 a They always play well, don't they?   No, they never win!
   b They usually win, don't they?   No, they never win!

4 a You need to practise more.   You need to practise more!
   b I practise quite a lot.   You need to practise more!

5 a I don't do any sports.   So what do you do then?
   b I think everybody should play a sport.   So what do you do then?

41 // <u>Schwartz</u> // <u>Pedro</u> Schwartz //
Emphasising added details

A 🔊 C6 Listen to the way the speaker emphasises certain words in this text.

// My name's <u>Schwartz</u> // <u>Pedro</u> Schwartz //
// I'm from <u>Chile</u> // the <u>south</u> of Chile //
// I live in <u>Puerto Montt</u> // <u>well</u> // <u>near</u> Puerto Montt //
// <u>Actually</u> // I live on an <u>island</u> // an island called <u>Chiloé</u> //
// My grandparents were <u>German</u> // <u>well</u> // <u>Swiss</u>-German, in fact //

In the first line, both speech units contain the name *Schwartz*.
In the first unit, the speaker emphasises this word because it is new information. But in the second speech unit, he doesn't, because now it is old information. The new information in the second phrase is *Pedro*, so the speaker emphasises this.

NEW	OLD
My name's <u>Schwartz</u>,	<u>Pedro</u> Schwartz.
	NEW

There is a similar pattern in each of the other lines in the text.

B 🔊 C7 In the speech above, the same speaker gives information and then adds new details. But in a conversation, one speaker can give information and *the other* can add new details. In both cases, the speaker emphasises the added detail.

Listen to this example.

A: // I hear you've got a <u>boat</u> //
B: // A <u>small</u> boat // <u>yes</u> //
A: // And a big <u>house</u> //
B: // <u>Well</u> // it's <u>quite</u> big // I sup<u>pose</u>.
A: // And you live in <u>Hollywood</u> //
B: // Well, <u>near</u> Hollywood // <u>yes</u> //
A: // So you must be <u>rich</u> then? //
B: // <u>Well</u> // <u>quite</u> rich I guess //

C 🔊 C8 Listen to these two short conversations.

question	response
1 // Where are you <u>from</u>? //	// South <u>India</u> //
2 // Which part of <u>India</u> are you from?//	// <u>South</u> India//

In 1, the question shows that the speaker doesn't know anything about where the person comes from. In 2, the question shows that the speaker knows the other person is from India, but not which part. This explains why the person answering the question emphasises different words in the two responses.

Exercises

41.1 Use the words from the box to add details to the sentences below. Underline the added detail. Say your sentences out loud.

car~~ ~~ plastic   James   French   very   central

EXAMPLE   It's a radio … *a car radio* .

1 It's cold … .
2 It's a bag … .
3 My name's Bond … .
4 It's in Asia … .
5 He's a composer … .

41.2 🔊 C9 Listen and underline the words which B emphasises.

A: // It's very <u>quiet</u> //
B: // <u>Too</u> quiet //
A: // I think something's <u>wrong</u> //
B: // Very wrong //
A: // I don't <u>like</u> it //
B: // I don't like it at all //
A: // Let's get <u>out</u> of here //
B: // Let's get out fast! //

Follow-up: Listen again and repeat B's lines.

41.3 🔊 C10 The responses to the pairs of questions a and b below are the same, but the speaker emphasises a different word each time. For example, in the response to Example a, the speaker emphasises 'Vettori' but in b, she emphasises 'Clara'. Read the other questions and underline the words in the responses the speaker will stress. Then listen and check.

EXAMPLE   **a** What's your name?   Clara <u>Vettori</u>.
               b What's your full name, Ms Vettori?   <u>Clara</u> Vettori.

	question	response
1	**a** Do you live in Milan?	// Near Milan // <u>yes</u> //
	b Do you live near Milan?	// Near Milan // <u>yes</u> //
2	**a** What do you do?	// I'm a graphic designer //
	b What kind of designer are you?	// I'm a graphic designer //
3	**a** Do you have your own home?	// <u>Yes</u> // a very nice flat //
	b Do you have a nice flat?	// <u>Yes</u> // a very nice flat //
4	**a** What do you do in the evenings?	// <u>Well</u> // I'm learning French //
	b Do you speak French?	// <u>Well</u> // I'm learning French //
5	**a** Do you know London?	// <u>Yes</u> // I lived there for a year //
	b You lived in London, didn't you?	// <u>Yes</u> // I lived there for a year //
6	**a** Do you have any brothers or sisters?	// <u>Yes</u> // two brothers //
	b You have some brothers, don't you?	// <u>Yes</u> // two brothers //
7	**a** What kind of music do you like?	// I like jazz and classical //
	b Which do you prefer, jazz or classical?	// I like jazz and classical //

Follow-up: Play the recording again and repeat the answers

42 // What do you do? //
Main stress in questions

A

[C11] Sometimes, a conversation begins like a game of tennis: one person serves the ball across the net and the other person returns it. In a conversation, one person 'serves' a question and the other person answers and 'returns' it, as in the example below.

Notice how the same question is pronounced differently in the 'serve' and 'return'.

A: (serve)   // What do you <u>do</u>? //
B: // I'm a <u>student</u> //
   (return) // What do <u>you</u> do? //
A: // I'm an ac<u>coun</u>tant //

In the 'serve' question, the speaker stresses the last content word. This is the normal pronunciation, with no special meaning (see Unit 39). In the 'return' question, the speaker emphasises *you*. This pronunciation gives the question a special meaning: the speaker is contrasting *you* with *I* in order to direct the conversation to the other person.

Listen and compare.

'serve' question	'return' question

// What's your <u>name</u>? //
 // What do you <u>do</u>? //
 // Where do you <u>come</u> from? //
	// What's <u>your</u> name? //
	 // What do <u>you</u> do? //
	 // Where do <u>you</u> come from? //

B

[C12] Often, one person 'serves' several questions before the other person 'returns' the question. The questioner can use emphasis to direct the conversation.

Listen to this conversation and notice the word which is emphasised in each question.

A: // What do you <u>do</u>? //
B: // I'm a <u>student</u> //
A: // Me <u>too</u> // What do you <u>study</u>? //
B: // Modern <u>languages</u> //
A: // Oh <u>right</u> // And <u>where</u> do you study? // <u>Here</u>? //

B: // Not <u>here</u> // <u>no</u> //
A: // So where <u>do</u> you study? //
B: // <u>Belfast</u> // What about <u>you</u>?
    // Where do <u>you</u> study? //
A: // I'm at <u>Leeds</u> University //

C

[C13] The questioner may emphasise any of the words in the question to create different meanings. Listen to questions 1–4. It is the same question, but with a different word emphasised each time.

	A question word	B opposite	C person	D action
1	Where	do	you	<u>study</u>?
2	Where	do	<u>you</u>	study?
3	Where	<u>do</u>	you	study?
4	<u>Where</u>	do	you	study?

Notice that:

- In 1, the questioner emphasises the last content word to focus on the action. This is the normal place to stress the question. (What could have come before: *I hear you're at university* …)

- In 2, the questioner emphasises the pronoun to focus on the person who does the action, contrasting with another person such as *I* or *he*. (What could have come before: *I study at Leeds University* …)

- In 3, the questioner emphasises the auxiliary to contrast with a negative or opposite such as *don't*. (What could have come before: *So you don't study at this university* …)

- In 4, the questioner emphasises the question word to contrast with other question words such as *what* or *when*. (What could have come before: *I know that you study modern languages, but* …)

Exercises

42.1 **C14** Listen to eight questions similar to the ones in Section A opposite. Decide if they are 'serve' or 'return' questions.

1 <u>return question</u> ....
2 ....
3 ....
4 ....

5 ....
6 ....
7 ....
8 ....

> **Follow-up:** Listen again and repeat the questions.

42.2 **C15** Read the conversation. Look at the questions in blue and underline the words you think the speaker will emphasise. Then listen and check your answers. Then listen again, pause after each line and repeat.

A: // Where do you <u>live</u>? //
B: // I live with my <u>parents</u> // And <u>you</u>? //
Where do you live? //
A: // I <u>don't</u> live with my parents //
B: // So where do you live? //
A: // In student accommo<u>da</u>tion //
B: // Why did you leave home? //
A: // Last Sep<u>tem</u>ber //
B: //<u>No</u> // Why did you leave home? //
A: //<u>Oh</u> // I just wanted to be inde<u>pen</u>dent//

42.3 **C16** Listen to the questions. Underline the word the speaker emphasises in each.

	A question word	B opposite	C person	D action
1	<u>Where</u>	do	you	study?
2	Where	are	you	staying?
3	When	was	she	born?
4	Why	did	they	leave?
5	What	shall	we	do?
6	How	does	he	feel?
7	Where	will	I	sleep?
8	What	have	you	done?

42.4 The sentences / phrases below have now been added to the questions from 42.3. Underline the word the speaker would emphasise in each question in these different contexts. The blue clues will help you.

1 (opposite) So you don't study in this university. Where <u>do</u> you study?
2 (person) I'm staying in a youth hostel. Where are you staying?
3 (question) I know where she was born, but when was she born?
4 (action) They seemed to be enjoying it, so why did they leave?
5 (person) Everyone else is going home. What shall we do?
6 (action) So you've visited Simon in hospital. How does he feel?
7 (person) If you're sleeping on the sofa, where will I sleep?
8 (opposite) You haven't done any of your homework; so what have you done?

43

// I think you're in <u>my</u> seat //
Main stress for contrasting information

 Listen to this conversation.

A: // Ex<u>cuse</u> me // I think you're in **my** seat //

B: // <u>Sorry</u> // but it says seven **<u>A</u>** on my boarding card //

A: // <u>Oh</u> // er … <u>right</u> // I asked for a <u>win</u>dow seat you see //

B: // <u>Yeah</u> // so did <u>I</u> // What's **your** seat number? //

A: // Let's <u>see</u> // <u>Oh</u> // it's **eight** A //

B: // So I guess you're in the seat be<u>hind</u> me //

A: // Oh <u>yes</u> // <u>Sorry</u> about that //

Notice that:

- Normally, speakers put the main stress on the last content word in a speech unit (see Unit 39). However, in the blue speech units in this conversation, the speakers emphasise a different word.

- Speakers may emphasise a word to contrast it with another word. For example, in the speech unit // it's **eight** A //, the speaker emphasises *eight* to contrast with *seven* earlier in the conversation.

- Sometimes, speakers emphasise a word for contrast but the contrast is hidden. For example, in the speech unit // I think you're in **my** seat //, the speaker emphasises *my* to contrast with *your*, even though nobody said *your* earlier in the conversation. Here, the contrast is in the speaker's mind, not in the conversation.

B

C18 Listen and compare the sentences in A and B below. The speech units are identical, but with different words emphasised. This is because the context in each speaker's mind (shown in blue) is different.

A	B
// Could I have a glass of <u>water</u> // <u>too</u>, please? //	// Could <u>I</u> have a glass of water // <u>too</u>, please? //
A passenger is getting a coffee and now wants water too.	A passenger asked for water and now the next passenger is asking for the same.
// You have to check in at <u>five</u> //	// You have to check <u>in</u> at five //
A travel agent is telling a customer the check-in time.	A person thinks their flight is at five but actually it's at six – they only have to check in at five.

C

C19 Listeners often decide what is in the speaker's mind from the emphasis. If you emphasise the wrong word by mistake, a listener may misunderstand you.

Listen to this conversation.

A: // Would you like another <u>drink</u>? //

B: // I'd like a **hot** coffee please //

A: // I'm <u>sorry</u> // Was the last one <u>cold</u>? //

B: (*confused*) // <u>No</u> // it was very <u>good</u> //

 Note: In the speech unit // I'd like a **hot** coffee please //, the normal place to put the main stress would be on *coffee*. Here, Speaker B emphasises the word *hot* by mistake. As a result, Speaker A thinks B is complaining that the last coffee was cold.

Exercises

43.1 〇C20 Read the conversation. Look at the speech units in blue and underline the words you think the speaker will emphasise. Listen and check your answers. Then listen again, pause after each line and repeat.

A: // Is this your <u>first</u> trip to Spain? //

B: // <u>Well</u> // I've been to the islands a few times //

A: // So you don't know <u>Madrid</u> then //

B: // <u>No</u> // Do you know Madrid? //

A: // <u>No</u> // It's my first time // as <u>well</u> //

B: // So what are you going to do in the city? //

A: // <u>Well</u> // if it's <u>wet</u> // I'll probably do some <u>art</u> galleries //

B: // And if it's not wet? //

A: // I'll go to the <u>beach</u> //

B: // There isn't a beach //

A: // <u>Ah</u>! // Can I borrow your <u>guide</u>book a moment? //

43.2 〇C20 (cont.) Listen to the sentences in the box and decide if you hear A or B first. Write A – B or B – A. B – A

EXAMPLE .... **1** .... **2** .... **3** .... **4** ....

A	B
// I <u>think</u> that's my bag //	// I think that's <u>my</u> bag //
She's not completely sure that it's her bag.	Another person is picking up her bag.
1 // Is that your <u>phone</u>? //	// Is that <u>your</u> phone? //
He can hear an electronic sound from someone's pocket.	He can see somebody's mobile phone on the seat.
2 // Is your seat <u>29</u>F? //	// Is your seat 29<u>F</u>? //
She is not sure she heard the number correctly.	She is not sure she heard the letter correctly.
3 // Is there a bank in <u>this</u> terminal? //	// Is there a <u>bank</u> in this terminal? //
He knows there is a bank in the other terminal but not if there is one in this terminal	He is looking for a bank.
4 // Where's the women's <u>toilet</u>? //	// Where's the <u>women</u>'s toilet? //
She is looking for the toilet.	She can see the men's toilet, but not the women's.

Follow-up: Record yourself saying the sentence for either context A or B. Make a note of which one you choose. Then listen to your recording in about two weeks and decide if you said A or B.

44 // <u>Fifty</u>? // <u>No</u> // fif<u>teen</u>! //
Emphasising corrections

C21 When we hear an error and we correct it, we emphasise the correct information.

Listen to this conversation. Notice how Andy emphasises the words which Bella has heard incorrectly.

Andy: // Let's meet <u>up</u> tonight //
Bella: // O<u>K</u> // When and <u>where</u>? //
Andy: // How about the Blues <u>Café</u>? //
Bella: // The Mews <u>Café</u>? // Don't <u>like</u> that place //
Andy: // No, the **Blues** Café // In Rawton <u>Road</u> //
Bella: // Where's Lawton <u>Road</u>? //
Andy: // Not **Law**ton Road // **Raw**ton Road //
   you <u>know</u> //
Bella: // Ah <u>yes</u> // O<u>K</u> // What <u>time</u>? //
Andy: // How about nine fif<u>teen</u> //
Bella: // Five fif<u>teen</u>? // That's too <u>early</u> //
Andy: // No, **nine** fifteen // What's wrong with
   your <u>ears</u> today?! //

B

C22 If only a part of a word or phrase is not heard correctly, we emphasise only that part when we correct. Listen to these examples.

A: // My nephew's fif<u>teen</u> //
B: // Thir<u>teen</u>? //
A: // <u>No</u> // **fif**teen! //

A: // You must be more <u>care</u>ful! //
B: // <u>Careless</u>? //
A: // <u>No</u> // care**ful**! //

A: // Her room is really un<u>tidy</u> //
B: // <u>Tidy</u>? //
A: // <u>No</u> // **un**tidy! //

A: // I saw a <u>black</u>bird // in the <u>garden</u> //
B: // A <u>black</u>board? //
A: // <u>No</u> // a black**bird**! //

C

C23 In the examples above, the mistake was that one of the speakers did not hear correctly. But we can also use extra stress when correcting other kinds of mistakes, for example if the information is wrong. Listen to this example.

A: // The Amazon's the longest river in the <u>world</u> //
B: // <u>Oh</u> // I thought the **Nile** was the longest river //

Exercises

44.1 **●C24** Read this phone conversation. Notice the words which are emphasised by Sylvia and decide whether Joe says phrase **a** or phrase **b**. Underline the correct answer. Then listen and check.

EXAMPLE   **Sylvia:** Hello, Joe, I'm coming to visit next month.
             Joe: You're coming **a** <u>this month?</u> **b** next week?
         Sylvia: No, <u>**next**</u> month. Can you meet me? I'll be on the evening plane.

1   **Joe:** On the **a** morning plane? **b** evening train?
    Sylvia: No no. On the evening <u>plane</u>. On Sunday the third.

2   **Joe:** On **a** Sunday the first? **b** Monday the third?
    Sylvia: No no, <u>Sun</u>day the third. At nine fifteen.

3   **Joe:** At **a** five fifteen? **b** nine fifty?
    Sylvia: No no, nine fif<u>teen</u>. You'll know it's me.
             I'll have a blue jacket.

4   **Joe:** **a** new jacket? **b** blue packet?
    Sylvia: No no, a <u>blue</u> jacket. See you there. Bye.

44.2 **●C24 (cont.)** Read these short conversations. Which syllable do you think the speaker will emphasise in each blue speech unit? Underline it.

EXAMPLE   **A:** // I disagree with you //
            B: // You agree? //
            A: // No // I <u>dis</u>agree! //

1 **A:** // He's in the <u>bath</u>room //
   B: // In the <u>bed</u>room? //
   A: // <u>No</u> // the bathroom! //

2 **A:** // My father's re<u>tired</u> //
   B: // <u>Why</u> is he tired? //
   A: // <u>No</u> // he's retired! //

3 **A:** // I bought a <u>book</u>shelf //
   B: // A <u>book</u>shop? //
   A: // <u>No</u> // a bookshelf! //

4 **A:** // But that's im<u>poss</u>ible! //
   B: // You think it's <u>poss</u>ible? //
   A: // <u>No</u> // I said impossible! //

5 **A:** // The kitchen's down<u>stairs</u> //
   B: // Up<u>stairs</u>? //
   A: // <u>No</u> // downstairs! //

Follow-up: Listen. You will hear the first two lines and then a pause before the third line. Say the third line with the stress you underlined. Then listen and check if you were right.

45 Bear! ↘ Bear? ↗
Rising and falling tones

A

🔊 C25 At the end of every speech unit, the voice goes up or down. This is very clear in the conversation below because there is only one word in each of the speech units.

Listen and notice the rising ↗ or falling ↘ tones.

A: // Shh! //
B: // What? ↘ //
A: // Bear! ↘ //
B: // Bear? ↗ //
A: // Bear! ↘ //
B: // Where? ↘ //
A: // There! ↘ //
B: // Far? ↗ //
A: // No! ↘ //
B: // Near? ↗ //
A: // Yeah! ↘ //
B: // Run? ↗ //
A: // Run! ↘ //

B

Very often, the tones follow the grammar of the sentence:

statement = ↘
open question = ↘
yes / no question = ↗

(Open questions begin with a question word, e.g. *who, where, what, how*, etc. Yes / no questions begin with an auxiliary verb, e.g. *is*, and the answer usually begins with *yes* or *no*.)

The conversation in A above follows this pattern. This is clearer if the conversation is expanded so that the speech units are complete sentences, e.g.

A: // Shh! //
B: // What <u>is</u> it? ↘ //
A: // There's a <u>bear</u>! ↘ //
B: // Did you say <u>'bear'</u>? ↗ //
A: // <u>Yes</u> ↘ // There's a <u>bear</u>! ↘ //
B: // Where <u>is</u> it? ↘ //
A: // It's over <u>there</u>! ↘ //
B: // Is it <u>far</u>? ↗ //
A: // <u>No</u> ↘ // it <u>isn't</u>! ↘ //
B: // Is it <u>near</u>? ↗ //
A: // <u>Yes</u> ↘ // it <u>is</u>! ↘ //
B: // Shall we <u>run</u>? ↗ //
A: // <u>Yes</u> ↘ // Let's <u>run</u>! ↘ //

Notice that:

- The falling or rising tone begins on the underlined word and continues to the end of the speech unit. For example, in the speech unit // Where <u>is</u> it? ↘ //, the falling tone begins on *is* and continues across *it* to the end.

- In a rising tone, the voice may fall first and then rise, or simply rise. In this book, we do not separate these two kinds of rising tone; we use the symbol ↗ for both of them.

C

A speaker's choice of a falling or rising tone often reflects the grammar of the sentence, as explained in B above. However, a speaker may choose to use any kind of tone in any kind of sentence, and this can give a special meaning to a speech unit. In this book, we do not expect you to learn how to use tones in this way, but Units 51–55 will help you to understand these special meanings as a listener.

Exercises

45.1 `C26` Listen and write the symbol ↘ or ↗ in each gap. Then listen again, pause and repeat after each line using the same tone.

A: // <u>Quick</u>! ...↘... //
B: // <u>What</u>? .... //
A: // <u>Train</u>! .... //
B: // <u>Train</u>? .... //
A: // <u>Train</u>! .... //
B: // <u>Why</u>? .... //
A: // <u>Leaving</u>! .... //
B: // <u>Already</u>? .... //
A: // <u>Gone</u>! .... //
B: // <u>Gone</u>? .... //
A: // <u>Gone</u> .... //
B: // What <u>now</u>? .... //
A: // <u>Bus</u>? .... //
B: // <u>Bus</u>. .... //

45.2 `C27` Read the conversation. Decide which tone the speakers use for each speech unit. Write the symbol ↘ or ↗ in each gap. Then listen and check.

A: // Are you <u>new</u> here? ...↗... //
B: // <u>Yes</u> .... // And <u>you</u>? .... //
A: // <u>No</u> .... // I've been here two <u>years</u> .... //
B: // Do you <u>like</u> it? .... //
A: // <u>No</u> .... // I <u>don't</u> .... //
B: // Why <u>not</u>? .... //
A: // The boss is <u>awful</u>! .... //
B: // <u>Who</u>? .... // Do you mean Mr <u>Collins</u>? .... //
A: // <u>Yes</u> .... // Mr <u>Collins</u> .... // He's <u>awful</u> .... //
B: // You don't <u>really</u> think that .... // <u>do</u> you? .... //
A: // <u>Yes</u> .... // I <u>do</u> .... //
B: // ... //
A: // <u>What</u>? .... // Did I say something <u>funny</u>? .... //
B: // It's Mr <u>Collins</u>! .... //
A: // <u>Where</u>? .... //
B: // <u>Behind</u> you! .... //

> **Follow-up:** Play the recording and pause and repeat after each line.

46

// Ehm••• // Well••• //
Thinking time

🔊C28 An interviewer on an English local radio station is talking to nutritionist Candace Surman. Read a simplified, written version of the first part of the interview below.

Interviewer: My first question is this: Has our nutrition really got so bad that we need extra help deciding what to eat?

Candace: Well, in society today, a lot of people don't have much time to think about what they're eating, and there are a lot of things that are quick to get hold of. But nutrition plays a big role in our health. At the end of the day, what we put into our bodies is what we get out. You know, the adage, 'You are what you eat'. So from that point of view, it's important to think about what you're putting into your body. That's what I can help with.

adage = expression

Now listen to the full interview. Notice that spoken language is different from written language because the speaker has to think about what to say and say it at the same time:

- It's not clear where sentences begin and end.

- Speakers may insert thinking noises such as *ehm* and fillers such as *you know*.

- Speakers may make mistakes and start again, for example *I'm … I think it's great.*

- Speakers vary their speed, sometimes speaking very fast and sometimes slowly.

🔊C29 Listen to Candace answering the question with the audio slowed down and read the transcript of her actual speech below.

// Ehm••• // Well••• // I think••• // ehm society today••• // there's••• //
// you know // a lot of people don't have an awful lot of time //
// to think about••• // ehm••• // maybe what they're eating //
// There's a lot of things ••• // that are very quick to••• // get hold of //
// ehm••• // and••• // I think••• //
// you know // nutrition plays a big role in our health //
// At the end of the day // what we put into our bodies really is what we get out //
// you know // If ⊠ if you like, the adage we are ⊠ you are what you eat //
// Ehm••• // and I think••• // you know // from that point of view //
// it is ⊠ it is very important // to think about••• //
// you know // wha ⊠ what you're putting into your body and nutrition //
// An ⊠ and that's really what I can help with //

Explanation of symbols

••• = The speaker speaks slowly and makes words longer while she thinks about what she will say next.
⊠ = The speaker makes a mistake and starts again.
// you know // = The speaker says these speech units quickly and in a low voice. These kinds of speech unit are called 'fillers' because they do not really add to the meaning; they just fill a gap.

🔊C30 You can tell from the pronunciation whether or not a speaker:

- is planning to continue
- is using an expression as a filler (in a separate speech unit).
- has completed a speech unit

Listen to the difference.

// It is very important to think about // (the speaker has finished the sentence)
// It is very important to think about••• // (the speaker plans to continue the sentence)

// Ehm // Well // I think you know // (*you know* isn't a filler)
// Ehm // Well // I think // you know // (*you know* is a filler)

Exercises

46.1 [●C31] In the next part of the interview, the interviewer asks Candace if his diet of microwave meals is good for him. Listen to Candace's reply. How many times do you hear her use // Ehm••• // for thinking time?

46.2 [●C31 (cont.)] Listen again to a slower version and read the text below. Show where Candace says *ehm* with the symbol ∧.

Possibly not the best, no. (*laughs*)∧They tend to be quite high in sugar and salt which

can obviously have implications for people so, so yeah certainly balance that with a lot

of good sort of healthy vegetables and fruit really, is ideal, if you can.

46.3 [●C32] Listen to these sentences. Has speaker B finished talking or is she planning to continue? Write a full stop or ••• in each gap.

1 **A:** How's your diet going?
   B: Well •••
2 **A:** What do you eat?
   B: Beans, rice, fruit and vegetables ....
3 **A:** Don't you miss eating meat?
   B: It's not something I think about ....
4 **A:** I suppose it's a healthy diet, really.
   B: That's what I think ....
5 **A:** Why don't you stop drinking coffee?
   B: I don't really want to ....
6 **A:** When do you bake bread?
   B: On Sundays ....

46.4 [●C33] You will hear four people speaking. What are their favourite fillers? Write the correct filler next to each name.

1 Frank: ..I mean.............   3 Kimberly: ....
2 Debbie: ....   4 Greg: ....

46.5 [●C34] Listen to the sentences. Is the word or phrase in blue a part of the speech unit or a filler? Underline the correct option.

	A = part of speech unit	B = filler
1	// I didn't meet anyone <u>you know</u> //	// I didn't meet anyone // you know //
2	// You know I can't eat cheese //	// You know // I can't eat cheese //
3	// It's just like a sweet potato //	// It's just // like // a sweet potato //
4	// My brother's like a top class cook //	// My brother's // like // a top class cook //
5	// That's the place I mean // It's really nice //	// That's the place // I mean // It's really nice //
6	// This is not the one I mean // It's horrible //	// This is not the one // I mean // It's horrible //
7	// It's like a kind of vegetable //	// It's like a // kind of // vegetable //

47

// I mean // and just kind of //
Unstressed words in conversation

A

🔊 **C35** A male interviewer on an English local radio station is talking to singer Faryl Smith about a time when she performed in front of the queen. A female interviewer is also in the studio.

Listen to the first part of the interview and read the transcript below. (⟨☒⟩ is used to show when the speaker stops and corrects him- or herself.) Notice how the function words in blue are often difficult to hear because they are very unstressed.

Interviewer:
// <u>Ehm</u> // How do you pre<u>pare</u> // for such an ⟨☒⟩ such an <u>event</u>? //
// Don't you worry about••• // forgetting <u>words</u> // or your <u>voice</u> crackling //
// or <u>anything</u> like that? //

Singer:
// <u>Ehm</u> // I *do* get very nervous // I <u>mean</u> // what<u>ever</u> I do // I get <u>nervous</u> //
// Ehm // if I do <u>interviews</u> // if I <u>sing</u> // I <u>mean</u> // but when you ⟨☒⟩ on the <u>stage</u> //
// and you're doing big <u>shows</u> like that // it is very very <u>nerve</u>-racking //
// but I usually just try and block everything <u>out</u> // and just kind of ⟨☒⟩ //
// they ⟨☒⟩ they <u>always</u> say // Get into your own <u>bubble</u> //
// and just go <u>out</u> // and just <u>do</u> it // and don't think of <u>anything</u> //

Listen again to a slowed-down version of the same recording.

B

🔊 **C36** Listen to these fragments from the interview and read how they are pronounced. You will hear each fragment repeated slowly three times. Notice how the unstressed words in blue join up with the words before and after them.

interview fragment	pronunciation
such an event	/sʌtʃə nəˈven/
if I sing I mean	/ifʌ ˈsɪŋʌ ˈmin/
on the stage and you're doing	/ɒnðə ˈsteɪ dʒən jə ˈduːɪn/
but I usually just try and	/bʌʔʌ ˈjuːzlɪ dʒʌs traɪən/
and just kind of	/ən dʒʌs kæn dəv/
and just go out and just do it	/ən dʒəs gəʊ ˈɑʊʔ ən dʒəs ˈduː ɪʔ/

 Note:

- The symbol /ʔ/ is a stop. The speaker closes her throat for a very short time so that the letter T in *but, out* and *it* is replaced by a very short stop.

- The words *an* and *and* are pronounced the same: /ən/.

C

🔊 **C36** In conversation, function words are normally unstressed (see Unit 32 for a list of function words). Fillers are also often very unstressed. Fillers are words and phrases which do not have an exact meaning in the context; they just fill gaps in the flow of speech. In the recording, fillers include *mean*, *just* and *kind*.

Listen again and notice that these fillers join together with other unstressed words before or after them. These joined-together phrases may sound like a single unstressed word:

I mean = amin
kind of = canduv
and just = unjuss

 Note: When you first hear a speaker saying these unstressed filler phrases, it may be confusing. Try to ignore them and focus on the stressed words instead.

Now listen to 🔊 **C35** again and notice all these features at full speed.

Exercises

47.1 **⚫C37** Listen to another part of the interview with the same singer. Fill the gaps in the text below with the correct unstressed words. Then listen to a slowed-down version of the same text and check your answers.

// I mean it ⊠ // I got to meet ......*her*...... // as well at
[1]................... Royal Variety //
// and // they // had in [2].................... dressing rooms // about
stuff that you could do [3]................... // that you couldn't do
// and I mean I [4]................... so nervous // because there's
things like //
// she has to talk [5].................. you first // and ⊠ and things
like that //
// and there was like [6].................. list // and // it ⊠ it just
made me really nervous //
// 'cause I thought // 'Oh no // I'm going to get [7]...................
all wrong! // I'm gonna talk to her!' //
// and oh // and then // but it was fine [8].................. the end
// but we [9].................. all so // nervous //

47.2 **⚫C38** Listen to these fragments from the interview and write what you hear. You will hear each fragment repeated slowly three times. Use the phonemic spellings below to help you.

1 /ʌgɒʔtə'miːʔə rəz'wel/   I got to meet her as well ....
2 /'stʌf ðəʔ jəkʊ 'duː ən/   ....
3 /'ʃiː hæs tə tɔːʔ tə juː/   ....
4 /'nəʊm gʌnə geʔ ɪʔ ɔːl 'rɒŋ/   ....
5 /bʌdɪʔ wəz 'faɪ nɪn ðɪ end/   ....

47.3 **⚫C39** Read these fragments from the interview. They are written incorrectly. Listen and write the correct version. You will hear each fragment repeated quickly three times.

1 Amina were so nervous   I mean I was so nervous ....
2 an things at that   ....
3 an those lack a list   ....
4 itches may be rilly nervous   ....

48

Scuba‿diving‿course
Listening to connected speech

🔊C40 Listen to a man telling a longer version of the joke below. Notice the way that his speech is divided into connected groups of words. In these groups, all of the words are connected together with no gaps between them.

Why do scuba divers always go off the boat backwards to get into the water? Because if they went forwards, they'd just land in the boat!

🔊C41 Listen to the first half of the joke again, slowed down. The connected groups of words are numbered 1–10 in the transcript below. The symbol ‿ shows which words are connected together.

¹A‿friend‿of‿mine‿went‿to‿eh   ²Ireland‿on‿a   ³scuba‿diving‿course

⁴and‿ehm   ⁵about‿three‿days‿into‿the‿course‿eh

⁶every‿day‿they‿went‿out‿and   ⁷did‿eh   ⁸you‿know

⁹on‿the‿boat‿and   ¹⁰went‿in‿the‿water‿and

Notice that:

- If a word ends with a consonant sound and the next word begins with a vowel sound (highlighted in yellow), the consonant is often connected to the vowel. For example,

- *went out and* sounds like *wen tou tand* /wen taʊ tən/. (For more on this, see Unit 25.)

- In group 1, *friend of* is pronounced /fre nəv/; the letter *d* is cut.

- In groups 4 and 5, we see that consonants are also connected to thinking noises *ehm* and *eh*.

🔊C42 Listen to the second half of the joke again, slowed down. The connected groups of words are numbered 10–22 in the transcript below.

¹⁰went‿in‿the‿water‿and‿w   ¹¹one‿day‿he‿asked‿the‿eh

¹²the‿instructor   ¹³he‿said‿why‿do‿we‿always‿go‿in

¹⁴you‿know   ¹⁵go‿in‿the‿water‿backwards

¹⁶you‿know   ¹⁷scuba‿diving‿and‿he‿said‿eh

¹⁸the‿instructor‿said‿well   ¹⁹if‿you‿go‿in‿forwards   ²⁰you'd

²¹just   ²²be‿in‿the‿boat

Notice that:

- If a word ends with a vowel sound and the next word begins with a vowel sound (highlighted in green), a slight consonant sound may be added to the beginning of the second word. For example:

  water and sounds like *water rand* /wɔːtə rən/

  (In this speaker's accent, the /r/ sound is not pronounced at the end of a word, so words such as *water* end with a vowel sound: /ˈwɔːtə/.)

  /r/ is added in group 10, /j/ is added in groups 11, 12, 18 and 22, /w/ is added in groups 13, 15 and 19. (For more on this, see Unit 26.)

- The words *the* and *to* have a different vowel sound if they come before a word beginning with a vowel sound:

before a consonant sound	before a vowel sound
the water /ðə wɔːtə/ to the boat /tə ðə bəʊt/	the instructor /ðiː ʲinstrʌktə/ to Ireland /tʊ ʷaɪələnd/

In group 11, we see that a consonant is also added to the thinking sound *eh*.

Exercises

48.1 ● C43 Listen to the first half of a joke and read the transcript. The connected groups of words are numbered 1–13.

¹I heard a really sad story   ²it was about these two old hunters who eh
³went out in the woods one day   ⁴to eh shoot a few bears or whatever
⁵you know   ⁶and anyway so they were walking around in the woods
⁷and then suddenly without any kind of warning
⁸one of them just drops on the ground   ⁹dead   ¹⁰you know   ¹¹so obviously
¹²the other guy was a bit upset about this   ¹³as you can imagine

48.2 In the transcript in 48.1, there are many examples where the consonant at the end of one word is connected to the start of the next word. Read the phonemic spellings, identify the phrase in the group and write it.

EXAMPLE   /hɜː də/ (group 1) = <u>heard a</u>

1 /wə zəbaʊt/ (group 2) = ...

2 /wen taʊ tɪn/ (group 3) = ...

3 /ʃuː tə/ (group 4) = ...

4 /wɪðaʊ tenɪ/ (group 7) = ...

5 /drɒp sɒn/ (group 8) = ...

6 /wə zə bɪ təpset/ (group 12) = ...

48.3 ● C44 Listen to the second half of the joke and read the transcript. The connected groups of words are numbered 1–22.

¹Anyway   ²he didn't know what to do about it
³so he phones 112 to ask for advice   ⁴and the person who answers is a woman
⁵and so he tells her everything   ⁶and she asks him   ⁷if he's sure about it
⁸you know   ⁹maybe he's alive   ¹⁰and he says   ¹¹no he isn't sure   ¹²so she says
¹³OK the first thing you have to do is make sure he's dead
¹⁴and the old hunter says   ¹⁵OK I'll just do that   ¹⁶and after a few seconds
¹⁷the woman hears a loud bang   ¹⁸you know   ¹⁹like a shot from a gun
²⁰and finally the old guy comes back on the phone and says   ²¹OK I've done that
²²What do I do next?

48.4 In the transcript in 48.3, which words ending with a vowel sound are connected to following words beginning with a vowel sound? Find the examples in the groups given. The slight consonant sound which is used to connect them is also given.

Note:

- In this speaker's accent, the sound /r/ is not usually pronounced at the end of a word, so words such as *after* end with a vowel sound: /ˈæftə/.
- This speaker sometimes cuts the /h/ sound from *he* so that *he* starts with a vowel sound.

1 Group 2: /ʷ/ = <u>do about</u>

2 Group 3: /ʷ/ = <u>so he</u>   /ʳ/ = <u>for advice</u>

3 Group 5: /ʳ/ = ...

4 Group 6: /ʲ/ = ...

5 Group 7 /ʳ/ = ...

6 Group 11 /ʲ/ = ...

7 Group 16 /ʳ/ = ...

8 Group 22 /ʷ/ = ...

48.5 Read the phrases below. Underline the blue word which has a different vowel sound.

EXAMPLE   in the woods   on the ground   <u>the</u> old hunter

1 the other guy	the woman	on the phone
2 to shoot a few	what to do	to ask
3 the start	the end	the beginning
4 to phone	to explain	to make sure
5 the airport	the station	the university
6 to visit	to invite	to help

49 White_bread or brown_bread?
Connected speech: sound changes

A

⏺C45 Two friends, Laurence and Vanessa, are discussing what meal they could make from the food in the kitchen.

Listen to the conversation. Notice the connection between the words shown by the symbol ‿.

Laurence: Well_we've_got_some_bread, brown and white, and peppers, and_we've_got_a _tin_of_sweet_corn …

Vanessa: We_could_mix_the_sweet_corn_with_the_tuna, and_salad_cream and have_sandwiches …

Laurence: We_don't_have_any_eggs so_we_can't_make_an_omelette … ehm, sandwiches sound like_a_really_good_idea. Do_you_like_baked_beans?

Vanessa: Yep. Beans_on_toast? We_could_toast_the_bread?

Laurence: Do_you_like_white_bread or_brown_bread?

Vanessa: I_like_brown_bread. What_about_you?

Laurence: I_like_brown_as_well.

baked beans = white beans cooked in tomato sauce and tinned
yep = informal version of yes

B

⏺C46 Listen to the word *sandwiches* taken from the conversation above. The speakers pronounce it as /ˈsæmwɪtʃɪz/. To make the word easier to say, the speakers cut the *d*. They also change the *n* to /m/ because this leaves the lips in a better position to pronounce the /w/ afterwards.

C

⏺C47 Speakers also cut or change sounds across more than one word. For example, listen to the words *sweet corn* from the conversation. To make the phrase easier to say, the speaker changes the *t* in *sweet* to /k/ because this leaves the mouth in the right position to say the *c* in *corn*. The phrase sounds like 'sweek corn'.

Here are some more examples from the conversation:

baked beans sounds like 'bake beans'
white bread sounds like 'wipe bread'
brown bread sounds like 'browm bread'

 Note: Speakers don't always make these changes. When people are speaking carefully, they may not change these sounds.

D

⏺C48 The sounds at the end of words which are most often cut or changed are /t/, /d/ and /n/.

Listen to these phrases first in careful speech and then in fast speech.

A careful speech	B fast speech
	sounds changed
white bread	white → 'wipe'
white coffee	white → 'wike'
red pepper	red → 'reb'
red cabbage	red → 'reg'
green pepper	green → 'greem'
green grapes	green → 'greeng' /griːŋ/
	sounds cut
sliced bread	sliced → 'slice' /slaɪst/
boiled potato	boiled → 'boil' /bɔɪld/

Exercises

49.1 🔊 **C49** Listen to this conversation. Underline the words which sound like the 'words' in the box.

EXAMPLE *could* in *could make* sounds like '*coub*', so underline <u>could</u>.

| 'coub' /kʊb/ (x 4) 'frook' (x 2) 'greem' 'jackip' |

Laura: We <u>could</u> make some cakes with the margarine. Some fruit cake?
Andy: Yeah. I dunno though. Dunno if I fancy fruit cake.
Laura: Or we could make a salad with the green peppers and the salad cream.
Andy: Yeah, I suppose so.
Laura: Or we could make a potato salad, if that would be more interesting?
Andy: Yeah. Or we could just do a jacket potato.
Laura: We haven't got any cheese though.
Andy: That's true. But you could put the beans on the pot … eh on the potato.

jacket potato = a potato baked in its skin

49.2 Which word is written incorrectly, i.e. as it sounds? Underline it and write the correct word.

EXAMPLE You can't <u>cup</u> bread with a spoon! .... cup ⟶ cut ....

1 We drank coffee and ape biscuits. ....
2 I went to a grape party last weekend. ....
3 I had a bag cold so I went to bed. ....
4 Jim's got a sung called Tom. ....
5 Were you talk cookery at school? ....
6 I got ache questions correct out of ten. ....

49.3 In these phrases, how is the sound at the end of the first word often changed in fast speech? Underline the correct option.

A careful speech	B fast speech
a sweet corn **b** sweet potato	sweet → 'sweep' / '<u>sweek</u>' sweet → '<u>sweep</u>' / 'sweek'
1 eight grapes **2** eight pears **3** salad cream **4** salad bowl **5** bad milk **6** bad cream **7** one pizza **8** one cake **9** ten carrots **10** ten potatoes	eight → 'ache' / 'ape' eight → 'ache' / 'ape' salad → 'salag' / 'salab' salad → 'salag' / 'salab' bad → 'bag' / 'bab' bad → 'bag' / 'bab' one → 'wung' / 'wum' one → 'wung' / 'wum' ten → 'teng' / 'tem' ten → 'teng' / 'tem'

49.4 🔊 **C50** Listen to the phrases in 49.3 spoken twice, once in careful speech and once in fast speech. Write the order you hear them in, using C for *careful*, F for *fast*.

EXAMPLE **a** .... C, F ....
         b .... F, C ....

1 ....
2 ....
3 ....
4 ....
5 ....
6 ....
7 ....
8 ....
9 ....
10 ....

50 // Do you actually know //
Fast and careful speech

🔊 C51 Words which are very common in conversation are often made shorter. For example, the word *actually* may be pronounced with /ˈæk.tʃu.ə.li/ (four syllables) in careful speech. However, normally it is made shorter, for example /ˈæ.tʃli/ or even /ˈæ.tʃi/ (two syllables).

Listen to six conversation fragments containing *actually*. In the first, *actually* is pronounced carefully. In the others, it is made shorter.

🔊 C52 You will hear part of a radio show about the dangers of giving too much personal information on the website **Facebook**. Mike is the presenter and Nic and Mel are two guests on the show. Notice Mike's pronunciation of the blue questions (**bold** shows careful speech).

Mike: **// How many people // ehm // does the average person have as friends //**
// on Facebook? //

Nic:	// Six hundred //	Mel:	// Ooh no // I think it's less than that //
Nic:	// Really? //	Mel:	// I'd say two fifty //

Mike: // The average person // how many friends do you think they have on Facebook? //
// is that your final answer? //
// Two fifty // and six hundred //

Nic:	// Six hundred //	Mel:	// Yeah //
Mike:	// It's actually ninety //		
Nic:	// Uh //	Mel:	// Really? //
Mike:	// Yeah // ninety //		
Nic:	// We're above average //	Mel:	// That we are Nicola // That we are! //

Notice that:

- Mike uses careful speech to make sure his guests hear the question properly. The speech units are well separated.

- Mike uses fast speech to repeat the question. He doesn't need to speak so carefully because his guests already know what he said. In the second version of the question, there are fewer speech units and some of the words are very reduced, for example *do you think*.

🔊 C53 Listen to the next part of the show, which includes a section of very fast speech. Notice there are a lot of false starts shown by ⌫.

Mike: **// But //** don't you think even ⌫ I think even that ⌫ I think it was ninety or //
// it could have been wrong // hundred and twenty // could be wrong //
// I think it was ninety // ehm // don't quote me on that // I'll just ⌫ I just ⌫ //
Nic: // You are full of //
Mike: // I was adam ⌫ //
Nic: // solid gold information //
Mike: // adam it ⌫ adamant that it was ninety //
// and now I'm thinking // was it one twenty? //
Mel: // Was it really? //
Mike: // but I ⌫ but I remember this morning them saying //
// I do remember them saying // you know // even ninety // right //
// Do you really know // ninety people? //

adamant = very sure

Mike's speech is full of ⌫ because:
- he is correcting himself or starting again
- he is being interrupted by the other speakers.

These features are typical of fast conversation and can make it difficult to follow. However, notice that after this section of fast speech, Mike returns to the main topic with a question in careful speech.

Exercises

50.1 🔊 C54 Listen to the next part of the show. How many times do you hear the word *actually*?

....

50.2 🔊 C54 Listen to the recording in 50.1 again. The speakers ask three questions using careful speech to make sure that their listeners understand. Write down the three questions.

1 ....

2 ....

3 ....

50.3 🔊 C55 Listen to the next part of the show without reading the transcript. Then read the transcript below and tick the best sentence to describe yourself.

When I listened, I

a) understood everything.
b) understood the main points.
c) understood a few words.
d) understood very little because
   it was too fast.

Mel:
// I na ⊠ I ⊠ I must have about <u>five</u> hundred // <u>six</u> // maybe even <u>more</u> people //
// and I go <u>through</u> it all the time // and <u>think</u> // 'I don't <u>speak</u> to you' // de<u>lete</u> //
// 'I don't even speak to <u>you</u>' // de<u>lete</u> // you don't <u>know</u> her // <u>like</u> //
// you <u>knew</u> them once in a lifetime // but you <u>don't</u> know them any more //
// and you don't <u>speak</u> to them // so what's the point in <u>keep</u>ing them? //
// it's ⊠ it's <u>stupid</u> //

Mike:
// And if you <u>think</u> // <u>right</u> // they can just look at <u>anything</u> // that you <u>post</u> on there //
// they can <u>see</u> // all ⊠ everything that you put <u>up</u> on there // all your nights <u>out</u> //
// all your <u>writing</u> on people's walls // about your <u>life</u> // they can see <u>anything</u> //
// but you don't <u>know</u> // as you <u>say</u> // if you don't know five <u>hund</u>red of them you ⊠ //
// what's to say <u>one</u> of them // doesn't use that the wrong <u>way</u>? //

50.4 🔊 C56 Some phrases in the conversation in 50.3 are very fast. If you listen to them on their own, they sound like completely different phrases. Listen, find the phrases you hear in the transcript in 50.3 and write them below. The phonemic spellings will help you.

EXAMPLE /ˈaɪmə stævə baʊt/ ..<u>I must have about</u>......................

1 /θruː ɪʔ ʌðə saɪmən θɪŋk/ ....

2 /əˈdəʊ nɪvə spɪktə ˈjuː/ ....

3 /deɪkət siː ˈenəhɪŋ/ ....

4 /ɪfjə dəʔ nəʊ faɪvʌnədʊɪ/ ....

51 // The kitchen ↗ // the garden ↗ // and the grounds ↘ //

Continuing or finishing tones

A

[●C57] In Unit 45, we saw that statements often have a falling tone ↘. However, speakers may also choose a rising tone ↗.

Listen to four fragments of a conversation. Notice the intonation of the final phrase in each fragment, shown below. In the first two fragments, the tone rises at the end. In the second two fragments, the tone falls at the end.

↗ (rising tone)	↘ (falling tone)
… into my gar^b … who'll do tha^t	… half past t$_{en}$ … twenty pe$_{ople}$

B

[●C58] Read the background information. Then read and listen to part of a radio interview. Notice that each speech unit has a rising or falling tone, or ••• (a tone which shows the speaker is thinking about what to say next; see Unit 46).

Charlie works as a guide at Glastonbury Abbey in south-west England. He and the other guides wear the historical clothes of the monks who used to live at the abbey, in order to give visitors an impression of what it was like 500 years ago. He shows the visitors different parts of the abbey, such as the abbot's kitchen, and explains what used to happen there.

Interviewer:
// What does the job en<u>tail</u> then? ↘ // Tell ⊠ Talk us through a typical day ↗ //
// for a monk ↗ // at the abbey ↗ // on a Saturday ↗ //

Charlie:
// Right ↘ // well ↘ // ehm••• // I get there about ten o'clock ↗ //
// and then get changed into ⊠ eh••• // into my garb ↗ // ehm ••• //
// and then the first talk is in the abbot's kitchen at half past ten ↘ //
// and so it'll be either myself or a colleague ↘ // who'll do that ↗ //
// and it'll just be talking to••• // perhaps••• // sometimes••• //
// at that time in the morning it's about twenty people ↘ //
// at most ↗ // perhaps in the summer ↗ // eh••• //
// you just tell them••• // about twenty minutes talking ↗ //
// about the eh abbot's kitchen ↗ // and what happens in there ↗ //

abbey = church and buildings for living in
abbot = the person in charge of an abbey
monk = religious man
garb = clothes, costume

C

When we say a list, we often use ↗ to show that the list is to be continued and ↘ to show that it is complete:

// the kitchen ↗ // the garden ↗ // and the grounds ↘ //

Charlie's description of his typical day is a list of actions, and he uses ↗ and ↘ as explained above:

// I get there about ten o'clock ↗ //

This is the first action on a list, and the ↗ shows he is going to continue.

// and then the first talk is in the abbot's kitchen at half past ten ↘ //

The ↘ shows that he has completed the first part of his description.

Exercises

51.1 ⏺C59 Listen to more fragments from Charlie's radio interview. Is there a rising or falling tone at the end? Put ↗ or ↘.

EXAMPLE   perhaps at 12 o'clock there's another talk [↗]

1 the whole tour round the grounds ☐
2 eh, around the grounds ☐
3 whatever they're interested in ☐
4 that's about 45 minutes ☐
5 some are just more interested in general history ☐
6 ehm, and then that's just repeated through the day ☐

51.2 ⏺C60 Listen to the next part of the interview. Put ↗ or ↘ in gaps 1–7. Put ↘ if the speech unit sounds complete. Put ↗ if it sounds like Charlie is going to continue.

// so it's ⊠ that's how it <u>starts</u> .....↗..... // and then after <u>that</u>
[1]............ //
// perhaps at twelve o'clock there's a<u>no</u>ther talk ↗ // ehm //
// <u>gen</u>erally [2]............ // I won't be doing <u>that</u> one ↗ //
// as I do a tour at about <u>quar</u>ter past twelve [3]............ //
// eh // around the <u>grounds</u> ↘ // which is a <u>bit</u> longer than the talk [4]............ //
// that's about forty-<u>five</u> minutes ↘ // the whole tour round the <u>grounds</u> ↗ //
// ehm //well // depending on <u>ques</u>tions asked [5]............ //
// that can take up to an <u>hour</u> or whatever ↗ // so an hour <u>round</u> the grounds [6]............ //
// just talking to <u>them</u> ↗ // whatever they're <u>inte</u>rested in ↗ //
// some people go there for King <u>Arthur</u> [7]............ //
// some are just more interested in general <u>his</u>tory ↗ //
// ehm // and then that's just repeated through the <u>day</u> ↘ //

51.3 In these lists, put // to show speech units and ↗ or ↘ to show tone. Practise saying the lists using the intonation you have marked.

EXAMPLE   I got up had a shower got dressed had breakfast and went out

// I got up ↗ // had a shower ↗ // got dressed ↗ // had breakfast ↗ // and went out ↘ //

| **1** | The | tours | start | at | twelve | one | thirty | three | o'clock |
| | and | five | thirty | | | | | | |

| **2** | I | arrive | at | work | sign | in | put | on | my | uniform |
| | and | have | a | coffee | | | | | | |

| **3** | You | can | swim | go | walking | visit | the | sights | or |
| | just | relax | | | | | | | |

| **4** | You | can | choose | small | medium | or | large | with | milk |
| | or | without | milk | | | | | | |

Follow-up: Practise describing your typical day. List your actions using ↗ and ↘ tones.

52 // It's about four hours ↗ //
Sure and unsure tones

A 🔊C61 In Unit 45, we saw that open questions often have a falling tone ↘ and yes/no questions usually have a rising tone ↗.

Listen to four questions. Notice the intonation at the end of each question. The movement up or down begins on the syllable with the main stress, which is <u>underlined</u>.

↗ (rising tone)	↘ (falling tone)
Did you have to leave <u>ear</u>ly?	How far a<u>way</u> was it?
And did it cost you a lot of <u>mon</u>ey?	How long did it <u>take</u>?

 Note:

- A tone may rise a lot or only a little bit, or it may fall first and then rise. In this book, we do not separate these different rising tones; we use the symbol ↗ for all of them.

- A speaker can use the rising tone to make a statement into a question, e.g.

  // You got back late? ↗ // (meaning: *Did you get back late?*)

- Rising tones are also quite common for open questions. It makes the question sound more like a conversation and less like an interview, e.g.

  // What time did you get back? ↗ //

B 🔊C62 Read the background information. Then read and listen to part of the conversation.

Laura and Andy, who live in south-east England, have been talking about Andy's recent excursion to a place called Alton Towers. Laura is asking about the journey time and the price.

Laura: // How far a<u>way</u> was it? ↘ // How long did it <u>take</u>? ↘ //
Andy: // Eh••• // It's a<u>bout</u> four hours ↗ // <u>may</u>be ↗ // yeah three four hours ↗ //
Laura: // OK ↗ // so it's quite a long <u>trip</u> ↘ //
Andy: // Yeah ↘ // and it's in the middle of <u>no</u>where ↘ // as <u>well</u> ↘ //
Laura: // Did you have to leave <u>ear</u>ly? ↗ //
Andy: // <u>Yeah</u> ↘ // We ehm••• // We wha ⊠ // We got <u>up</u> ⊠ // I <u>think</u> it opens ↗ //
  // about nine o'<u>clock</u> ↘ // <u>so</u> ↘ // <u>yeah</u> ↘ // We got up about six o'clock ↘ //
  // to <u>get</u> there ↗ //
Laura: // And did it cost you a lot of <u>mon</u>ey? ↗ //
Andy: // Ehm••• // It's about••• // It's <u>quite</u> dear ↗ // It's twenty-<u>five</u> ↗ // thirty <u>quid</u> ↗ //
  // a <u>head</u> ↗ // But it's well <u>worth</u> it ↘ //

dear = expensive   *quid* = pounds   *a head* = per person

In Unit 45, we saw that statements often have a falling tone ↘. However, speakers may choose a rising tone ↗ to show they are not sure about the information. The rising tone makes some of Andy's statements sound like questions. For example, in the statements below, it seems Andy is not sure and he's asking himself the hidden questions.

unsure statement	hidden question
// four <u>hours</u> ↗ //	// Is it four hours? //
// thirty <u>quid</u> ↗ //	// Is it thirty quid? //

C 🔊C63 The hidden question depends on the context. Listen to these examples.

// I spent about sixty pounds ↗ //
(Possible hidden question: *Was it sixty pounds?*)

// Last week I went to London Fashion Weekend ↗ //
(Possible hidden question: *Have you heard of London Fashion Weekend?*)

Exercises

52.1 [C64] Read the questions below and decide if they will finish with a rising tone or a falling tone. Put ↗ or ↘. Then listen and check.

EXAMPLE   So have you been anywhere interesting lately? [↗]

1 How often do you dance? ☐
2 Was it expensive? ☐
3 What time's it open? ☐
4 But do they really not know? ☐
5 What could we do with them? ☐

6 Did it take you long to get there? ☐
7 What makes you laugh? ☐
8 How often do you go shopping? ☐
9 What's there to do there? ☐
10 It was just you and your partner? ☐

52.2 [C65] Andy is telling Vanessa about his trip to Alton Towers. Listen and notice the pronunciation of the speech units in blue. Put a rising tone ↗ or a falling tone ↘ in the gaps.

Andy: // I went to Alton <u>Towers</u> // the other day //
Vanessa: // <u>Oh</u> yeah // Where <u>is</u> it? ....↘.... //
Andy: // It's it's up <u>north</u> [1]// It's sort of in the middle of <u>nowhere</u> .... //
// Up near Stoke-on-<u>Trent</u> // I think // It's great <u>fun</u> //
Vanessa: [2]// What do you <u>do</u> there? .... //
Andy: // Oh [3]// It's a <u>theme</u> park .... // So //
// I think it's generally regarded as the best in <u>England</u> //
// Ehm and // You know // You've [4]// It's about twenty-five quid to get <u>in</u> .... //
// I <u>think</u> // per <u>head</u> // And I think <u>family</u> tickets // ehm //
// If you're to go with a <u>family</u> // are maybe about <u>seventy</u> //
Vanessa: [5]// What time does it <u>open</u>? .... //
Andy: // Ehm [6]// About nine in the <u>morning</u> .... // I <u>think</u>//
Vanessa: // Is it open in the <u>evening</u> // the <u>park</u>? //
Andy: // Yeah // Closes about eight o'clock at <u>night</u> // I <u>think</u> //
Vanessa: // Did you drive back the same <u>night</u>? //
Andy: // Yeah [7]// It was hard <u>work</u> .... //
Vanessa: // What time did you get <u>back</u>? //
Andy: // Ehm [8]// Probably about one in the <u>morning</u> .... //

52.3 [C66] Listen to the sentences and decide if the intonation rises or falls at the end. Put ↗ or ↘.

EXAMPLE   [↗] (The speaker is asking herself, 'Was it six o'clock?')

1 ☐
2 ☐
3 ☐
4 ☐
5 ☐

6 ☐
7 ☐
8 ☐
9 ☐
10 ☐

11 ☐

Follow-up: If the intonation rises, what do you think is the speaker's hidden question?

53 // Do I press 'enter'? ↗ //
Intonation in instructions

A 🔊C67 Cindy is explaining to Sue how to look at a video on the Internet. Listen and read their conversation below. Notice that there are a lot of rising tones ↗ in the conversation.

Cindy: // So we can get ⊗ // so if we're going to try to look at a video ↘ //
// on YouTube ↘ // we can either ehm go straight there ↗ // or use Google ↘ //
// to find ↘ // YouTube's address ↘ // ehm··· //

Sue: // I ↘ // know ↘ // Google ↗ // so should I go there? ↗ //

Cindy: // So maybe if you go to the top address bar ↗ //
// and type www dot google dot com ↗ //

Sue: //www dot google dot com // And ↗ // do I press enter? ↗ //

Cindy: // Yes ↘ // I think that ⊗ // I think that's right ↗ //

Sue: // Here we go ↘ //

Cindy: // Perfect ↗ // perfect ↗ // so now there should
be the Google search bar ↗ // // and so if you
enter YouTube ↗ // I think it can be either ↘ //
one word or two ↗ //

Sue: // Oh it comes up ↘ // in a menu thing ↘ //

Cindy: // Ah hah ha excellent ↗ // well ↗ // if it looks ⊗
if it looks right ↗ // // you can go ahead and use
their suggestion ↗ //

B 🔊C68 Listen again to these speech units from the conversation.

instruction	response
// So maybe if you go to the top address bar ↗ // // and type www dot google dot com ↗ //	// And ↗ // do I press enter? ↗ //

Notice that:

- Cindy gives instructions using a rising tone to show that there will be more to follow.

- Sue responds using a rising tone to show that she expects more to follow.

- Other common responses include acknowledgements such as *Ok, right, uh huh*. All of these can be said with a rising tone if the speaker expects more instructions to follow.

C 🔊C69 Laura has been explaining to Andy how he can check his emails. Listen to the end of their conversation.

instruction	response
1 // And then you enter your username in the box ↗ // **2** // and then your password ↘ // **3** // and then you should be logged into your emails ↘ //	// Ah! ↘ //

Notice that:

- Laura uses a rising tone in 1 to show she is going to continue.

- Laura uses falling tones in 2 and 3 to show that her instructions are complete.

- Andy's response also has a falling tone to show he understands that the instructions are complete.

Exercises

53.1 **●C70** Read the next part of the conversation between Cindy and Sue. Decide if the tones are rising or falling and put ↗ or ↘ in gaps 1–10. Then listen and check.

Sue: // Should I go YouTube U̲K̲ ↘ // i̲s̲ it ↗ //
Cindy: // Ehm••• // I think it's out of America but it probably shouldn't m̲atter [1].......... //
// but you can ⊠ // I g̲uess just regular YouTube ↘ // is probably the b̲est [2].......... //
Sue: // And and••• // y̲es ↘ //
Cindy: // So n̲ow what came up? [3].......... //
Sue: // Y̲ouTube came up ↘ // G̲reat [4].......... //
Cindy: // E̲xcellent ↘ // so I guess if you just click on the first o̲ne [5].......... // that ehm••• //
Sue: // Double c̲lick? [6].......... //
Cindy: // P̲erfect [7].......... //
Sue: // OK ↗ // R̲ight ↘ //
Cindy: // So n̲ow what do you see? [8].......... //
Sue: // Ah // W̲ell [9].......... // the••• // YouTube ehm••• // homep̲age I can see ↘ //
Cindy: // E̲xcellent [10].......... //
// and is there anywhere that you can see to s̲earch for something ↘ //
Sue: // To s̲earch ↘ // so y̲es ↘ // near the••• add•••ress b̲ox ↗ //

53.2 **●C71** Put the conversation in order by numbering the lines. Use the intonation to help you. Then listen and check.

☐1 // Could you put those photos on my pen drive? ↗ //

☐ // Oh ↘ // Right ↘ //

☐5 // OK ↗ // And does the icon come up on the screen? ↗ //

☐ // OK ↗ // So just move the file of photos over the icon ↗ // And that's it ↘ //

☐ // Sure ↘ // How do I do that? ↘ //

☐4 // Uh huh ↗ // OK ↗ //

☐ // Well ↘ // if you plug it into the computer ↗ //

☐ // Yeah ↗ // Uh huh ↗ //

53.3 **●C72** Listen and decide if the speaker is going to continue or has finished. Put ↗ or ↘.

EXAMPLE   You type in 'intranet'   ☐↗

1 Click that button and then save   ☐

2 Click that link that says 'check your mail'   ☐

3 The link is if you click in that text box   ☐

4 And then you should be logged into your emails   ☐

5 A: And then enter? B: Yeah, and then enter   ☐

6 You've requested an encrypted page   ☐

7 And then hit 'return'   ☐

8 If you scroll back up   ☐

9 And then it should give you a bunch of results   ☐

10 So if you just click on one   ☐

54

// He's quite rude ↘ // isn't he? ↘ //
Intonation in opinions

[C73] Sue is discussing well-known British comedians with Laura and Cindy. Listen and read their conversation below. Notice the intonation in the blue speech units.

Sue: // Ooh // I tell you <u>one</u> comedian ↗ // that <u>I</u> don't like ↗ // that's Russell <u>Brand</u> ↘ //
// But I don't know what <u>you</u> think to him ↗ // But oof! ↘ //

Laura: // I think he's quite <u>funny</u> ↗ // I think that he he's very hyper<u>ac</u>tive ↘ //
// And I I think that he's quite difficult to watch too <u>much</u> of ↘ //
// But I think <u>some</u>times he can be quite funny ↗ //

Sue: // <u>Right</u> ↘ // <u>Right</u> ↘ //

Cindy: // What sort of stuff does he <u>do</u>? ↗ //

Sue: // Ehm // One-<u>li</u>ners ↗ //

Laura: // He's quite <u>rude</u> ↘ // <u>isn</u>'t he? ↘ //

Sue: // Yes ↘ //

one-liner = very short joke

Notice that:

- Sue uses a falling tone to give a definite opinion.

- Laura uses a rising tone to show her opinion is less sure. This tone suggests that there is a hidden 'but':

opinion	hidden **'but'**
I think he's quite funny ↗	(but he's also quite rude)

[C74] The hidden *'but'* tone falls before it rises. Sometimes the fall is bigger than the rise; the final rise may be very small and difficult to notice.

Listen to the sentence below slowed down.

// But I think sometimes he can be quite funny // (hidden *'but'*: *but not all the time*)

Notice that the tone movement begins at the syllable with the main stress. In the example above, the speaker stresses *sometimes*, perhaps to contrast with *all the time*. The word *sometimes* is quite a long way from the end of the sentence, so the tone moves across all of the last six words in the speech unit.

[C75] Notice that, in the conversation in A, Laura expresses an opinion using a tag question *isn't he?* Although this appears to be a question, it is really an opinion, so she uses a falling tone.

// He's quite <u>rude</u> ↘ // <u>isn</u>'t he? ↘ //

 Note: Tag questions may also be used when the speaker is really asking a question, as in the example below. In this case, the tone rises.

// So you'd be OK with that then ↘ // would you? ↗ //

Listen to the example sentences above and compare the intonation.

Exercises

54.1 🔊 C76 Listen. Put ↘ if the speaker is definite or ↗ if they are expressing a 'hidden *but*'.

EXAMPLE   I really like John Bishop ↘

1 I've seen it advertised ☐

2 I know a <u>bit</u> about it ☐

3 I like him because he's so intelligent as well ☐

4 I mean I agree I don't I don't <u>like</u> *Big Brother* ☐

5 Yeah, 'cause I watched the <u>first</u> series ☐

6 It was so different from these you know big Hollywood blockbusters ☐

7 I thought the book was really really good ☐

8 I <u>kind</u> of enjoyed it ☐

54.2 🔊 C77 Read the sentences and the hidden *'buts'*. Underline the word with the main stress in each sentence and draw the intonation arrow from that word to the end. Then listen and check.

EXAMPLE   I <u>think</u> it's based on a book. (*but I'm not sure*)

1 I saw the first programme in the series (*but I didn't see the rest*)

2 I quite like Woody Allen films (*but I'm not crazy about them*)

3 I've never actually seen *Big Brother* (*but I've heard about it*)

4 I don't usually like thrillers (*but I liked that one*)

5 I think sometimes they can be quite interesting (*but usually they aren't*)

6 I think I've read most of her books (*but not all of them*)

54.3 🔊 C78 Listen to some short fragments from conversations. Which tag questions do you hear?

| isn't it? x5   isn't he?   do you?   wasn't it?   didn't it?   don't you? |

EXAMPLE   .... *isn't it?* ....

1 ....   **4** ....   **7** ....
2 ....   **5** ....   **8** ....
3 ....   **6** ....   **9** ....

54.4 🔊 C79 Complete the sentences with the tag questions from the box. Then decide if they are opinions ↘ or real questions ↗. Listen and check.

is it?	EXAMPLE You aren't hungry, ... *are you?* .... ↗
isn't it?	**1** How's your headache? It isn't getting worse, ... ☐
is she?	**2** Those flowers are lovely, ... ☐
isn't he?	**3** You haven't seen my glasses anywhere, ... ☐
~~are you?~~	**4** Torsen's a great player, ... ☐
aren't they?	**5** I'm not sure. He was from Brazil, ... ☐
was it?	**6** I can't quite remember. You need 40 points to win, ... ☐
wasn't he?	**7** Tennis is so boring, ... ☐
don't you?	**8** She isn't a very good swimmer, ... ☐
doesn't it?	**9** I'm not sure. It starts at nine, ... ☐
have you?	**10** It wasn't a very interesting game, ... ☐

55

// It's • absolutely • stun̲ning ↘ //
Showing enthusiasm

A

🔊C80 Read and listen to the first part of a radio interview with a woman who is talking about her recent cruise to the fjords of Norway.

Interviewer: // Ehm••• // Have you be̲en anywhere since th ⊠ ↗ // Were y ⊠ //
// You were going to Nor̲way ↘ // we̲ren't y ⊠ ↗ //

Ava: // I **have** ↘ // yes ↘ // I was ⊠ eh // I went on a Fred Olsen cruise ↗ //
// out of Sou̲thampton ↗ // at the end of eh A̲ugust ↗ // and eh ••• //
// we had an eight-day cruise up to Nor̲way ↘ // up to the fj̲ords ↘ //
// and eh••• // o̲h my goodness ↘ //
// I can certainly recom ⊠ recon ⊠ recommend that to **an**̲ybody ↘ //
// an̲yone thinking about the fjords ↘ // • **do**̲ it! ↘ //

Notice that:

- Ava gives a lot of emphasis in her answer // I **have** ↘ // yes ↘ //to the interviewer's first question. The word is said at a high pitch. As a result, the ↘ is stronger, because it starts from higher. This high fall tone is used to express enthusiasm: Ava h̲as been somewhere, and she is very keen to talk about it.

- Ava gives a lot of emphasis to *do it*: // an̲yone thinking about the fjords ↘ // • **do**̲ it! ↘ //. The word *do* is stressed, and there is a dramatic pause before it. (The symbol • shows the dramatic pause.) This emphasis shows that Ava's recommendation is strong and enthusiastic.

B

🔊C81 Read and listen to the next part of the interview.

Ava: // OK well ↗ // the the Flåm r̲ailway ↗ // is ehm // it's ⊠ they they bi̲ll it ↘ //
// as being unp̲aralleled experience in Europe ↗ // and I think that's pretty f̲air ↗ //
// ehm // it's at a place called Fl̲åm ↗ // we ⊠ we would say Fl̲am ↘ // F-L-A-M̲ ↘ //
// but it's actually Fl̲åm // it's ehm // it's got a ⊠ it goes up to what, two thousand eight hundred and thirty-eight fe̲et ↗ // but it has a gradient of one in eigh̲teen ↘ //
// so it's a p̲retty steep climb ↘ //

Notice that words like *pretty*, *just* and *quite* can make statements weaker or stronger. In // and I think that's pretty f̲air ↗ //, *pretty* makes the statement weaker: *pretty fair* = a little bit fair. In // so it's a p̲retty steep climb ↘//, it makes the statement stronger: *pretty steep* = very steep. This difference in meaning is clear in the pronunciation. Here, *pretty* is stressed and the speech unit has a high fall tone.

C

🔊C82 Read and listen to the next part of the interview.

Ava: // And eh••• // in order to get thr̲ough ↗ // eh to get u̲p to that height ↗ //
// it goes through tu̲nnels that have been pulled out ↗ // you know //
// sort of carved out in the mountains••• // and it's • absolutely • stu̲nning ↘ //

Notice that when she says // and it's • absolutely • stu̲nning ↘ //

Ava expresses an enthusiastic opinion with an extreme adjective, *stunning*, and adds emphasis with *absolutely*. Her pronunciation supports her enthusiasm: she uses both a high fall tone and dramatic pauses.

If speakers use extreme adjectives such as *stunning* wi̲thout enthusiastic pronunciation, such as in the response below, the meaning may be the opposite. Listen; here the speaker is being sarcastic.

Question: // What was the fi̲lm like? ↘ //
Response: // It was stu̲nning ↘ // I fell asl̲eep ↘ //

Exercises

55.1 **●C83** Read the next part of the interview. Guess where Ava will use a high fall tone and dramatic pauses to show enthusiasm, and circle the phrases. Find three more examples. Listen and check.

// and it's (absolutely stunning) // to go up there // as you rise //

// as it as it rises it gets a bit chillier // obviously // but it's just fabulous //

// it's very expensive // for what it is // it costs about eh thirty // thirty-six pounds //

// something like tha ⊠ // thirty-four // thirty-five // thirty-six pounds // for a return trip //

// you can obviously do it with the cruise companies // I should say that //

// and then they'll treat you to lunch // and everything // as well //

// but if you want to do it on your own // you can // but it was stunning //

// and eh // there's a massive waterfall // 'bout three-quarters of the way up //

// and it's ⊠ it's quite reminiscent // obviously much much smaller //

// but quite reminiscent // actually // of eh ⊠ of Niagara //

55.2 **●C84** Listen to the enthusiastic fragments from 55.1 again. You will hear each fragment three times. Now try saying these fragments with the same intonation.

55.3 Which of these sentences would you say with enthusiastic intonation? Which would you say with a normal intonation? Write E (enthusiastic) or N (normal).

EXAMPLE   It's just fabulous. ....E.........
                    It's just around the corner. ....N.........

1 We were just a bit surprised. ....
2 We were just amazed. ....
3 The view was quite nice. ....
4 The view was quite stunning. ....
5 The food was pretty amazing. ....
6 The food was pretty good. ....

55.4 **●C85** In the responses to statements a and b below, one response has an enthusiastic intonation and the other does not. Write E (enthusiastic) or N (normal). Then listen and check.

EXAMPLE
a We had to stay in a five-star hotel.
b We had to spend two days in the airport.

Responses
How awful for you! ....N.........
How awful for you! ....E.........

1 a Forget the beach; it's raining again!
   b They say we don't have to pay; it's free.

Brilliant! ....
Brilliant! ....

2 a I got an A in the exam!
   b I've crashed the car again!

Well done! ....
Well done! ....

3 a I can count to 3 in German.
   b I learnt how to fly a plane while we were on holiday.

Amazing! ....
Amazing! ....

4 a We could pick fresh fruit off the trees in the garden.
   b We had a tiny bit of cheese on a dry, old piece of bread.

Delicious! ....
Delicious! ....

5 a Frank says he'll take us to the airport.
   b The car's broken down and there are no taxis.

Excellent! ....
Excellent! ....

56 Finders keepers
Accent variation relating to R

A 🔊C86 Listen and notice how the speakers pronounce the letter R after a vowel. For example, compare the way Cindy and Sue pronounce the word *losers*: Cindy pronounces the letter R but Sue doesn't.

Cindy is American and Sue is English. They are playing a game: Cindy must try to explain an expression in English and Sue must try to guess what it is. The expression is 'Finders keepers, losers weepers*'.

Cindy: So the first word of this expression is *finders*.
  Sue: Ah, two words, is it?
Cindy: Ah, well it's, so you're looking for …
  Sue: *Finders keepers*? No?
Cindy: Yeah, well that's the first half.
  Sue: *Finders keepers.*
Cindy: And what happens to the previous owner? *Losers* …
  Sue: *Losers* … lose? No! *Losers* … lost? Eh …
Cindy: *Losers weepers!*

* = People who find something can keep it, people who lose something can only weep (cry).

B We can classify accents into two general types:

Silent R accents	R accents
SE Aus NZ	Am Scot Can I

SE = Southern English   Aus = Australian   Scot = Scottish
Am = American   NZ = New Zealand   Can = Canadian   I = Irish

In Silent R accents such as SE (the model in this book), the sound /r/ only occurs *before* a vowel sound. Otherwise, the letter R is 'silent'. For example, in *boring* /bɔːrɪŋ/ we hear the sound /r/, but in *bored* /bɔːd/ the letter R is silent. In R accents, the letter R is pronounced in both words.

 Note: The same rule applies across gaps between words. In Silent R accents, the R is silent in *far to go*, but it is pronounced in *far away* because there is a vowel sound after it. (See Unit 26.)

C 🔊C87 There are certain vowel sounds which always or usually have an R in the spelling but which are pronounced very differently in Silent R accents and R accents. These sounds are shown in blue in the box below.

Listen to the phrases spoken in four different accents: SE , Am , Aus and Scot.

Vowel sounds almost always spelt with an R		
1 /ɜː/	**2** /eə/	**3** /ɪə/
The first word	Fair hair	Near here
Vowel sounds very often spelt with an R		
4 /ɑː/	**5** /ɔː/	**6** /ə/ (word-final)
A large car	Four doors	Finders keepers

Notice that the /r/ is not pronounced / sounded in the SE and Aus accents but is pronounced / sounded in the Am and Scot accents.

 Note: When there is an R in the spelling of a word, many learners of English (and speakers with R accents) expect to hear it and may be confused when it is silent. For this reason, in international English, it may be better to pronounce it. (See Section E5 for more on this.)

Exercises

56.1 Read the conversation between two colleagues who work as nurses at a hospital. Look at all the examples of the letter R in blue. Circle them if they are silent in Silent R accents.

Mark: Listen, Claire. I'm having a party on Thursday. Would you like to come?

Claire: I'm sorry, Mark, I can't. My brother's visiting on Thursday ...

Mark: Bring your brother along – the more the merrier!

Claire: Oh, OK, great! What's the party for?

Mark: It's my birthday. I'll be thirty-four.

Claire: Thirty-four! Poor you – one foot in the grave already!

Mark: You're a nurse, Claire – I expected a bit more sympathy!

Claire: Sorry, Mark, just joking. I'm thirty-something myself. Where's the party?

56.2 ◉C88 Listen to the conversation in 56.1. Who has a Silent R accent and who has an R accent?

56.3 Find a route from A to B. You may only go through a word if the R is silent in Silent R accents.

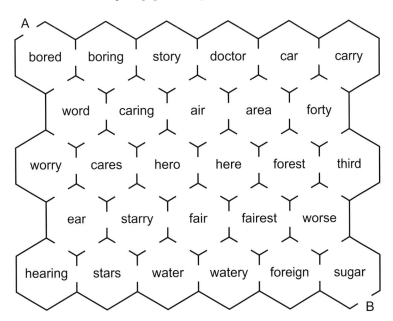

56.4 ◉C88 (cont.) Put the words from the correct route in 56.3 under the correct vowel sound in the box below. Then listen and check your answers. You will hear the words first in a Silent R accent and then in an R accent.

1 /ɜː/	2 /eə/	3 /ɪə/
word	cares	ear
4 /ɑː/	**5 /ɔː/**	**6 /ə/ (word-final)**
stars	bored	water

57 We had a cat
Vowel sound variation in different accents

A Vowel sounds vary a lot across different accents of English. You need to be flexible when listening and not expect words to always be pronounced in the same way you learnt. In this unit, we will compare the vowel sounds of speakers with five different accents:

SE = Southern English NE = Northern English Scot = Scottish
Am = American NZ = New Zealand

Perhaps the biggest variation in these accents is in the pronunciation of vowels which are spelt with the letters A and O. Here are some of the example words we will hear. The phonemic symbols show the pronunciation of the vowel in a SE accent.

1 /æ/	2 /ɑː/	3 /ɔː/	4 /ɒ/	5 /əʊ/
had bad cat	fast laugh dance	walk bought	hot shop not o'clock	cold slowly go

B **New Zealand**

C89 Listen. You will hear two people asking each other the question, 'Have you ever had a dog or a cat?' The first speaker has a SE accent and the second speaker has a NZ accent. Notice that the NZ speaker pronounces *had* and *cat* like *head* or 'ket' in the SE speaker's accent.

C **Northern English**

C90 Listen. You will hear two people asking each other the question, 'How do you walk – slow or fast?' The first speaker has a SE accent and the second speaker has a NE accent. Notice that the NE speaker pronounces the vowel in *fast* so it sounds like the vowel in *fat* in the SE speaker's accent.

D **American**

C91 Listen. You will hear two people asking each other the questions, 'What weather do you prefer – hot or cold?' and 'How do you walk – slow or fast?' The first speaker has a SE accent and the second speaker has an Am accent. Notice that the Am speaker pronounces the same vowel sound in both *hot* and *walk*. It is similar to the vowel sound in *heart* in a SE speaker's accent (/ɑː/), but shorter.

E **Scottish**

C92 Listen. You will hear two people asking each other the question, 'What weather do you prefer – hot or cold?' The first speaker has a Scot accent and the second speaker has a SE accent. Notice that the Scot speaker pronounces *cold* so it sounds like *called* in a SE speaker's accent. The vowel sound in *hot* is longer than in a SE speaker's accent.

⚠ **Note:** In international English (see Section E5), you don't need to worry too much about pronouncing vowels exactly as they do in one particular accent of English. However, it may be better to choose one accent as a model to aim for.

Exercises

57.1 A [NZ] speaker said the sentences below and a [SE] speaker wrote them down wrongly because of the different accent. Underline one or two mistakes in each sentence and write the correct spellings.

EXAMPLE   We need a new frying <u>pen</u>. ....*pan*....

⚠️ **Note:** the [NZ] speaker pronounced *pan* so it sounded like *pen* in a [SE] speaker's accent.

1 I set on the sofa and head a cup of coffee. ....

2 The film was so said that everybody cried. ....

3 I saw an old men carrying a heavy beg. ....

4 My mum and dead decided to merry in 1970. ....

5 I wanted a nice ten but I got a bed sunburn instead. ....

57.2 🔊C93 [SE] speakers say the words *laugh* and *dance* with the long vowel sound /ɑː/. [NE] speakers say these words with the short vowel sound /æ/. Listen and decide if the speakers have [SE] or [NE] accents.

1 ....*SE*....   **3** ....   **5** ....   **7** ....

2 ....   **4** ....   **6** ....   **8** ....

57.3 Which sentence ending rhymes in an American accent and which rhymes in an English accent? Pay attention to the words in blue. Write [SE] or [Am].

EXAMPLE   The visitor thought   **a** the room was hot. ....*Am*....

                                   b he'd enjoy the sport. ....*SE*....

⚠️ **Note:** For an [Am] speaker, *thought* rhymes with *hot*; for a [SE] speaker, *thought* rhymes with *sport*.

1 I went for a walk   **a** in the streets of New York. ....

                               b at eleven o'clock. ....

2 The fish you caught   **a** is now in the pot. ....

                               b was really short. ....

3 Life was calm   **a** when I lived on the farm. ....

                               b where my mother was from. ....

4 When she started to talk **a** I dropped my fork. ....

                               b it was quite a shock. ....

57.4 🔊C94 Listen to a female [SE] speaker and a male [Am] speaker saying the sentences in 57.3 and check your answers.

57.5 🔊C94 (cont.) Listen to a conversation between Mark and Shirley and fill in the missing words. Shirley is from Scotland.

Mark: How do you walk – fast or slow?

Shirley: I'd like to say medium, but my dog ......*walks*...... so slowly sometimes I have to
¹.................................. ².............................. to just be with her.

Mark: What time do you get up and go to bed?

Shirley: I ³.......................... to bed about midnight and I get up about nine ⁴.......................... .

Mark: How often do you go shopping?

Shirley: I ⁵.......................... like ⁶.......................... and I try ⁷.......................... to do it.

Mark: And you don't remember the last time you went or the last thing you bought?

Shirley: Oh yeah, I ⁸.......................... a pair of ⁹.......................... in Mallorca.

58 Rita's writing a book
Consonant sound variation in different accents

A

Consonant sounds are generally similar across different accents of English, but there are a few important variations. In this unit, we will compare the consonant sounds of speakers with four different accents:

| SE | = Southern English | J | = Jamaican | C | = Cockney (London)
| Am | = American

Perhaps the biggest variation in these accents is in the pronunciation of consonants which are spelt with the letters TH and T, as well as a sound which is cut in many accents: /h/.

Here are some of the example words we will hear. The phonemic symbols show the pronunciation of each consonant in a SE accent.

1 /θ/	**2** /ð/	**3** /t/	**4** /h/
thought three	than those	writing butter	his hear hair

B

🔊C95 Listen to SE , J and C speakers saying the sentences below. Notice the pronunciation of the consonants in blue.

1 My mother and brother are both taller than my father.
2 There are three things that we always do on Thursday.
3 I think you should thank Mathew and Thelma for their help.

Notice that:

- The J speaker replaces /θ/ and /ð/ with /t/ and /d/, so *three* sounds like *tree* and *than* sounds like *Dan*.

- The C speaker replaces /θ/ and /ð/ with /f/ and /v/, so *three* sounds like *free* and *than* sounds like *van*.

 Note: Because most world languages and many varieties of English do not have the sounds /θ/ and /ð/, it is perhaps not important to spend a lot of time trying to pronounce these sounds accurately for international English. (See Section E5.)

C

🔊C96 Listen to this short conversation and compare the pronunciation of the letter T.

SE : What are Tom and ehm Rita doing these days?
Am : Well, last I heard, Tom's retired and Rita's writing a book.
SE : Writing a book? Wow!

Notice that the Am speaker pronounces *Rita's writing* so it sounds like *reader's riding* in a SE speaker's accent. In the Am speaker's accent, T only sounds like D before an unstressed syllable (except when T is part of a consonant group, e.g. *poster*). Before a stressed syllable, it is still /t/, for example *Tom* and *retired*.

Listen to a C speaker saying the same sentence as the Am speaker above. Notice that this speaker pronounces the T before an unstressed syllable as a short silence or *stop* /ʔ/, so *writing* sounds like *wri'ing* /raɪʔɪŋ/. This is common in many British accents.

D

🔊C97 Listen to this short conversation and compare the pronunciation of the letter H.

SE : Hi. What are you doing, sitting here in your coat and hat?
C : Well, it's freezing. There's no heating in here!

Notice that the C speaker pronounces *heating in here* so it sounds like *eating in ear* in a SE speaker's accent. Other SE speakers may also cut the /h/ when speaking in relaxed and informal contexts.

Exercises

58.1 🔊C98 Listen to two speakers saying the text below and fill the gaps with the missing words. First you will hear a ☐J☐ speaker and then you will hear a ☐C☐ speaker.

> When I was a kid I ....*thought*............ my parents were [1]................................... the same age, but actually my [2].................................'s ten years older [3].................................... my [4]................................... . She was only twenty-[5].................................... when they got married and he was [6]...................................-[7].................................... . I was their [8]................................... child – I've got [9]................................... older [10]................................... .

58.2 🔊C98 (cont.) Listen to an ☐Am☐ speaker saying the words below. Underline the one in which the speaker pronounces the T as /t/.

EXAMPLE   butter   <u>guitar</u>   heating   water

1 photos	letters	bottle	hotel
2 doctor	waiter	babysitter	daughter
3 better	faster	lighter	hotter
4 hated	wasted	waited	voted

58.3 An ☐Am☐ speaker and a ☐C☐ speaker said the sentences below (☐Am☐ 1–5; ☐C☐ 6–10) and a ☐SE☐ speaker wrote them down wrongly because of the different pronunciations of the letters T and H. Underline one or two mistakes in each sentence and write the correct spellings.

EXAMPLES   ☐Am☐ We need a <u>leader</u> of milk. ....*litre*............
            ☐C☐ I can't <u>ear</u> my <u>art</u> beating! ....*hear, heart*...........

1 Don't worry – it doesn't madder. ....
2 I need reading glasses because I'm short-sided. ....
3 Come on – what are you wading for? ....
4 My grandfather's hair gets wider every year. ....
5 I don't like being seeded by the door in a restaurant. ....
6 I ate getting my air cut. ....
7 You should old it with both ands. ....
8 My airbrush is in my andbag. ....
9 Newtown's in a valley between eye ills. ....
10 Don't worry – is dog's armless. ....

58.4 🔊C99 Look at the photo and read the description. Which words contain a T which would be pronounced as a /ʔ/ in a ☐C☐ accent? Which words contain an H which would be cut? Underline them. Now listen and check.

In this picture we can see a waiter holding a bottle of water. You can see both his hands but you can't see his face. You can also see a woman with long hair sitting at a table – you can just see the back of her head.

58.5 🔊C99 (cont.) Listen to two recordings of the description in 58.4. Is the speaker ☐Am☐ or ☐SE☐?

1 ....
2 ....

59

Hello. I'm from …
English from around the world

Most of the English speakers in the world do <u>not</u> come from English-speaking countries such as the UK, the USA, Australia, etc. Here are three examples.

A   A multilingual speaker of English

D1 Duffy is from Kenya. She has spoken English all her life, along with Swahili and Luhya (a local language in Western Kenya). Her accent is slightly different from the British model used in this book. For example, she doesn't reduce the vowel to /ə/ in function words (see Unit 32). This does not make her English less clear; in fact, it probably makes it clearer. Listen.

Duffy: Eh hello. My name is Duffy. I'm from Kenya. I'm from the capital city, which is Nairobi. I've been living in Spain for about ten years now. Even though I'm from the capital city, my family is initially from a small village on the west of Kenya, in the west of Kenya. It's called Busia. I've been living here for about eh, as I said before, eleven years and I really like it. I have a job in a good company so initially I have no intentions of going back.

B   A non-native speaker of English

D2 Gianluca is from Italy. He has studied English for many years and he has lived in English-speaking countries. He speaks English with an Italian accent. For example, if a word finishes with a consonant sound (e.g. in *called* and *coast*), he sometimes adds a slight vowel sound after it. However, this does not make his English less clear; it is simply part of his accent. Listen to him talking to Duffy.

Gianluca: Well, I eh come from Italy.
Duffy: Oh yeah? What part of Italy?
Gianluca: It's eh a small city, Bari it's called. It's eh in the south of Italy.
Duffy: Oh, I don't know about Bari. I've been to eh Rome, personally.
Gianluca: To Rome? That's the capital. It's quite far from Bari, but it eh it's a lovely place.
Duffy: Is Bari anywhere near Sicily, or more to the south or …
Gianluca: Oh no no no, not at all. It's on eh the Adriatic eh coast.

C   A learner of English

D3 Yoko is from Japan. She is studying English at the moment. Her speech contains some pronunciation features which could make it more difficult to understand. For example, her pronunciation of the sound /l/ in *kilometre* and *language* sounds more like the sound /r/. The listener will probably need some time to get accustomed to her speech. Listen.

Yoko: Hello. My name is Yoko Yabusaki. I'm from Japan. I come from Shizuoka, which is a small city where is a 200 kilometres from Tokyo, and with eh Mount Fuji. My first language is Japanese.
I also speak Spanish and English. I'm a coordinator for travel agency. I live in the centre of Madrid. I live here in Spain for ten years. I love Spain. I want to retire here.

Exercises

59.1 🔊 D4 Listen to Duffy talking to Gianluca. What do they say about these things?

59.2 🔊 D5 Listen to Yoko talking to Duffy.

1 Where does Yoko want to go?
2 Why does she want to go there?
3 What does she *not* want to see?

59.3 🔊 D6 Listen to two learners of English called Laura and Kasia. Answer the questions.

1 Where are they from?
2 Where are they working?

Are there any parts of Laura and Kasia's pronunciation which were difficult to understand?
Look at the script on p.198 and listen again. Underline the parts which you found difficult.

59.4 Complete the text below for yourself. Record yourself saying it.

Hello, my name's .... (name)
I'm from .... (country)
I come from .... (place, e.g. *a small town in the north of the country*)
My first language(s) is / are .... (language)
I also speak (a little) .... (other languages)
I'm a .... (job)

59.5 Imagine you are speaking English to Duffy, Gianluca or Yoko. Think about your own pronunciation of English. Which features of your speech:

1 are part of your English accent?
2 could make it difficult for the other person to understand?
3 are you happy with?
4 would you like to change?

60 Fairtrade
Pronunciation objectives: clarity or speed?

A

⏺ D7 Sophie is a French speaker of English. She is explaining to a radio interviewer the meaning of the Fairtrade label shown in the photograph. Listen and read her explanation.

Sophie: // OK // so the Fairtrade <u>mark</u> // is a guarantee for con<u>sum</u>ers //
// that ehm // the producers have received a fair <u>price</u> // for their <u>prod</u>ucts //
// So <u>this</u> is done // ehm// by an agreed stable <u>price</u> // which covers the cost of pro<u>duc</u>tion //
// and it enables <u>far</u>mers // to provide for their <u>fam</u>ilies //
// And what is also ehm <u>good</u> // as part of this <u>scheme</u> // is that there is a <u>prem</u>ium //
// which <u>farm</u>ers can spend // can rein<u>vest</u> // in <u>any</u> community project // that they
<u>want</u> to // // and there <u>is</u> also a guarantee // that minimum <u>health</u> and safety //
// and environmental standards are <u>met</u> //

Notice that Sophie uses short, clear speech units (shown by //) which make her speech clear and easy to understand. She doesn't use features of pronunciation which native speakers often use to make it easier to speak quickly.

B

Many good speakers of English change their speech according to the context. For friendly conversation, they may use features of pronunciation that enable them to speak fast, but when it is very important to be clearly understood, they may *not* use these. Here are some examples from Sophie's speech where she does *not* use the features of fast speech. This probably makes her sound less like a native speaker, but probably makes her easier to understand in international communication.

- In // the producers have received a fair <u>price</u> //, Sophie separates the word *received* from *a*, rather than joining them together.
- She pronounces *have* as /hæv/ instead of reducing it to /əv/.
- She doesn't reduce the first vowel sound in *consumers* to the weak vowel /ə/.
- She pronounces *families* as three syllables, rather than cutting the second syllable: *fam·lies*.

 Note: The collection of pronunciation features which are important for clarity in international communication has been called the Lingua Franca Core (LFC). See Section E5.

C

Pronunciation objectives may be divided into features which:

- make your speech easier to understand (clarity)
- make it easier for you to speak quickly (speed).

If your main priority is to be understood in international communication, then you could focus on clarity. If you are planning to spend a lot of time in an English-speaking environment, you could also focus on speed. Here is a summary:

A Clarity = easier to understand	B Speed = easier to say quickly
short and clear speech units (shown by //) (Unit 37)	joining words together (e.g. *walked_away* Unit 25)
clear main stress (shown by <u>underlining</u>) (Unit 39)	reducing function words (e.g. *her* = /ə/, Unit 33)
consonants clearly distinguished, (e.g. *price* v *prize*, Unit 4)	reducing unstressed vowels (e.g. *banana* = /bənɑːnə/, Unit 7)
careful pronunciation of consonant groups (e.g. *products*, Unit 22)	cutting sounds and syllables (e.g. *friends* = /frenz/, Unit 50)
vowel sounds clearly distinguished (e.g. *cost* v *coast*, Unit 16)	

Exercises

60.1   **D8** Listen and read another part of the interview.

Sophie explains that Fairtrade products are a bit more expensive than normal products, and the interviewer asks if this means that people won't want to buy Fairtrade products. Here is Sophie's response:

// I think this is quite a possi<u>bili</u>ty // but we we ran an e<u>vent</u> // last <u>Sa</u>turday //
// which involved a Fairtrade ba<u>nana</u>-eating challenge //
// and we fou <u>found</u> that // a <u>lot</u> of people // were very re<u>cep</u>tive // ehm //
// and they showed a great <u>inter</u>est // in Fairtrade <u>prod</u>ucts // so ehm //
// I <u>think</u> // a <u>lot</u> more Fairtrade products // are being <u>sold</u> in the UK // at the <u>mom</u>ent //
// but only <u>one</u> in four bananas // sold in the UK is <u>Fair</u>trade // so there <u>is</u> //
// eh room for im<u>prove</u>ment //

Underline the correct options below.

EXAMPLE   Sophie joins / <u>doesn't join</u> together the words *lot more* so they sound like '*lop ͜ more*'.

1 Sophie uses / doesn't use a slight /r/ to join the words *banana ͜ ʳ ͜ eating*.
2 Sophie pronounces / doesn't pronounce the consonant group /lvd/ at the end of *involved*.
3 Sophie pronounces *were* as /wɜːr/ / /wə/.
4 Sophie puts / doesn't put the main stress on the most important words in each speech unit.
5 Sophie pronounces *banana* as /bæˈnænæ/ / /bəˈnɑːnə/.
6 Sophie uses / doesn't use short, clear speech units.

60.2   Read the objectives of these learners of English. Decide whether they should focus on C (Clarity) or S (Speed).

EXAMPLE   I don't have a lot of time to study pronunciation, so I just want to learn the most important features. ....C......

1 I can already make myself understood, but I would like to be able to speak more quickly. ....
2 I don't want to sound like a native speaker – I just want to be understood. ....
3 I live in an English-speaking country and I would like to sound more like a local. ....
4 I would like to use English to communicate effectively with people from all over the world. ....

60.3   Read these pronunciation tips taken from this book and decide if they are mainly about C (Clarity) or S (Speed).

EXAMPLE   Spelling is not always a good guide to pronunciation. *Shoe* does not rhyme with *toe* even though the spelling of the end of the word is the same. ......C.....

1 In the sound /p/, there is no voice from the throat. Instead, there is a small explosion of air when the lips open. ....
2 The /h/ is often dropped from the beginning of pronouns, so *thanked him* sounds like *thank Tim*. ....
3 You should be sure to pronounce the *final* consonant in a consonant group because this may change the meaning. ....
4 In very fast speech, four-syllable questions may be pronounced with only three syllables, e.g. *What do you want?* /ˈwɒt dʒə ˈwɒnt/ ....
5 By changing the way we divide a message into speech units, we can change its meaning. ....
6 The word *actually* may be reduced to /ˈæ.tʃli/ or even /ˈæ.tʃi/. ....
7 To make *sweet corn* easier to say, the speaker changes the *t* in *sweet* to /k/ because this leaves the mouth in the right position to say the *c* in *corn*. ....

Introduction to phonemic symbols
The phonemic alphabet

/æ/ apple	/e/ egg	/ɪ/ insect	/ɒ/ orange	/ʌ/ umbrella	/ʊ/ book
/aː/ arm	/ɜː/ earth	/iː/ eagle	/ɔː/ organ	/uː/ two	
/eə/ aeroplane	/ɪə/ ear	/aɪ/ eye	/eɪ/ eight	/ɔɪ/ coin	
/əʊ/ oval	/aʊ/ owl	/ə/ banana			

/b/ bird	/tʃ/ chair	/d/ dog	/f/ fish	/g/ girl	/h/ heart
/dʒ/ jar	/k/ key	/l/ leaf	/m/ monkey	/n/ nine	/ŋ/ ring
/p/ pear	/r/ rose	/s/ sofa	/ʃ/ sheep	/ʒ/ television	/t/ table
/ð/ mother	/θ/ thirteen	/v/ volcano	/w/ web	/j/ yacht	/z/ zebra

Exercises

Phonemic spellings which are the same as normal spellings

E1.1 In each of these groups of words, one word is exactly the same as in normal letters. Underline it. Then write the others in normal letters.

Example *Furniture:* /ˈteɪbəl <u>bed</u> ˈsəʊfə tʃeə/
 table *sofa* *chair*

1 *For writing:* /ˈpensəl ˈpeɪpə pen ˈnəʊtbʊk/

2 *In the office:* /desk fæks kəmˈpjuːtə ˈtelɪfəʊn/

3 *Body parts:* /nek hed hænd leg/

4 *Farm animals:* /hen læm ʃiːp caʊ/

5 *Colours:* /griːn bluː red blæk/

6 *Verbs:* /get teɪk gɪv gəʊ/

7 *Numbers:* /ˈsevən ten θriː faɪv/

Phonemic spellings which are very different from normal spellings

E1.2 Some phonemic spellings are surprisingly different from normal spellings. For example, in phonemic spelling, quick is /kwɪk/. Can you find all the words in this wordsearch? The words are horizontal → or vertical ↓ . Use all the letters.

tʃ	eə	ɪ	ŋ	g	l	ɪ	ʃ
m	k	w	e	s	tʃ	ə	n
ɪ	k	n	j	uː	z	b	s
k	w	k	əʊ	s	f	r	ɪ
s	ɪ	w	ʃ	k	j	iː	k
t	k	aɪ	ə	uː	uː	ð	s
e	dʒ	t	n	l	tʃ	z	θ
dʒ	uː	s	ʃ	uː	ə	ð	əʊ

breathes ocean
chair question
edge ~~quick~~
English quite
future school
juice shoe
mixed sixth
news though

Phonemic symbols for vowels

E1.3 Complete these phonemic crosswords. The words in normal spelling are next to the crosswords. You need to write one of these consonant symbols in each empty square. You can use the symbols more than once.

/b d f g h k l m n p r t v w z/

1 Long vowel crossword

rain   ~~bike~~   warm   boot
late   leave   five   room
woke   born   bean   phone

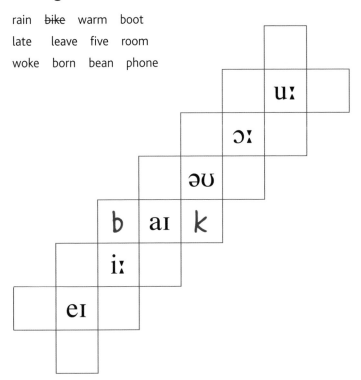

2 Short vowel crossword

hat   put   ~~fit~~   lip   gone
fun   pet   pack   get   look
cot   cup

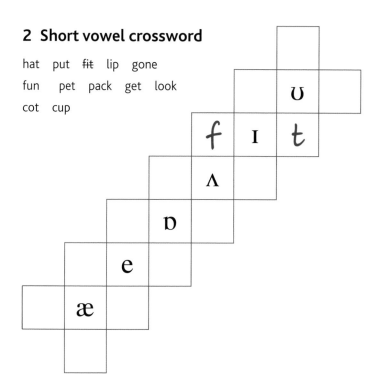

3 Vowels before R crossword

port   hairs   bears   ~~hears~~
heard   card   beard   heart
hers   court

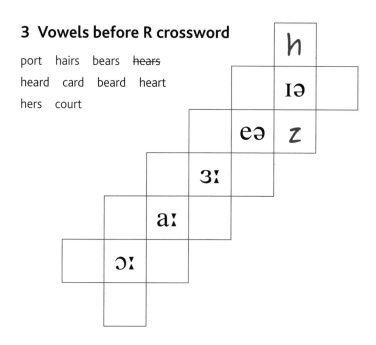

Phonemic consonants which are different from normal consonants

E1.4 Here is a list of different activities. For each activity, one of the words is written with phonemic symbols. Write it in normal letters. Use the table to help you.

Example

/wɒtʃɪŋ/ .....*watching*..... television

1 ski /dʒʌmpɪŋ/ ....

2 /wɒʃɪŋ/ .... the dishes

3 /juːzɪŋ/ .... a computer

4 sun /beɪðɪŋ/ ....

5 /sɪŋɪŋ/ .... songs

6 /θɪŋkɪŋ/ .... about something

7 /pleɪjɪŋ/ .... games

phonemic symbol	usual spelling
ʃ	SH
dʒ	G or J
tʃ	CH
ŋ	NG
j	Y or U
θ	TH
ð	TH

E1.5 Put these words in the correct square in the table. Do not write in the shaded squares.

boy here share shy she toy hair high he bore
pier bear buy be pour tea tie pair deer pea we die
pie dare door fear four wear why fair wore tear

	ɔɪ	ɔː	ɪə	eə	aɪ	iː
w						
f						
d						
p						
t						
b	boy					
h			here			
ʃ						

E1.6 Find phonemic spellings for these thirteen different foods in the wordsearch.
The words are horizontal → or vertical ↓ . Use all the letters.

h	æ	m	b	ɜː	g	ə	s
p	r	f	b	r	e	d	t
æ	aɪ	ɪ	tʃ	ɪ	p	s	r
s	s	ʃ	m	iː	t	ɒ	ɔː
t	k	æ	r	ə	t	r	b
ə	ʌ	n	j	ə	n	ɪ	r
t	ə	m	ɑː	t	əʊ	n	ɪ
b	ə	n	ɑː	n	ə	dʒ	z

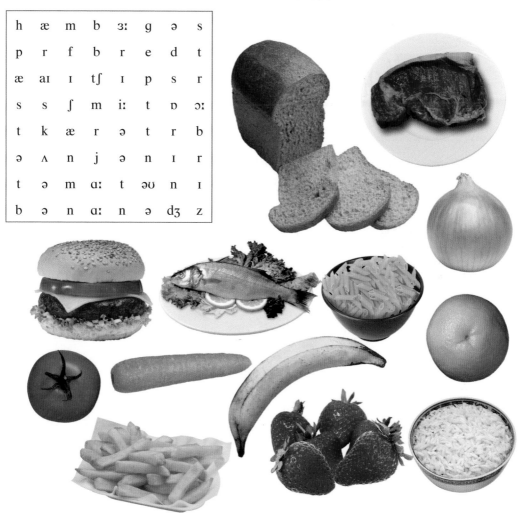

E1.7 Find phonemic spellings for thirteen jobs in the wordsearch. The words are horizontal → or vertical ↓ . Use all the letters.

k	d	ɒ	k	t	ə	n
ʊ	d	r	aɪ	v	ə	ɜː
k	p	eɪ	n	t	ə	s
m	ə	k	æ	n	ɪ	k
f	e	n	dʒ	ɪ	n	ɪə
ɑː	v	r	aɪ	t	ə	g
m	e	s	ɪ	ŋ	ə	ɑː
ə	t	w	eɪ	t	ə	d

E1.8 Here is a word square making the words *can*, *cap*, *not* and *pot*.

c	a	n
a	█	o
p	o	t

Here is a phonemic word square making the words *beach*, *bean*, *cheese* and *knees*.

b	iː	tʃ
iː	█	iː
n	iː	z

Now complete these word squares to make the four words underneath each one.

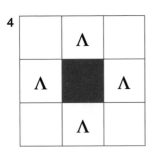

1 rhyme might tight write

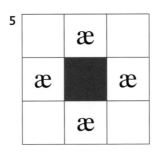

2 laws cause tall talk

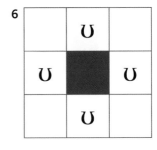

3 shop wash what top

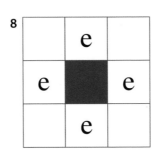

4 cut come touch much

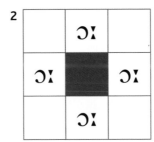

5 back tap cap bat

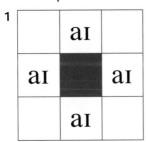

6 could bush should book

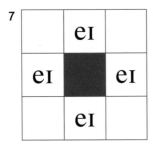

7 pain page jail nail

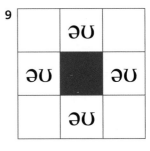

8 yes sell tell yet

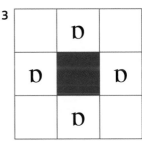

9 wrote roll loan tone

E2 Pronunciation test

Sections A, B and C of this test correspond to Sections A, B and C of the book. If you find one of the test sections more difficult than the others, you can spend more time on the units in the corresponding section of the book.

Section A Sounds

A1   Underline the word with a different vowel sound.

EXAMPLE   hot   <u>hold</u>   gone   swan

1 black	want	mad	hand
2 case	lake	name	care
3 soap	hope	sold	soup
4 what	hot	most	watch
5 foot	look	blood	push
6 rude	luck	run	but
7 leave	beach	bread	clean

My score = ____/7

A2   Underline the word if one of the consonant letters is not pronounced.

EXAMPLE   camp   crisp   <u>climb</u>   cost

1 lamb	label	cable	cab
2 recipe	repeat	receipt	rope
3 listen	winter	eaten	after
4 hour	hate	home	hill
5 old	pile	half	help
6 cold	calm	fold	film
7 hurry	hairy	hungry	here

My score = ____/7

A3   Add the consonant sound to the word to make another word (sometimes with a different spelling).

EXAMPLE   /g/ + eight = <u>gate</u>

1 /k/ + aim = ...

2 /k/ + ache = ...

3 /l/ + eight = ...

4 /r/ + owes = ...

5 /w/ + eight = ...

6 /s/ + eyes = ...

7 /h/ + eye = ...

8 /b/ + air = ...

9 /b/ + earn = ...

My score = ____/9

A4 🔊 D9 Listen and underline the word you hear.

   1 Have you got a *pan / pin / pen* I could borrow?
   2 We should clean the *cut / cat / cot* first.
   3 You won't be able to *fill / feel / fail* this.
   4 I think that's the *west / worst / waist*.
   5 The *cot / coat / court*'s too small.
   6 I don't think it's *far / fur / fair*, you know.
   7 What time did the *woman / women* arrive?
   8 The *officer's / office's* here.
   9 I used to have a *bet / vet / pet*.
  10 I got a good *price / prize* for it.
  11 They didn't *suit / shoot* him.
  12 I think that's the *code / coat / coach*.
  13 That's a *fine / vine / pine* tree.
  14 His *back / bag* was broken.
  15 You can smell it in the *air / hair*.
  16 You'll have to *watch / wash* the baby.
  17 They're *singing / sinking*.
  18 I'll *collect / correct / connect* it tomorrow.

My score = _____/18

A5 🔊 D10 Listen and underline the word you hear.

   1 The *glass / gas* is green.
   2 The *tooth / truth* is out!
   3 I can't *sell / smell* anything.
   4 They *need / needed* more time.
   5 I think they *want / wanted* to talk.
   6 There are *thirty / thirteen* people in my class.
   7 Alice *is / was* here.
   8 The books *are / were* cheap.
   9 I think there are some pears *and / or* grapes.
  10 What *does / did* she say?
  11 *That smile / That's a mile*.
  12 We need more *sport / support*.
  13 It's all in the *past / pasta* now.
  14 Our *guests / guest* came late.

My score = _____/14

A6 Which word has a different number of syllables from the others? Underline it.

EXAMPLE   snakes   sheep   <u>foxes</u>   cats

1 likes	wants	talks	washes
2 wanted	walked	saved	brushed
3 chicken	chocolate	afternoon	different
4 about	around	asleep	asked
5 fourteen	forty	fortieth	hundred
6 builds	rebuild	builder	building
7 supermarket	waterfall	holiday	hairdresser
8 school	texts	over	sports

My score = _____/8

Section B Stress

B1 Underline the word with the stress pattern given.

EXAMPLE ●● enjoy relax <u>visit</u> explain

1 ●●●	hamburger	potato	onions	sandwiches
2 ●●	question	answer	mistake	number
3 ●●●	American	European	Chinese	Japanese
4 ●●●	weekend	Saturday	Sunday	Tuesday
5 ●●	arrive	begin	finish	decide
6 ●●●●	communicate	communication	educate	education
7 ●●●●	photograph	photography	national	nationality

My score = ____/7

B2 Put the phrases from the box in the correct part of the table according to the stress patterns. There are two phrases in each section.

Where do you live? Go and see. Close the door. I'm cold and tired.
What would you like? Pleased to meet you. Call and thank him. I'd like to help.

●●●●	●●●●	●●●	●●●●
Where do you live?			

My score = ____/7

B3 All the words or expressions in each group have the same number of syllables. Underline the one with the stress in a different place.

EXAMPLE October November December <u>January</u>

1 Saturday	holiday	tomorrow	yesterday
2 morning	fifty	fifteen	August
3 He told me.	I like it.	She finished.	Close the door.
4 Go to bed!	Don't worry!	What's the time?	fish and chips
5 table	tourist	tunnel	today
6 mistake	famous	become	remove
7 playground	shoe shop	first class	handbag
8 economics	economy	education	scientific
9 It isn't true.	I'll see you soon.	No, it isn't.	He's not at home.

My score = ____/9

Section C Intonation

C1 **D11** Listen. **Which sentence do you hear? Tick (✓) a or b.**

EXAMPLE **a** Was that the question he asked? ✓
b 'Was that the question?' he asked.

1 a We walked carefully downstairs. It was dark.
b We walked carefully. Downstairs it was dark.

2 a I saw her clearly. She was hungry.
b I saw her. Clearly, she was hungry.

3 a The word he said was right.
b The word he said was 'right'.

4 a It was cold last night. The roads were icy.
b It was cold. Last night, the roads were icy.

5 a 'Who?' said Martin.
b Who said 'Martin'?

6 a What she said was good.
b What she said was, 'Good'.

7 a Let's go home later. We can have a pizza.
b Let's go home. Later we can have a pizza.

My score = ____/7

C2 **D12** Listen. **You will only hear the response. Which one is it? Tick (✓) a or b.**

EXAMPLE **a** – The train leaves at eleven fifteen. **b** – The train leaves at twelve fifty.
– No it doesn't, it leaves at twelve fifteen. – No it doesn't, it leaves at twelve fifteen. ✓

1 a – Where are you from? **b** – Which part of Africa are you from?
– North Africa. – North Africa.

2 a – Do you have any brothers or sisters? **b** – You have some brothers, don't you?
– Yes, two brothers. – Yes, two brothers.

3 a – Would you like anything to drink? **b** – Would you like black or white?
– I'd like black coffee, please. – I'd like black coffee, please.

4 a – Malaga's in the south of Italy. **b** – Malaga's in the north of Spain.
– No it isn't, it's in the south of Spain. – No it isn't, it's in the south of Spain.

5 a – Let's go tomorrow. **b** – When is it closed?
– It's closed tomorrow. – It's closed tomorrow.

6 a – What's upstairs? **b** – Where's menswear?
– Menswear is upstairs. – Menswear is upstairs.

7 a – We had to stay in a five-star hotel. **b** – We spent two days in the airport.
– How awful for you! – How awful for you!

8 a – I got an A in the exam! **b** – I've crashed the car again.
– Well done! – Well done!

My score = ____/8

C3   🔊D13 Listen and underline the option you hear.

EXAMPLE   All right.   <u>All right?</u>

1 Now!	Now?
2 Tonight.	Tonight?
3 Five o'clock.	Five o'clock?
4 Here.	Here?
5 Coffee.	Coffee?
6 Milk and sugar.	Milk and sugar?
7 You're tired.	You're tired?

My score = _____/7

Section D Understanding pronunciation in use

D1   🔊D14 Listen to these sentences. Is the expression in blue a 'filler' (said fast and in a low voice) or part of the sentence? If it is 'throw away', underline it. Note that the punctuation is not written, so you must decide from the pronunciation.

EXAMPLE I was born in Scotland <u>you know</u>

1 I don't think these are the men you know
2 I've taught you everything you know
3 Do you know the place I mean it's just over there
4 She's not the one I mean she's too tall
5 They're like wild animals
6 This is like Arctic weather

My score = _____/6

D2   🔊D15 Listen. How does the speaker sound? Underline the best option. Note that the punctuation is not written, so you must decide just from the pronunciation.

EXAMPLE	*The speaker sounds as if he / she…*
Nice day isn't it	… *is /* <u>*isn't*</u> asking a question
1 She plays a lot of instruments piano guitar	… *is / isn't* going to continue the list.
2 Well that is truly amazing	… *is / isn't* really amazed.
3 You're coming here tomorrow	… *is / isn't* asking a question.
4 Oh, thank you very much	… *does / doesn't* really mean it.
5 Next to the supermarket	… *is / isn't* asking a question.
6 I got up had a shower and got dressed	… *is / isn't* going to continue the list.
7 Oh really how interesting	… *is / isn't* really interested.
8 You're from Brazil aren't you	… *is / isn't* asking a question.
9 I think that's my bag	… *is / isn't* sure about it.
10 Yes it's quite good	… *is / isn't* going to say 'but…'

My score = _____/10

D3   **D16** Listen to these sentences. Is the accent from America (the letter R is pronounced after the vowel) or the South of England (the letter R is not pronounced after the vowel)? Write Am or SE.

EXAMPLE   He asked her to dance. SE

1 We started in March. ....

2 It's a fast car. ....

3 My heart's strong. ....

4 Where's the bar? ....

5 It stops and starts. ....

6 A glass of water. ....

7 Was his hair dark or fair? ....

8 It's hard work, of course. ....

9 Are you sure? ....

10 I walk to work. ....

11 Law and order. ....

12 I saw the bird fall. ....

13 He was born on Thursday the thirty-first. ....

14 She taught German. ....

15 I learned to surf in Brazil. ....

16 'Caught' and 'court' sound the same in my accent. ....

My score = ____/16

E3 Guide for speakers of specific languages

Note: It has not been possible to include all languages in this section.

Arabic

From Section A *Letters and sounds* (Units 1–20), you could leave out these units:
2, 4, 5, 14, 18, 20
From Section E4 *Sound pairs*, it would probably be useful for you to do these sound pairs:
4, 13, 14, 23, 28, 35, 36, 37, 40, 41, 44, 45, 46, 48

Chinese

From Section A *Letters and sounds* (Units 1–20), you could leave out these units:
14, 19, 20
From Section E4 *Sound pairs*, it would probably be useful for you to do these sound pairs:
1, 2, 3, 10, 14, 15, 19, 23, 28, 31, 33, 34, 35, 37, 38, 39, 40, 41, 43, 44, 45, 50

Dravidian languages e.g. Tamil

From Section A *Letters and sounds* (Units 1–20), you could leave out these units:
6, 10, 11, 12
From Section E4 *Sound pairs*, it would probably be useful for you to do these sound pairs:
3, 10, 12, 14, 17, 19, 23, 28, 30, 31, 34, 35, 40, 45, 48

Dutch

From Section A *Letters and sounds* (Units 1–20), you could leave out these units:
15, 20
From Section E4 *Sound pairs*, it would probably be useful for you to do these sound pairs:
1, 7, 10, 13, 15, 17, 19, 20, 26, 31, 32, 33, 34, 37, 38, 39, 40, 44, 45

Farsi

From Section A *Letters and sounds* (Units 1–20), you could leave out these units:
3, 4, 5, 6, 8, 9, 12
From Section E4 *Sound pairs*, it would probably be useful for you to do these sound pairs:
1, 9, 10, 12, 14, 19, 23, 24, 25, 35, 38, 48

French

From Section A *Letters and sounds* (Units 1–20), you could leave out these units:
3, 4, 5, 6, 8, 9, 14, 15, 20
From Section E4 *Sound pairs*, it would probably be useful for you to do these sound pairs:
1, 2, 3, 4, 10, 15, 17, 19, 21, 28, 31, 33, 34, 35, 37, 39, 40, 41, 44, 45

German

From Section A *Letters and sounds* (Units 1–20), you could leave out these units:
11, 15, 20
From Section E4 *Sound pairs*, it would probably be useful for you to do these sound pairs:
1, 5, 15, 17, 28, 31, 33, 34, 37, 38, 39, 40

Greek

From Section A *Letters and sounds* (Units 1–20), you could leave out these units:
5, 8, 9, 13, 17, 20
From Section E4 *Sound pairs*, it would probably be useful for you to do these sound pairs:
1, 2, 3, 8, 10, 11, 12, 14, 17, 19, 23, 31, 32, 41, 44, 46, 47, 48

Italian

From Section A *Letters and sounds* (Units 1–20), you could leave out these units:
6, 8, 9, 10, 12, 13, 14, 19
From Section E4 *Sound pairs*, it would probably be useful for you to do these sound pairs:
1, 2, 4, 10, 14, 17, 23, 28, 31, 34, 35, 37, 40, 45

Japanese

From Section A *Letters and sounds* (Units 1–20), you could leave out these units:
3, 6, 12, 20
From Section E4 *Sound pairs*, it would probably be useful for you to do these sound pairs:
2, 6, 9, 17, 24, 25, 27, 29, 32, 33, 36, 43, 46, 48, 49, 50

Korean

From Section A *Letters and sounds* (Units 1–20), you could leave out these units:
10, 15, 20
From Section E4 *Sound pairs*, it would probably be useful for you to do these sound pairs:
1, 9, 10, 12, 14, 17, 19, 23, 26, 28, 29, 30, 31, 32, 33, 34, 35, 37, 40, 45, 46, 50

Malay / Indonesian

From Section A *Letters and sounds* (Units 1–20), you could leave out these units:
13, 15, 16, 20
From Section E4 *Sound pairs*, it would probably be useful for you to do these sound pairs:
1, 10, 19, 23, 28, 30, 31, 32, 34, 35, 37, 40, 44, 45

Polish

From Section A *Letters and sounds* (Units 1–20), you could leave out these units:
8, 18
From Section E4 *Sound pairs*, it would probably be useful for you to do these sound pairs:
1, 3, 10, 17, 26, 28, 31, 32, 33, 34, 35, 36, 39, 40, 41, 44, 45, 46, 47, 48

Portuguese

From Section A *Letters and sounds* (Units 1–20), you could leave out these units:
8, 20
From Section E4 *Sound pairs*, it would probably be useful for you to do these sound pairs:
1, 2, 3, 8, 10, 19, 23, 28, 31, 33, 34, 35, 36, 40, 46, 48, 49

Russian

From Section A *Letters and sounds* (Units 1–20), you could leave out these units:
4, 8, 11, 15, 20
From Section E4 *Sound pairs*, it would probably be useful for you to do these sound pairs:
1, 3, 10, 12, 14, 17, 21, 23, 24, 25, 26, 27, 28, 32, 33, 34, 38, 40, 41, 46, 47, 48

Scandinavian languages

From Section A *Letters and sounds* (Units 1–20), you could leave out these units:
6, 8, 15, 20
From Section E4 *Sound pairs*, it would probably be useful for you to do these sound pairs:
1, 10, 15, 16, 18, 31, 33, 35, 38, 39, 42, 45, 46

South Asian languages e.g. Hindi, Urdu, Bengali, Gujarati

From Section A *Letters and sounds* (Units 1–20), you could leave out these units:
15, 18
From Section E4 *Sound pairs*, it would probably be useful for you to do these sound pairs:
1, 4, 7, 17, 22, 28, 30, 32, 34, 35, 38, 40, 45, 46, 47

Spanish

From Section A *Letters and sounds* (Units 1–20), you could leave out these units:
17, 20
From Section E4 *Sound pairs*, it would probably be useful for you to do these sound pairs:
2, 3, 9, 10, 12, 14, 19, 21, 23, 24, 25, 26, 27, 28, 29, 34, 35, 40, 41, 42, 44, 45, 46, 47, 48, 49

Swahili

From Section A *Letters and sounds* (Units 1–20), you could leave out these units:
4, 8, 15, 20
From Section E4 *Sound pairs*, it would probably be useful for you to do these sound pairs:
1, 2, 3, 4, 9, 10, 13, 14, 17, 19, 21, 23, 28, 32, 33, 34, 35, 40, 41, 45, 50

Thai

From Section A *Letters and sounds* (Units 1–20), you could leave out these units:
3, 6, 10, 11, 15, 18, 19
From Section E4 *Sound pairs*, it would probably be useful for you to do these sound pairs:
3, 5, 6, 17, 30, 31, 33, 34, 35, 36, 38, 40, 45, 50

Turkish

From Section A *Letters and sounds* (Units 1–20), you could leave out these units:
4, 9, 16
From Section E4 *Sound pairs*, it would probably be useful for you to do these sound pairs:
1, 5, 11, 17, 19, 28, 34, 35, 38, 45, 47, 48, 49

West African languages

From Section A *Letters and sounds* (Units 1–20), you could leave out these units:
8, 10, 11, 12, 20
From Section E4 *Sound pairs*, it would probably be useful for you to do these sound pairs:
1, 2, 3, 9, 10, 12, 14, 17, 19, 22, 23, 28, 31, 34, 35, 37, 40, 45, 48, 50

E4 Sound pairs

If you have problems in hearing the difference between individual sounds in Section A of the book, you will be directed to one of the exercises in this section.

or

Look in E3 *Guide for speakers of specific languages*, find the sound pairs recommended for speakers of your language, and do these.

In order to remember which sound pairs you have done, put a tick in the boxes. If you have completed it but you still find it difficult, tick 'visited'. If you are sure you know it, tick 'understood'. If you have recorded yourself saying the words correctly, tick 'recorded'.

D17 Sound pair 1: /æ/ and /e/

For more on these sounds, see Units 2, 6.

Listen to the words in the box.

man – men	had – head
gas – guess	sad – said

Listen. The speaker will say two words from the box.
If you hear the same word twice, write S (same).
If you hear two different words, write D (different).

1 .... 2 .... 3 .... 4 .... 5 .... 6 .... 7 ....

Listen. Circle the word you hear.

8 *bad / bed*
9 *dad / dead*
10 *sat / set*
11 *marry / merry*
12 Talk to the *man / men*.

visited	
understood	
recorded	

D18 Sound pair 2: /æ/ and /ʌ/

For more on these sounds, see Units 2, 18.

Listen to the words in the box.

ran – run	cat – cut
match – much	sang – sung

Listen. The speaker will say two words from the box.
If you hear the same word twice, write S (same).
If you hear two different words, write D (different).

1 .... 2 .... 3 .... 4 .... 5 .... 6 .... 7 ....

Listen. Circle the word or phrase you hear.

8 *fan / fun*
9 *cap / cup*
10 *rang / rung*
11 She's got a *cat / cut* on her arm.
12 *He's sung / He sang* in public.

visited	
understood	
recorded	

D19 Sound pair 3: /æ/ and /ɑː/

For more on these sounds, see Units 2, 14.

Listen to the words in the box.

(Note: In accents where the R is pronounced, these are not minimal pairs.)

hat – heart	had – hard
match – March	pack – park

Listen. The speaker will say two words from the box. If you hear the same word twice, write S (same). If you hear two different words, write D (different).

1 .... **2** .... **3** .... **4** .... **5** .... **6** .... **7** ....

Listen. Circle the word or phrase you hear.

8 *cat / cart*
9 *match / March*
10 *had a / harder* problem
11 He always *packs / parks* slowly.
12 She put her hand on her *hat / heart*.

visited	
understood	
recorded	

D20 Sound pair 4: /eɪ/ and /e/

For more on these sounds, see Units 2, 6.

Listen to the words in the box.

main – men	weight – wet
late – let	pain – pen

Listen. The speaker will say two words from the box. If you hear the same word twice, write S (same). If you hear two different words, write D (different).

1 .... **2** .... **3** .... **4** .... **5** .... **6** .... **7** ....

Listen. Circle the word you hear.

8 *gate / get*
9 *paper / pepper*
10 *waste / west*
11 What would happen if we *fail / fell*?
12 I've got a *pain / pen* in my hand.

visited	
understood	
recorded	

D21 Sound pair 5: /eɪ/ and /eə/

For more on these sounds, see Units 2, 14.

Listen to the words in the box.

(Note: In accents where the R is pronounced, these are not minimal pairs.)

way – wear	pays – pears
they – there	stays – stairs

Listen. The speaker will say two words from the box. If you hear the same word twice, write S (same). If you hear two different words, write D (different).

1 .... **2** .... **3** .... **4** .... **5** .... **6** .... **7** ....

Listen. Circle the word or phrase you hear.

8 *they / their*
9 *stays / stairs*
10 *hey / hair*
11 I don't want *to pay / a pear*.
12 There's *no way / nowhere* to go.

visited	
understood	
recorded	

⊙D22 Sound pair 6: /eə/ and /ɑː/

For more on these sounds, see Unit 14.

Listen to the words in the box.

fare – far	stairs – stars
bear – bar	care – car

**Listen. The speaker will say two words from the box.
If you hear the same word twice, write S (same). If you hear
two different words, write D (different).**

1 .... **2** .... **3** .... **4** .... **5** .... **6** .... **7** ....

Listen. Circle the word you hear.

8 *fare / far*
9 *bare / bar*
10 *cares / cars*
11 I don't think it's *fair / far*.
12 We slept under the *stairs / stars*.

visited	
understood	
recorded	

⊙D23 Sound pair 7: /ɑː/ and /ɔː/

For more on these sounds, see Units 14, 19.

Listen to the words in the box.

farm – form	part – port
bar – bore	star – store

**Listen. The speaker will say two words from the box.
If you hear the same word twice, write S (same). If you hear
two different words, write D (different).**

1 .... **2** .... **3** .... **4** .... **5** .... **6** .... **7** ....

Listen. Circle the word you hear.

8 *farm / form*
9 *park / port*
10 There are thousands of *stars / stores*.
11 You can visit any *part / port*.
12 I don't think it's *far / four*.

visited	
understood	
recorded	

⊙D24 Sound pair 8: /eə/ and /ɪə/

For more on these sounds, see Units 6, 14.

Listen to the words in the box.

hair – here	fair – fear
chairs – cheers	pair – pier

**Listen. The speaker will say two words from the box.
If you hear the same word twice, write S (same).
If you hear two different words, write D (different).**

1 .... **2** .... **3** .... **4** .... **5** .... **6** .... **7** ....

Listen. Circle the word you hear.

8 *where / we're*
9 *dare / dear*
10 *chairs / cheers*
11 *hair / hear*
12 There's something in the *air / ear*.

visited	
understood	
recorded	

D25 ## Sound pair 9: /ʌ/ and /ɑː/

For more on these sounds, see Units 14, 18.

Listen to the words in the box.

| come – calm | much – March |
| duck – dark | cut – cart |

(Note: In accents where the R is pronounced, some of these are not minimal pairs.)

Listen. The speaker will say two words from the box. If you hear the same word twice, write S (same). If you hear two different words, write D (different).

1 .... **2** .... **3** .... **4** .... **5** .... **6** .... **7** ....

Listen. Circle the word you hear.

8 *hut / heart*
9 *much / March*
10 *duck / dark*
11 *cut / cart*
12 Try to *come / calm* down.

visited	
understood	
recorded	

D26 ## Sound pair 10: /ɪ/ and /iː/

For more on these sounds, see Units 6, 11.

Listen to the words in the box.

| hit – heat | rich – reach |
| chip – cheap | live – leave |

Listen. The speaker will say two words from the box. If you hear the same word twice, write S (same). If you hear two different words, write D (different).

1 .... **2** .... **3** .... **4** .... **5** .... **6** .... **7** ....

Listen. Circle the word or phrase you hear.

8 *chip / cheap*
9 *fit / feet*
10 He doesn't want to *live / leave*.
11 Can you *fill / feel* it?
12 Do you want *to sit / a seat*?

visited	
understood	
recorded	

D27 ## Sound pair 11: /iː/ and /ɪə/

For more on these sounds, see Unit 6.

Listen to the words in the box.

| knee – near | pea – pier |
| he – here | tea – tear |

(Note: In accents where the R is pronounced, these are not minimal pairs.)

Listen. The speaker will say two words from the box. If you hear the same word twice, write S (same). If you hear two different words, write D (different).

1 .... **2** .... **3** .... **4** .... **5** .... **6** .... **7** ....

Listen. Circle the word you hear.

8 *we / we're*
9 *knee / near*
10 *pea / pier*
11 *feed / feared*
12 Who is *he / here*?

visited	
understood	
recorded	

D28 ## Sound pair 12: /e/ and /ɜː/

For more on these sounds, see Units 6, 19.

head – heard	west – worst
bed – bird	feather – further

Listen to the words in the box.

(Note: In accents where the R is pronounced, these are not minimal pairs.)

Listen. The speaker will say two words from the box. If you hear the same word twice, write S (same). If you hear two different words, write D (different).

1 .... **2** .... **3** .... **4** .... **5** .... **6** .... **7** ....

Listen. Circle the word you hear.

8 *ten / turn*
9 *lend / learned*
10 *Jenny / journey*
11 That's a nice *bed / bird*.
12 This is the *west / worst* side.

visited	
understood	
recorded	

D29 ## Sound pair 13: /ɪ/ and /e/

For more on these sounds, see Units 6, 11.

did – dead	lift – left
sit – set	bill – bell

Listen to the words in the box.

Listen. The speaker will say two words from the box. If you hear the same word twice, write S (same). If you hear two different words, write D (different).

1 .... **2** .... **3** .... **4** .... **5** .... **6** .... **7** ....

Listen. Circle the word you hear.

8 *miss / mess*
9 *bill / bell*
10 *will / well*
11 Who dropped the *litter / letter*?
12 You should take the *lift / left*.

visited	
understood	
recorded	

D30 ## Sound pair 14: /ɒ/ and /əʊ/

For more on these sounds, see Unit 16.

want – won't	cost – coast
not – note	shone – shown

Listen to the words in the box.

Listen. The speaker will say two words from the box. If you hear the same word twice, write S (same). If you hear two different words, write D (different).

1 .... **2** .... **3** .... **4** .... **5** .... **6** .... **7** ....

Listen. Circle the word you hear.

8 *not / note*
9 *rob / robe*
10 *goat / got*
11 They *want / won't* sleep.
12 The *cost / coast* is clear.

visited	
understood	
recorded	

ⓓ D31 Sound pair 15: /ɒ/ and /ʌ/

For more on these sounds, see Units 16, 18.

Listen to the words in the box.

lock – luck	shot – shut
gone – gun	not – nut

**Listen. The speaker will say two words from the box.
If you hear the same word twice, write S (same).
If you hear two different words, write D (different).**

1 ....   2 ....   3 ....   4 ....   5 ....   6 ....   7 ....

Listen. Circle the word or phrase you hear.

  8 *not / nut*
  9 *lock / luck*
10 They *shot / shut* the door.
11 This shirt has a horrible *collar / colour*.
12 Did you see *they're gone / their gun*?

visited	
understood	
recorded	

ⓓ D32 Sound pair 16: /əʊ/ and /uː/

For more on these sounds, see Units 16, 18.

Listen to the words in the box.

show – shoe	toe – two
blow – blue	soap – soup

**Listen. The speaker will say two words from the box.
If you hear the same word twice, write S (same).
If you hear two different words, write D (different).**

1 ....   2 ....   3 ....   4 ....   5 ....   6 ....   7 ....

Listen. Circle the word you hear.

  8 *soap / soup*
  9 *rule / roll*
10 There's water in my *boat / boot*.
11 He went to the north *pool / pole*.
12 We *grow / grew* strawberries.

visited	
understood	
recorded	

ⓓ D33 Sound pair 17: /əʊ/ and /ɔː/

For more on these sounds, see Units 16, 19.

Listen to the words in the box.

coat – caught	low – law
boat – bought	woke – walk

**Listen. The speaker will say two words from the box.
If you hear the same word twice, write S (same).
If you hear two different words, write D (different).**

1 ....   2 ....   3 ....   4 ....   5 ....   6 ....   7 ....

Listen. Circle the word you hear.

  8 *so / saw*
  9 *low / law*
10 *coal / call*
11 It's a new *bowl / ball*.
12 I *woke / walk* in the morning.

visited	
understood	
recorded	

●D34 ## Sound pair 18: /eʊ/ and /aʊ/

For more on these sounds, see Units 16, 20.

Listen to the words in the box.

| no – now   blows – blouse |
| phoned – found   tone – town |

Listen. The speaker will say two words from the box.
If you hear the same word twice, write S (same).
If you hear two different words, write D (different).

1 .... **2** .... **3** .... **4** .... **5** .... **6** .... **7** ....

Listen. Circle the word or phrase you hear.

8 *know / now*
9 *blows / blouse*
10 It isn't *a load / allowed.*
11 I don't want *to show her / a shower.*
12 Tim *phoned / found* her.

visited	
understood	
recorded	

●D35 ## Sound pair 19: /ʊ/ and /uː/

For more on these sounds, see Unit 18.

Listen to the words in the box.

| full – fool   pull – pool |
| look – Luke |

Listen. The speaker will say two words from the box.
If you hear the same word twice, write S (same).
If you hear two different words, write D (different).

1 .... **2** .... **3** .... **4** .... **5** .... **6** .... **7** ....

Listen. Circle the word or phrase you hear.

8 *Luke / look*
9 *full / fool*
10 *pull / pool*
11 *Should I? / shoe dye*
12 The *butcher / boots you* saw.

visited	
understood	
recorded	

●D36 ## Sound pair 20: /ʌ/ and /ʊ/

For more on these sounds, see Unit 18.

Listen to the words in the box.

| luck – look   bucks – books |

Listen. The speaker will say two words from the box.
If you hear the same word twice, write S (same).
If you hear two different words, write D (different).

1 .... **2** .... **3** .... **4** ....

Listen. Circle the word you hear.

5 *bucks / books*
6 *luck / look*

visited	
understood	
recorded	

Sound pair 21: /ʌ/ and /ɜː/

For more on these sounds, see Units 18, 19.

shut – shirt	suffer – surfer
such – search	ton – turn

Listen to the words in the box.

(Note: In accents where the R is pronounced, some of these are not minimal pairs.)

Listen. The speaker will say two words from the box. If you hear the same word twice, write S (same). If you hear two different words, write D (different).

1 .... **2** .... **3** .... **4** .... **5** .... **6** .... **7** ....

Listen. Circle the word or phrase you hear.

8 *but / Bert*
9 *hut / hurt*
10 *under / earned a*
11 *suffer / surfer*
12 It looks like the butcher's *shut / shirt*.

visited	
understood	
recorded	

Sound pair 22: /ʌ/ and /e/

For more on these sounds, see Units 6, 18.

won – when	study – steady
butter – better	nut – net

Listen to the words in the box.

Listen. The speaker will say two words from the box. If you hear the same word twice, write S (same). If you hear two different words, write D (different).

1 .... **2** .... **3** .... **4** .... **5** .... **6** .... **7** ....

Listen. Circle the word or phrase you hear.

8 *but / bet*
9 *study / steady*
10 *won / when*
11 He shot *a gun / again*.
12 This one's *butter / better*.

visited	
understood	
recorded	

Sound pair 23: /ɔː/ and /ɒ/

For more on these sounds, see Units 16, 19.

short – shot	order – odder
sport – spot	port – pot

Listen to the words in the box.

(Note: In accents where the R is pronounced, some of these are not minimal pairs.)

Listen. The speaker will say two words from the box. If you hear the same word twice, write S (same). If you hear two different words, write D (different).

1 .... **2** .... **3** .... **4** .... **5** .... **6** .... **7** ....

Listen. Circle the word or phrase you hear.

8 *short / shot*
9 *order / odder*
10 *sport / spot*
11 *water ski / what a ski*
12 There's coffee in the *port / pot*.

visited	
understood	
recorded	

⏺D40 ## Sound pair 24: /ɜː/ and /ɪə/

For more on these sounds, see Units 6, 19.

Listen to the words in the box.

bird – beard	her – hear
were – we're	fur – fear

**Listen. The speaker will say two words from the box.
If you hear the same word twice, write S (same).
If you hear two different words, write D (different).**

1 ....   2 ....   3 ....   4 ....   5 ....   6 ....   7 ....

Listen. Circle the word you hear.

  8 *bird / beard*
  9 *were / we're*
10 *fur / fear*
11 I can't see if it's *her / here*.
12 He has a black *bird / beard*.

visited	
understood	
recorded	

⏺D41 ## Sound pair 25: /ɜː/ and /eə/

For more on these sounds, see Units 14, 19.

Listen to the words in the box.

(Note: In accents where the R is pronounced,
some of these are not minimal pairs.)

her – hair	fur – fair
were – where	bird – bared

**Listen. The speaker will say two words from the box. If you hear the same word twice,
write S (same). If you hear two different words, write D (different).**

1 ....   2 ....   3 ....   4 ....   5 ....   6 ....   7 ....

Listen. Circle the word you hear.

  8 *were / where*
  9 *stir / stair*
10 *bird / bared*
11 I can't see if it's *her / hair*.
12 It isn't *fur / fair*.

visited	
understood	
recorded	

⏺D42 ## Sound pair 26: /ɜː/ and /ɔː/

For more on these sounds, see Unit 19.

Listen to the words in the box.

(Note: In accents where the R is pronounced,
some of these are not minimal pairs.)

worked – walked	shirt – short
burn – born	bird – bored

**Listen. The speaker will say two words from the box. If you hear the same word twice,
write S (same). If you hear two different words, write D (different).**

1 ....   2 ....   3 ....   4 ....   5 ....   6 ....   7 ....

Listen. Circle the word you hear.

  8 *bird / bored*
  9 *sir / saw*
10 *shirt / short*
11 You weren't *first / forced* to do it.
12 We *worked / walked* all day.

visited	
understood	
recorded	

D43 ## Sound pair 27: /ɜː/ and /ɑː/

For more on these sounds, see Units 14, 19.

hurt – heart	heard – hard
further – father	firm – farm

Listen to the words in the box.

Listen. The speaker will say two words from the box.
If you hear the same word twice, write S (same).
If you hear two different words, write D (different).

1 .... **2** .... **3** .... **4** .... **5** .... **6** .... **7** ....

Listen. Circle the word you hear.

8 *fur / far*
9 *hurt / heart*
10 *further / father*
11 The question wasn't *heard / hard.*
12 She owned a *firm / farm.*

visited	
understood	
recorded	

D44 ## Sound pair 28: /b/ and /p/

For more on these sounds, see Unit 3.

bill – pill	cubs – cups
back – pack	bin – pin

Listen to the words in the box.

Listen. The speaker will say two words from the box.
If you hear the same word twice, write S (same).
If you hear two different words, write D (different).

1 .... **2** .... **3** .... **4** .... **5** .... **6** .... **7** ....

Listen. Circle the word you hear.

8 *bill / pill*
9 *bush / push*
10 The soldiers lay on their *backs / packs.*
11 They tied the *robe / rope* round his neck.
12 There's a *bear / pear* in that tree.

visited	
understood	
recorded	

D45 ## Sound pair 29: /b/ and /v/

For more on these sounds, see Units 3, 8.

best – vest	bet – vet
cupboard – covered	

Listen to the words in the box.

Listen. The speaker will say two words from the box.
If you hear the same word twice, write S (same).
If you hear two different words, write D (different).

1 .... **2** .... **3** .... **4** .... **5** .... **6** .... **7** ....

Listen. Circle the word or phrase you hear.

8 *bet / vet*
9 *They've ached / They baked* all day.
10 *summer beach / some of each*
11 *Say 'boil'. / Save oil.*
12 *I brushed it. / I've rushed it.*

visited	
understood	
recorded	

Sound pair 30: /p/ and /f/

For more on these sounds, see Units 3, 8.

Listen to the words in the box.

pull – full	copy – coffee
wipe – wife	supper – suffer

Listen. The speaker will say two words from the box.
If you hear the same word twice, write S (same).
If you hear two different words, write D (different).

1 .... **2** .... **3** .... **4** .... **5** .... **6** .... **7** ....

Listen. Circle the word or phrase you hear.

8 *pool / fool*
9 *pine / fine*
10 He was driving *past / fast*.
11 *a nicer pear / a nice affair*
12 a change of *pace / face*

visited	
understood	
recorded	

Sound pair 31: /s/ and /z/

For more on these sounds, see Unit 4.

Listen to the words in the box.

place – plays	Sue – zoo
rice – rise	east – eased

Listen. The speaker will say two words from the box.
If you hear the same word twice, write S (same).
If you hear two different words, write D (different).

1 .... **2** .... **3** .... **4** .... **5** .... **6** .... **7** ....

Listen. Circle the word you hear.

8 *ice / eyes*
9 *sip / zip*
10 They *race / raise* horses here.
11 What's wrong with your *niece / knees* today?
12 I just want some *peace / peas* please.

visited	
understood	
recorded	

Sound pair 32: /s/ and /ʃ/

For more on these sounds, see Units 4, 12.

Listen to the words in the box.

same – shame	self – shelf
fist – fished	sell – shell

Listen. The speaker will say two words from the box.
If you hear the same word twice, write S (same).
If you hear two different words, write D (different).

1 .... **2** .... **3** .... **4** .... **5** .... **6** .... **7** ....

Listen. Circle the word you hear.

8 *sign / shine*
9 *mass / mash*
10 I didn't *save / shave* for years.
11 They didn't *suit / shoot* him.
12 They sat on the *seat / sheet*.

visited	
understood	
recorded	

D49 Sound pairs 33: /s/ and /θ/, /z/ and /ð/

For more on these sounds, see Units 4, 17.

Listen to the words in the box.

sink – think	worse – worth
bays – bathe	closed – clothed

Listen. The speaker will say two words from the box.
If you hear the same word twice, write S (same).
If you hear two different words, write D (different).

1 .... **2** .... **3** .... **4** .... **5** .... **6** .... **7** ....

Listen. Circle the word you hear.

  8 *sing / thing*
  9 *breeze / breathe*
 10 That's a funny *sort / thought*.
 11 Her *mouse / mouth* seems to be smiling.
 12 Are they *closed / clothed* yet?

visited	
understood	
recorded	

D50 Sound pair 34: /d/ and /t/

For more on these sounds, see Unit 5.

Listen to the words in the box.

hard – heart	road – wrote
dune – tune	die – tie

Listen. The speaker will say two words from the box.
If you hear the same word twice, write S (same).
If you hear two different words, write D (different).

1 .... **2** .... **3** .... **4** .... **5** .... **6** .... **7** ....

Listen. Circle the word you hear.

  8 *said / set*
  9 *down / town*
 10 I forgot the *code / coat*.
 11 It's a very *wide / white* beach.
 12 She started *riding / writing* young.

visited	
understood	
recorded	

D51 Sound pairs 35: /t/ and /θ/, /d/ and /ð/

For more on these sounds, see Units 5, 17.

Listen to the words in the box.

tree – three	boat – both
breed – breathe	dough – though

Listen. The speaker will say two words from the box.
If you hear the same word twice, write S (same).
If you hear two different words, write D (different).

1 .... **2** .... **3** .... **4** .... **5** .... **6** .... **7** ....

Listen. Circle the word you hear.

  8 *tree / three*
  9 *day / they*
 10 I don't want your *tanks / thanks*!
 11 That's what I *taught / thought*!
 12 They couldn't *breed / breathe* very well.

visited	
understood	
recorded	

🔊 D52   Sound pairs 36: /t/ and /tʃ/, /d/ and /dʒ/

For more on these sounds, see Units 5, 12.

Listen to the words in the box.

art – arch	what – watch
paid – page	head – hedge

Listen. The speaker will say two words from the box.
If you hear the same word twice, write S (same).
If you hear two different words, write D (different).

1 ....   **2** ....   **3** ....   **4** ....   **5** ....   **6** ....   **7** ....

Listen. Circle the word you hear.

  8   *taught / torch*
  9   *aid / age*
10   It's a tropical *beat / beach*.
11   He took the *coat / coach* all the way to London.
12   It went over my *head / hedge* into the next garden.

visited	
understood	
recorded	

🔊 D53   Sound pair 37: /f/ and /v/

For more on these sounds, see Unit 8.

Listen to the words in the box.

leaf – leave	half – halve
safer – saver	ferry – very

Listen. The speaker will say two words from the box.
If you hear the same word twice, write S (same).
If you hear two different words, write D (different).

1 ....   **2** ....   **3** ....   **4** ....   **5** ....   **6** ....   **7** ....

Listen. Circle the word or phrase you hear.

  8   *that sofa / that's over*
  9   This is where we *lift / lived*.
10   That's quite a *few / view*!
11   Ask your *wife's / wives'* friends.
12   a current *affair / of air*

visited	
understood	
recorded	

🔊 D54   Sound pair 38: /v/ and /w/

For more on these sounds, see Units 8, 10.

Listen to the words in the box.

vet – wet	veil – whale
invite – in white	verse – worse

Listen. The speaker will say two words from the box.
If you hear the same word twice, write S (same).
If you hear two different words, write D (different).

1 ....   **2** ....   **3** ....   **4** ....   **5** ....   **6** ....   **7** ....

Listen. Circle the word or phrase you hear.

  8   *made of air / made aware*
  9   Which is *verse / worse*?
10   He's not *all wet / a vet*.
11   It's in the *vest / west*.
12   *half a weight / half of eight*

visited	
understood	
recorded	

🔊 D55 Sound pairs 39: /f/ and /θ/, /v/ and /ð/

For more on these sounds, see Units 8, 17.

fin – thin	deaf – death
loaves – loathes	van – than

Listen to the words in the box.

Listen. The speaker will say two words from the box.
If you hear the same word twice, write S (same).
If you hear two different words, write D (different).

1 .... 　 2 .... 　 3 .... 　 4 .... 　 5 .... 　 6 .... 　 7 ....

Listen. Circle the word or phrase you hear.

 8 *first / thirst*
 9 I got these *free / three* gifts.
10 It's a *fort / thought*.
11 *What some of us / What's a mother's* first thought.
12 I don't know *Eva / either*.

visited	
understood	
recorded	

🔊 D56 Sound pair 40: /g/ and /k/

For more on these sounds, see Unit 9.

goat – coat	glass – class
log – lock	blog – block

Listen to the words in the box.

Listen. The speaker will say two words from the box.
If you hear the same word twice, write S (same).
If you hear two different words, write D (different).

1 .... 　 2 .... 　 3 .... 　 4 .... 　 5 .... 　 6 .... 　 7 ....

Listen. Circle the word you hear.

 8 The *gap's / cap's* too small.
 9 His *bag / back* was broken.
10 Did you see the *ghost / coast*?
11 There was a *guard / card* by the door.
12 Is it *gold / cold*?

visited	
understood	
recorded	

🔊 D57 Sound pair 41: /h/ and / /

For more on this sound, see Unit 10.

hill – ill	hold – old
hear – ear	hall – all

Listen to the words in the box.

Listen. The speaker will say two words from the box.
If you hear the same word twice, write S (same).
If you hear two different words, write D (different).

1 .... 　 2 .... 　 3 .... 　 4 .... 　 5 .... 　 6 .... 　 7 ....

Listen. Circle the word you hear.

 8 *hate / eight*
 9 *heart / art*
10 You can smell it in the *hair / air*.
11 She lost her *hearing / earring*.
12 They aren't *heating / eating* it properly.

visited	
understood	
recorded	

D58   ## Sound pair 42: /j/ and /dʒ/

For more on these sounds, see Units 10, 12.

Listen to the words in the box.

use – juice	your – jaw
yoke – joke	yet – jet

Listen. The speaker will say two words from the box.
If you hear the same word twice, write S (same).
If you hear two different words, write D (different).

1 ....   **2** ....   **3** ....   **4** ....   **5** ....   **6** ....   **7** ....

Listen. Circle the word or phrase you hear.

  8   *yet / jet*
  9   *until you lie / until July*
10   I don't see the *yoke / joke*.
11   Did you see *yours / Jaws*?
12   What's the *use / juice*?

visited	
understood	
recorded	

D59   ## Sound pairs 43: /h/ and /ʃ/, /h/ and /f/

For more on these sounds, see Units 8, 10, 12.

Listen to the words in the box.

hip – ship	hot – shot
horse – force	hate – fate

Listen. The speaker will say two words from the box.
If you hear the same word twice, write S (same).
If you hear two different words, write D (different).

1 ....   **2** ....   **3** ....   **4** ....   **5** ....   **6** ....   **7** ....

Listen. Circle the word you hear.

  8   I think the *holder's / shoulder's* broken.
  9   You have to *hold / fold* it there.
10   I can't sleep with this *heat / sheet*.
11   I don't think it's *hair / fair*.
12   The boss *hired / fired* me.

visited	
understood	
recorded	

D60   ## Sound pair 44: /tʃ/ and /ʃ/

For more on these sounds, see Unit 12.

Listen to the words in the box.

cheap – sheep	chair – share
watch – wash	witch – wish

Listen. The speaker will say two words from the box.
If you hear the same word twice, write S (same).
If you hear two different words, write D (different).

1 ....   **2** ....   **3** ....   **4** ....   **5** ....   **6** ....   **7** ....

Listen. Circle the word you hear.

  8   *choose / shoes*
  9   *chair / share*
10   I tried to *catch / cash* the cheque.
11   But there aren't any *chips / ships*!
12   You'll have to *watch / wash* the baby.

visited	
understood	
recorded	

D61 ## Sound pair 45: /tʃ/ and /dʒ/

For more on these sounds, see Unit 12.

Listen to the words in the box.

chin – gin	rich – ridge
chain – Jane	H – age

Listen. The speaker will say two words from the box.
If you hear the same word twice, write S (same).
If you hear two different words, write D (different).

1 .... 2 .... 3 .... 4 .... 5 .... 6 .... 7 ....

Listen. Circle the word you hear.

8 *chose / Joe's*
9 *cheap / jeep*
10 I dreamt of enormous *riches / ridges*.
11 Hair-loss starts with *H / age*.
12 I don't think it's in *tune / June*.

visited	
understood	
recorded	

D62 ## Sound pairs 46: /ts/ and /tʃ/, /dz/ and /dʒ/

For more on these sounds, see Unit 12.

Listen to the words in the box.

cats – catch	mats – match
raids – rage	aids – age

Listen. The speaker will say two words from the box.
If you hear the same word twice, write S (same).
If you hear two different words, write D (different).

1 .... 2 .... 3 .... 4 .... 5 .... 6 .... 7 ....

Listen. Circle the word you hear.

8 *arts / arch*
9 *aids / age*
10 *eats / each*
11 *Watch / What's* the time! / ?
12 They suffered the *raids / rage* of the bandits.

visited	
understood	
recorded	

D63 ## Sound pairs 47: /tr/ and /tʃ/, /dr/ and /dʒ/

For more on these sounds, see Units 12, 13.

Listen to the words in the box.

trees – cheese	train – chain
draw – jaw	drunk – junk

Listen. The speaker will say two words from the box.
If you hear the same word twice, write S (same).
If you hear two different words, write D (different).

1 .... 2 .... 3 .... 4 .... 5 .... 6 .... 7 ....

Listen. Circle the word you hear.

8 *trips / chips*
9 *drunk / junk*
10 The *train / chain* isn't moving.
11 There's something in the *trees / cheese*.
12 It's in the lower *drawer / jaw*.

visited	
understood	
recorded	

⏺D64 Sound pair 48: /n/, /ŋ/ and /ŋk/

For more on these sounds, see Unit 15.

Listen to the words in the box.

thin – thing	sinner – singer
thing – think	singing – sinking

Listen. The speaker will say two words from the box.
If you hear the same word twice, write S (same).
If you hear two different words, write D (different).

1 .... **2** .... **3** .... **4** .... **5** .... **6** .... **7** ....

Listen. Circle the word or phrase you hear.

8 *hand / hanged*
9 *win / wing*
10 *Robin Banks / robbing banks*
11 I *ran / rang* home yesterday.
12 They're *singing / sinking*.

visited	
understood	
recorded	

⏺D65 Sound pairs 49: /m/ and /n/, /m/ and /ŋ/

For more on these sounds, see Unit 15.

Listen to the words in the box.

some – sun	smack – snack
game – gain	some – sung

Listen. The speaker will say two words from the box.
If you hear the same word twice, write S (same).
If you hear two different words, write D (different).

1 .... **2** .... **3** .... **4** .... **5** .... **6** .... **7** ....

Listen. Circle the word or phrase you hear.

8 *term / turn*
9 *mice / nice*
10 The *son warned / sun warmed* me.
11 It's *mine / nine* already!
12 You have to *swim / swing* to the left.

visited	
understood	
recorded	

⏺D66 Sound pair 50: /l/ and /r/

For more on these sounds, see Unit 13.

Listen to the words in the box.

light – write	lock – rock
alive – arrive	flight – fright

Listen. The speaker will say two words from the box.
If you hear the same word twice, write S (same).
If you hear two different words, write D (different).

1 .... **2** .... **3** .... **4** .... **5** .... **6** .... **7** ....

Listen. Circle the word you hear.

8 They *played / prayed* for the team.
9 It wasn't *long / wrong*.
10 They *glow / grow* in the dark.
11 There were *flies / fries* all around my burger.
12 I'll *collect / correct* it tomorrow.

visited	
understood	
recorded	

E5 English as a Lingua Franca

Today, English is used as an international language or Lingua Franca. This means that it is often used for communication outside the countries where it is the native language, such as the USA, Britain, Australia, etc. Also, it is often used to communicate between people who are not native speakers of English. For example, a Spanish student in Denmark will probably attend lectures in English and use English to speak to Danish classmates.

If you are *not* planning to visit or live in an English-speaking country, think about these questions.

Will you be using English to communicate with people:

- via the Internet?
- at an event with visitors from many countries, e.g. a music festival or sports event?
- while travelling to other countries on holiday, for business or for any other reason?
- at university?
- at work, with visitors or clients phoning from other countries?
- from a non-English speaking country?

If you answered *yes* to some of the questions above, then you will probably be using English as a Lingua Franca, or ELF. If this is the kind of English that you most want to learn, then you should pay more attention to some aspects of pronunciation than others. On the next page is a list showing which units of *English Pronunciation in Use Intermediate* are most important for ELF.

Red = very important for ELF
Green = may be important for ELF
Black = not important for ELF

1	Playing with the sounds of English
2	The vowel sounds /eɪ/ and /æ/
3	The consonant sounds /b/ and /p/
4	The consonant sounds /s/ and /z/
5	The consonant sounds /d/ and /t/
6	The vowel sounds /iː/ and /e/
7	Unstressed vowels /ə/ and /ɪ/
8	The consonant sounds /f/ and /v/
9	The consonant sounds /g/ and /k/
10	The sounds /h/, /w/ and /j/
11	The vowel sounds /aɪ/ and /ɪ/
12	The consonant sounds /ʃ/, /dʒ/ and /tʃ/
13	The consonant sounds /l/ and /r/
14	The vowel sounds /ɑː(r)/ and /eə(r)/
15	The consonant sounds /m/, /n/ and /ŋ/
16	The vowel sounds /əʊ/ and /ɒ/
17	The consonant sounds /θ/ and /ð/
18	The vowel sounds /ʌ/, /ʊ/ and /uː/
19	The vowel sounds /ɜː(r)/ and /ɔː(r)/
20	The vowel sounds /ɔɪ/ and /aʊ/

27	Introducing word stress
28	Stress in two-syllable words
29	Stress in compound words
30	Stress in longer words 1
31	Stress in longer words 2
32	Introducing stress patterns
33	Pronouns in stress patterns
34	The verb to be in stress patterns
35	Auxiliary verbs in stress patterns
36	Pronouncing short words (a, of, or)

37	Dividing messages into speech units
38	Speech units and grammar
39	Introduction to main stress
40	Emphasising a contrasting opinion
41	Emphasising added details
42	Main stress in questions
43	Main stress for contrasting information
44	Emphasising corrections
45	Rising and falling tones

21	Consonant groups at the beginning of words
22	Consonant groups at the end of words
23	Words with -s endings
24	Words with -ed endings
25	Consonant sounds at word boundaries
26	Vowel sounds at word boundaries

Notes:

- The table is partially based on the ELF priorities given in *The Phonology of English as a Lingua Franca* (Jennifer Jenkins, OUP, 2000), but modified in some important ways for this book.

- Units 46–60 are not included here because these focus on pronunciation features for listening, not features you are expected to pronounce yourself.

Vowel sounds: It is not important to spend time trying to make your vowel sounds exactly the same as those of a native speaker. Your vowel sounds are part of your accent. However, research suggests that it is important to make a clear difference between long and short vowel sounds, e.g. *meet* and *met*. Also, it is important not to pronounce from spelling, for example by pronouncing the *ea* in *steak* as two vowel sounds rather than one.

Consonant sounds: It is important to pronounce most consonant sounds and consonant groups clearly. However, the consonant sounds spelt TH (/θ/ and /ð/) are not important. Many speakers of English, both native and non-native, are able to communicate without pronouncing these sounds. See Unit 58 for alternative ways of pronouncing TH.

Word stress: Research shows that people often understand each other successfully, even when their speech contains word stress errors. However, if your speech has wrong word stress and other errors as well, it can be difficult to understand.

Stress patterns: Using reduced forms of function words is important if you want to speak quickly and fluently, but they are not important in ELF, and too much reduction can make you *less* intelligible. Many ELF speakers do not use the weak vowel /ə/ (see Unit 7) but they still can still communicate clearly. However, stress patterns (i.e. the typical rhythms resulting from putting stress on content words and no stress on function words) may be important, because if you put stress on function words by mistake, it could sound like 'main stress' (see *Intonation* below).

Joining sounds (Units 25 and 26): Joining words is important if you want to speak quickly and fluently. However, in ELF, this may not make it easy for people to understand you; in fact, it may make it *more* difficult.

Intonation: Research suggests that it is important in ELF to divide what you are saying into speech units, and to use main stress to emphasise the most important word in each speech unit, depending on your meaning in context. However, it is not important to learn to use rising and falling tones like a native speaker.

accent An accent is the way the people of a place pronounce their language. For example, people in London and Sydney both speak English, but they have different accents. Accents are not only regional but may also reflect social differences such as urban / rural, working class / middle class, adult / teenager.

auxiliary verb An auxiliary verb is a verb which does not have a meaning by itself; it helps the grammar of the sentence. For example, in *Do you like music?*, *do* is an auxiliary verb.

careful speech / fast speech People pronounce sentences differently when they speak carefully. For example, you may use careful speech when you are talking in public or reading aloud. But in normal conversation you would use fast speech. See Unit 60 for the pronunciation features relating to careful speech (clarity) or fast speech (speed).

consonant sound A consonant sound is a sound we make by obstructing the flow of air from the mouth.

content words These are words which have a meaning on their own, e.g. nouns, verbs and adjectives. Compare with *function words*.

contraction A contraction is a short form of an auxiliary verb in writing, e.g. *are* is contracted to *re* in *they're*.

function words These are words which don't have a meaning on their own, but which give grammatical meaning in a sentence, e.g. pronouns, prepositions and auxiliary verbs. Compare with *content words*.

glottal stop A short silence made by closing the back of the throat, shown by the phonemic symbol /ʔ/. Some speakers use this sound instead of /t/ in words like *bottle*.

main stress In each speech unit, a speaker puts the main stress on one word. This is the word which they think is the most important in the message. Main stress can go on any word, depending on the context. We put main stress on words by pronouncing them louder, longer and / or higher.

minimal pair If two words are pronounced nearly the same, but they have just one sound different, they are a minimal pair. For example, in the pair *ship* /ʃɪp/ and *sheep* /ʃiːp/, only the second sound is different.

multilingual speaker If you are a multilingual speaker, you have been able to speak two, three or more languages since you were a young child.

native speaker If you are a native speaker of a language, that language is your first language, the language which you learnt as a young child.

non-native speaker If you are a non-native speaker of a language, it is not the language, or one of the languages, which you learnt first, as a young child.

phonemic symbol A phonemic symbol is a letter which represents a sound. For example, the first sound in *shoe* is represented by the phonemic symbol /ʃ/.

rhyme Two words rhyme if they have the same final vowel or vowel and consonant sounds. For example, *go* rhymes with *show* and *hat* rhymes with *cat*.

sound A sound is the minimum segment of the pronunciation of a word. For example, the word *this* has three sounds: /ð/, /ɪ/ and /s/.

speech unit When people speak, they divide their message into pieces called speech units. These help the speaker to communicate the meaning of what they want to say. Boundaries between speech units can be shown by the symbol //.

stress pattern The pattern of strong and weak syllables in a word or sentence is its stress pattern. In this book, stress patterns are represented by big and small circles. For example, the stress pattern of the sentence *How do you do?* is ●●●● (the first and last syllables strong, the second and third syllables weak).

syllable A syllable is a word or part of a word that has one vowel sound. It may also have one or more consonant sounds. For example, *ago* has two syllables. The first syllable is just one vowel sound. The second syllable is a consonant sound followed by a vowel sound.

tone A tone is the way your voice goes up or down when you say a sentence. This can change the meaning of the sentence.

unstressed An unstressed syllable is one which is not pronounced strongly.

voice Many pairs of consonant sounds are similar, but one of them is voiced and the other is not. For example, /d/ is similar to /t/, but /d/ is voiced and /t/ is not. A consonant is voiced when there is vibration in the throat.

vowel sound A vowel sound is a sound we make when we don't obstruct the air flow from the mouth in speaking.

weak vowels Unstressed syllables often contain a weak vowel. The most common weak vowel is /ə/. This is the first vowel sound in *about*, for example. The vowel /ɪ/ is also sometimes weak, in the second syllable of *orange*, for example.

word stress Word stress is the pattern of strong and weak syllables in a word. For example, the word *decided* has three syllables and the second one is pronounced more strongly. So *decided* has this word stress pattern: ●●●.

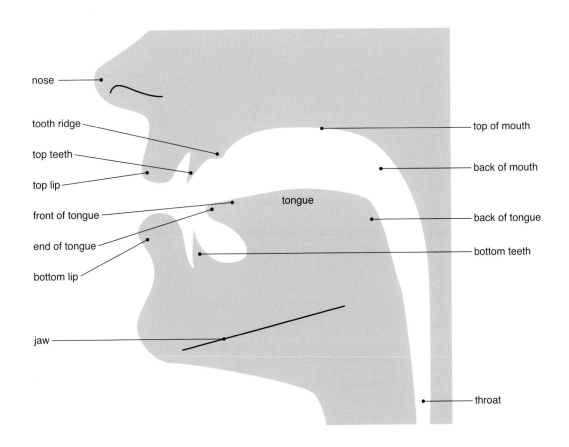

nose

tooth ridge

top teeth

top lip

front of tongue

end of tongue

bottom lip

jaw

tongue

top of mouth

back of mouth

back of tongue

bottom teeth

throat

Answer key

Section A

Unit 1

1.1
1 fun in the sun
2 high and dry
3 the name of the game
4 a man with a plan
5 chalk and talk
6 steer clear

1.2
1 go
2 magazine
3 Doll
4 goal
5 Slower
6 hour
7 wood
8 rude
9 sounds

1.3
1 war
2 cow
3 does
4 bear
5 early
6 close
7 move

1.4
B 3 key
Q 2 shoe
R car star
eye fly tie
10 N pen
Z bed head
9 sign line

Unit 2

2.1
Words with /eɪ/ = [cake], table, baby, eight, train, plate, nail, tail
Words with /æ/ = [apple], hat, hand, cat, rat, map, bag, pan, tap

2.2
1 /eɪ/ = [holiday], Spain, Jane, great, train, plane, staying, case, Kate, favour, days, okay
2 /æ/ = [plans], Jack, Manchester, plans, cash, actually, that, flat, cat, back, back, Saturday

2.3
1 man
2 cap
3 heart
4 pen
5 stare

Unit 3

3.1

Stef says:	Mel hears:
1 [pouring]	[boring]
2 bills	pills
3 wrap it	rabbit

3.2   A baboon goes into a pet shop to buy peanuts and bananas.
'Sorry,' says the shopkeeper, 'This is a pet shop – we only sell food for pets.'
'OK,' says the baboon, 'I'd like to buy food for my pet rabbit.'
'What does your pet rabbit eat?' asks the shopkeeper.
'Peanuts and bananas,' replies the baboon.

3.3
1 lamb
2 climb
3 cupboard
4 photo

5 receipt
6 psychology
7 combing

3.4
1 There's a bear in that tree.
2 He had the peach to himself.
3 They've earned it.
4 Say 'boil'.
5 This is a nice affair.
6 Would you like a coffee?

Unit 4

4.1   /s/ street, police, stopped, place, officer, straight, saw, said, yes
/z/ [was, zebra,] zoo, museum

4.2

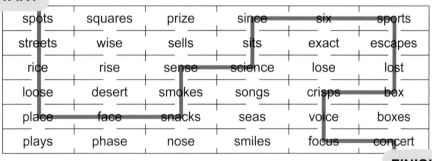

4.3
2 I'm not going to (advise) you, you never take my *advice*.
3 Your tooth is *loose*. You'll (lose) it if you're not careful.
4 The shop's very *close* to home, and it doesn't (close) till late.
5 I can't (excuse) people who drop litter. There's no *excuse* for it.

4.4
1 prize
2 he's at
3 suit
4 saved

5 think
6 clothed

Unit 5

5.1 There was a young lady called Kate,
Who always got out of bed *late*.
The first thing she *said*
When she lifted her *head*
Was: 'I thought it was better to *wait*.'

There was a young waiter called Dwight,
Who didn't like being *polite*.
If you asked him for *food*,
He was terribly *rude*
And invited you out for a *fight*.

5.2
2 wide
3 weighed
4 hurt
5 down
6 try
7 sent

5.3
1 It wasn't *built* in a day; it takes ages to *build* a cathedral like that.
2 When you're out in the mountains, you have to *try* to stay *dry*.
3 He *sent* it to the wrong address, so he had to *send* another copy.
4 It *hurt* my ears when I *heard* that noise.
5 The *white* sofa is too *wide* to go through that door.
6 We went *down* the hill and into the *town*.

5.4
1 whiter
2 dry
3 breeding
4 taught
5 aid
6 Watch

Unit 6

6.1 Words with /iː/ [green], leaf, feet, sweet, tree, key, seat, ski
Words with /e/ [pen], bed, red, bell, shell, tent, bread, head

6.2

present tense (vowel = /iː/)	sleep	meet	*feel*	*read*	leave	dream
past tense (vowel = /e/)	[slept]	*met*	felt	read	*left*	*dreamt*

The verb *read* is interesting because the spelling is the same for the present and past but the pronunciation is different.

6.3
1 met
2 felt
3 leave
4 left
5 Sleep
6 slept
7 dream
8 dreamt
9 read
10 read
11 feel

6.4 **1** men
2 pain
3 pier
4 leave
5 bird
6 left

Unit 7

7.1 pasta, faster
Rita, metre
daughter, water

7.2 **1** from Canada to China
2 The parrot was asleep.
3 The cinema was open.
4 the photographer's assistant
5 a question and an answer
6 a woman and her husband
7 a pasta salad

7.3

vowel in weak syllable = /ə/	vowel in weak syllable = /ɪ/
[woman], collect, asleep, salad, teacher, letter, sofa, quarter	[orange], return, market, begin, visit, teaches, needed, peaches, women

7.4 **1** lettuces
2 bananas
3 carrots
4 sausages
5 oranges
6 sugar
7 peppers
8 peaches

7.5 **1** address
2 way
3 teacher's
4 drive
5 office's
6 woman
7 driver's asleep

Unit 8

8.1 **1** 3   **2** 4   **3** 3   **4** 4   **5** 4

8.2 A giraffe goes into a café and asks for a coffee. The girl who is serving fetches the coffee and leaves the bill on the table. The giraffe finishes the coffee and looks at the bill – very expensive, at four pounds seventy-five.

He gives the girl a fiver to cover the bill and turns to leave. The girl says, 'You know, it's strange, but I've never seen a giraffe in here before.'

'That's not so strange,' says the giraffe, 'if you charge nearly five pounds for a coffee!'

8.3 **2** knives
3 thief's
4 halves
5 wife's
6 life's
7 loaf's

8.4 **1** The last loaf's; been
2 The footballer's wife's; –
3 It's autumn and the first leaves; have already
4 Be careful, your lives; are
5 In most matches, the second half's; usually

8.5 **1** thief's **4** vote
2 view **5** verse
3 copy **6** free

Unit 9

9.1 Douglas met a girl he knew,
Standing quietly in the queue.
In her bag, she had some eggs,
A box of figs and chicken legs,

A pack of burgers, tuna steaks,
Party snacks and chocolate cakes,
Pink ice cream, a box of dates,
Cans of drink and plastic plates.

Douglas looked. 'Oh', said he,
'You're having guests tonight, I see!'
The girl said: 'Yes, that's quite true.'
And then invited Douglas too.

9.2

Stef says:	Mel hears:
1 [glasses]	[classes]
2 bag	back
3 coat	goat

9.3 **1** coast **4** coat
2 glasses **5** blog
3 bag

Unit 10

10.1 **1** Your uniform used to be yellow. /j/ = 4
2 Haley's horse hurried ahead. /h/ = 4
3 This is a quiz with twenty quick questions. /w/ = 5
4 We went to work at quarter to twelve. /w/ = 5
5 New York University student's union /j/ = 5

10.2 [I], a, about, in, the, about, been, doing, Surfing, The
Wendy: Hi, Ewan! How's your wife?
Ewan: Hello, Wendy! Yolanda's well.
How's your husband? Well, I hope?
Wendy: Yes, Harry's well.
We heard you had a holiday?
Ewan: Yes, one whole week without worrying about work!
Wendy: Where were you?
Ewan: We went walking in Wales.
Wendy: How was the weather? Wet? Windy?
Ewan: We had wonderful weather.
What about you? What have you been doing?
Wendy: Surfing.
Ewan: Wow! Where?
Wendy: The world wide web!

10.3
1 under
2 whole
3 who
4 untie
5 honest
6 write

10.4
1 heart
2 earring
3 vest
4 aware
5 juice
6 sheet

Unit 11

11.1

word with /aɪ/	related word with /ɪ/
[light]	[lit]
1 child	children
2 bite	bit
3 drive	driven
4 hide	hid
5 crime	criminal
6 write	written
7 ride	ridden

11.2 Words with /aɪ/: wife, wide, light, life, line, lime, mice, mine, mile, mite, night, nice, nine, fight, fine, file, time, sight, side, site, quite (Also: lice, might, mime, Nile, tight, tile, tide)

Words with /ɪ/: will, wish, win, mill, fit, fill, fish, tin, sit, sin, quit (Also: wit, lit, nit, fin, till, sill, quill)

11.3
1 night
2 fly
3 nice
4 die
5 life
6 wish
7 time
8 light
9 arrived
10 dinner
11 give
12 like

11.4
1 live
2 feel
3 letter
4 lift

Unit 12

12.1

contains /dʒ/	contains /ʃ/	contains /tʃ/
[Belgian], German, Japanese	Polish, Turkish, Welsh, Russian	Chinese, Chilean, Dutch, French

12.2
1 much–change–job–brush–shape–page
2 jump–push–shirt–teach–child–dish
3 fridge–juice–switch–cheek–cash–sugar

12.3

Stef says:	Mel hears:
1 [wash]	[watch]
2 sheets	cheats
3 shoes	choose
4 cheap	sheep

12.4 **1** watch
       2 , Jane
       3 shave

       4 use
       5 What's; ?
       6 trees

Unit 13

13.1 Lilly lost her last umbrella.
       Left it on the train.
       Feeling really silly,
       She ran home in the rain.

       Rory felt so lucky,
       Walking in the rain.
       He'd found a large umbrella
       Lying on the train.

13.2 I worked *late* (rate) that day and I didn't *arrive* (alive) home until 10 o'clock. I was very wet
       because of the *rain* (lane). Then, to my *surprise* (supplies), my key didn't fit in the *lock* (rock).
       So I looked closely at my keys and saw that they were the *wrong* (long) ones. I had left my
       house keys at work. So I got back on my motorbike and *rode* (load) back to the office to *collect*
       (correct) them. I got home really tired, so I went to bed, *read* (led) for half an hour, switched
       off the *light* (right) and went to sleep.

13.3 **1** court
       2 folk
       3 hair

       4 should
       5 artist

13.4 **1** supplies
       2 correct
       3 flight

       4 cheese
       5 drawer

Unit 14

14.1

words with /ɑː/	words with /eə/
[bar], far, star, start, car, card, cart, calm, half, hard, chart, calf	[bare], rare, dare, fair, stair, square, care, hair, hare, chair, stare, fare

14.2 **1** chair
       2 star
       3 care
       4 chart

       5 square
       6 far
       7 stare / stair
       8 half

14.3 **1** [car], alarms, parts, cars, marketing, department, starting, calm, smart, dark, barber's, started
       2 [where], care, spare, fairly, wear, Wear, hair, hairdressers, there, chair

14.4 **1** heart
       2 no way
       3 far

       4 part
       5 pier
       6 come

Unit 15

15.1

Stef says:	Mel hears:
1 [rang]	[ran]
2 term	turn
3 nine	mine

15.2
I knew a you<u>ng</u> woma<u>n</u> called June
Whose m<u>um</u> used to sing 'Blue Moon'.
Her voice was stro<u>ng</u>
But the <u>n</u>otes were all wro<u>ng</u>
And she sa<u>ng</u> the whole so<u>ng</u> out of tu<u>n</u>e.

A slim you<u>ng</u> ma<u>n</u> called Tim
Spent all his ti<u>m</u>e in the <u>gym</u>.
He worked out for lo<u>ng</u>er;
Got stro<u>ng</u>er and stro<u>ng</u>er.
<u>N</u>ow Tim is no lo<u>ng</u>er so sli<u>m</u>.

15.3
1 finger
2 signs
3 kind
4 column
5 king
6 strange

15.4
1 Robin Banks
2 ran
3 swim
4 son warned
5 sinking

Unit 16

16.1

words with /əʊ/	words with /ɒ/
[bone], boat, bowl, comb, goal, road, toes, sofa	[lock], clock, box, doll, sock, frog, watch, cross

16.2
1 wrong
2 woke
3 cough
4 got
5 nose
6 body
7 know
8 cold
9 bone
10 Sorry
11 joking
12 home

16.3
1 come
2 most
3 love
4 cow
5 cloth
6 word
7 lost

16.4
1 coast
2 shut
3 boat
4 woke
5 found

Unit 17

17.1

START					
south	bath	bathing	thought	breath	youth
southern	third	their	through	though	thumb
path	cloth	mouth	fifth	with	worth
month	clothes	thousand	brother	that	teeth

FINISH

17.2 Arthur had a *brother*
And he didn't want *another*.
And of the brothers, *neither*
Wanted sisters, *either*.
The last thing on this *Earth*
They wanted was a *birth*.
So Arthur's mother *Heather*
Got them both *together*,
And told them all good *brothers*
Should learn to share their *mothers*.

17.3
1 bath
2 through
3 thin
4 thick
5 thought
6 death

17.4
1 use
2 taught
3 Free
4 clothed
5 breeding
6 These are

Unit 18

18.1
1 [studied], London, summer, months, pub, lunches, much
2 [school], two, June, July, food, true, too

18.2
2 The *month* /ʌ/ after *June* /uː/ is July.
3 My mother's other *son* /ʌ/ is my *brother* /ʌ/.
4 Brazil *won* /ʌ/ the World *Cup* /ʌ/ in 2002.
5 Fruit *juice* /uː/ is *good* /ʊ/ for you.
6 There is a *full* /ʊ/ *moon* /uː/ once a month.
7 You pronounce *wood* / *would* /ʊ/ exactly the same as *would* / *wood* /ʊ/.

18.3
1 book
2 rude
3 does
4 rule
5 shoulder
6 move
7 south

18.4
1 cat
2 calm
3 gun
4 shows
5 'Pool'
6 luck
7 shut
8 a gun

Unit 19

19.1

Stef says:	Mel hears:
1 [walking]	[working]
2 shorts	shirts
3 bored	bird

19.2
- **1** four
- **2** ball
- **3** wall
- **4** awful
- **5** returned
- **6** third
- **7** thought
- **8** girls
- **9** birds
- **10** called
- **11** more
- **12** working

19.3
- **1** far
- **2** worst
- **3** walk
- **4** shut
- **5** pot
- **6** beard
- **7** her
- **8** walked

Unit 20

20.1
- **1** boys /ɔɪ/
- **2** noise /ɔɪ/
- **3** found /aʊ/
- **4** point /ɔɪ/
- **5** how /aʊ/
- **6** boil /ɔɪ/
- **7** hour /aʊ/
- **8** flower /aʊ/
- **9** enjoy /ɔɪ/

20.2
I had an old teacher called Lloyd
Who everyone tried to *avoid*.
If ever the *boys*
Made any *noise*,
Lloyd was always *annoyed*.

I knew a young boy named McLeod
Whose voice was amazingly *loud*.
From north to *south*
You could hear his *mouth*
As loud as the sound of a *crowd*.

20.3
Words with /ɔɪ/: [enjoy], noisy, points, choice,
Words with /aʊ/: [down], town, loud, shout, out, around

20.4
- **1** toy
- **2** 'Good boy!'
- **3** found
- **4** tone

Unit 21

21.1
c = cloud, clock
d = dress, drawer
f = fly, fruit
g = glove, grape
p = plane, plate
t = train, tree

21.2 The brightest blue
The greyest cloud
The slowest queue
The greatest crowd

The greenest grass
The smallest grain
The cleanest glass
The quickest brain

The freshest breeze
The sweetest fruit
The tallest trees
The smartest suit

21.3 I was once on a short <u>f</u>light from France to <u>S</u>pain. It was only a small <u>p</u>lane and I was by the window. I could see the <u>s</u>now on the ground below. Just when we were <u>f</u>lying through a <u>c</u>loud, we heard one of the engines <u>s</u>top. I was really <u>s</u>cared, but a few moments later, we heard it <u>s</u>tart again. Everything was fine but I decided to return to France on the <u>t</u>rain, even though it was much <u>s</u>lower!

21.4 **1** B   **2** A   **3** A   **4** B   **5** A   **6** B   **7** B   **8** A

Unit 22

22.1 [first, What's, eighth, month], August, Correct, Second, what's, highest, Earth (some accents), Mount, Everest, Correct, Mount Everest, Next, furthest, east, Athens, Brussels, Budapest, Budapest, perhaps, Brussels, Athens, last, what's, biggest, land, world, elephant, correct, that's, percent

22.2 [watched / film]
missed;
start;
think / past / six;
asked;
old's;
it's / seventh / next;
played / cards;
went / watched;
worst;
switched

22.3 **1** cook   **5** guess
2 helper   **6** burnt
3 didn't   **7** pasta
4 learnt   **8** mix

Unit 23

23.1

-s = /ɪz/	[watches], dances, kisses, washes, closes, pushes
-s = /s/ or /z/	[sings], goes, gets, comes, sees, pulls

23.2 There's /z/ no life on the town's /z/ streets /s/any more. Nobody goes /z/ there. Nobody stops /s/ and talks /s/ while they're shopping – the shops /s/ have all closed. There used to be a butcher's, /z/ a green grocer's, /z/ a chemist's, /s/ a newsagent's, /s/ clothes /z/ shops, /s/ lots /s/ of small cafés /z/ – all gone. Now, everybody drives /z/ to the big shopping centres /z/ outside town.

23.3

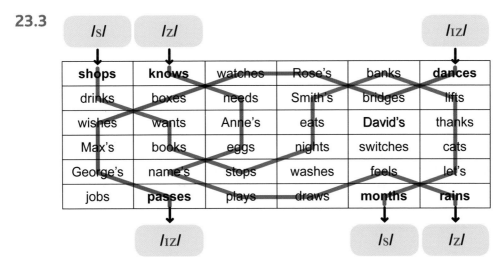

23.4

1 bird
2 guests
3 arms
4 song
5 car

6 books
7 bag
8 shop
9 class
10 boxes

Unit 24

24.1

1 syllable	[walked], washed, helped, phoned, danced, asked
-ed = extra syllable	[hated], needed, waited, wasted, tasted, ended

24.2

● ● ●	●●●●●● (-ed = extra syllable)
[Paul played games.] Ken *cooked* lunch. Fred *phoned* friends. Marge *mixed* drinks. Will *watched* films.	[Peter painted pictures.] Karen *counted* money. Stella *started* singing. Alice *added* sugar. Sheila *shouted* loudly.

24.3   **2** e   **3** g   **4** c   **5** i   **6** a   **7** j   **8** f   **9** b   **10** d

24.4

1 walked
2 want
3 laugh
4 danced

5 hated
6 help
7 enjoy
8 saved

Unit 25

25.1 **1** ~~Known uses~~ good news, as they say. *No news is*
2 Have you ~~phone jaw~~ parents this week? *phoned your*
3 I've never ~~her July~~ before. *heard you lie*
4 I think I ~~fell train~~; let's go inside. *felt rain*
5 These ~~ship steak~~ cars across the river. *ships take*
6 They ~~join does~~ for dinner. *joined us*
7 We ~~stop choosing~~ the typewriter when we got the computer. *stopped using*

25.2 There was ‿ an ‿ old man called Greg,
Who tried to break ‿ open ‿ an ‿ egg.
He kicked ‿ it ‿ around,
But fell ‿ on the ground,
And found that he'd broken ‿ a leg.

25.3 **1** Tim and Heather work~~ed~~ together, Heather never worked‿alone.
2 Susan ate six sweets /sɪks swiːts/ at six o'clock /sɪks‿ əˈklɒk/ and was sick.
3 Lenny talked‿a lot but he never talk~~ed~~ to Lottie.
4 Simon's shop sells‿only socks, Sara's shop sells skirts and tops

Unit 26

26.1 The sky ‿ above is grey ‿ and there's snow ‿ on the ground. /j/ /j/ /w/
Where ‿ am I? No ‿ idea. /r/ /w/
I'll find somewhere dry ‿ and try ‿ and make a fire. /j/ /j/
Oh – there's an old house. Is the door ‿ open? /r/
'Hello, is there ‿ anybody ‿ in there?' Can't hear ‿ anything. /r/ /j/ /r/
There's a chair ‿ and a few ‿ old books – and a fire ‿ in the fireplace. /r/ /w/ /r/
The owner can't be far ‿ away… /r/

26.2

/j/	/w/	/r/
me and you	[blue and green]	saw a film
tie a knot	true or false	draw a line
three or four	no idea	law against

26.3 **1 A:** You don't look well – are you ‿ all right? /w/
    B: No, I think I've got flu ‿ again. /w/
2 A: I saw ‿ a good film on Friday called *Titanic*. /r/
    B: Oh, that's so ‿ old! /w/
3 A: Would you like a cup of tea ‿ or something? /j/
    B: No thanks. I'm about to go ‿ out. /w/
4 A: Can you tell me ‿ a quick way to get to the beach? /j/
    B: Sure – I'll draw ‿ a map for you. /r/

26.4 (As the recording)

Section B

Unit 27

27.1

●●	●●	●●●	●●●	●●●
[Monday] Tuesday Thursday April August second thirty	today July thirteen thirteenth	Saturday holiday thirtieth seventy	tomorrow September October November eleventh	seventeen afternoon

27.2

1 Saturday
2 seventy
3 afternoon
4 eleventh

5 July
6 seventeen
7 tomorrow
8 holiday

27.3

B: On the thirtieth of August.
　　　　 ●●● 　　 ●●

A: That's next Saturday!
　　　　 ●●●

B: We're leaving in the afternoon.
　　　　　　 ●●●

A: And when are you coming back?

B: Saturday September the thirteenth.
　　　　 ●●● 　　　 ●●

A: Thirtieth?
　 ●●●

B: No, thirteenth!
　 ●●

27.4　**1** 17　**2** 14th　**3** 50　**4** 1916　**5** 30　**6** 80

Unit 28

28.1 This is a <u>picture</u> of a <u>kitchen</u>. There's a <u>basket</u> with <u>apples</u>, <u>lemons</u> and an <u>orange</u>. There are a few <u>onions</u> and <u>carrots</u>, and there's a <u>cupboard</u> with some <u>sugar</u> and <u>coffee</u>. There are <u>yellow</u> <u>curtains</u> with a <u>flower</u> <u>pattern</u> in the <u>window</u>. Outside, there's a <u>garden</u> and the <u>weather</u> is <u>sunny</u>.

28.2

Did you	[forget to cancel] agree to delay expect to repeat begin to enjoy offer to explain decide to return	the visit?

I	listened and answered received and copied arrived and entered relaxed and enjoyed tidied and repaired unlocked and opened	the questions. the document. the building. the film. the car. the door.

28.3

1 answer
2 mistake
3 copy
4 guitar

5 complete
6 promise
7 shampoo
8 reason

28.4

1 progressed = ●●   progress = ●●
2 import = ●●   export = ●●
3 protest = ●●   rebelled = ●●
4 desert = ●●   contrast = ●●
5 produce = ●●   objects = ●●

Unit 29

29.1

●●	●●●	●●●●
[bookshops] shoe shops snack bars something playground handbag	[anything] post office hairdresser's everything hamburger sports centre swimming pool credit card	[shopping centre] travel agent's supermarket

29.2

1 second-hand
2 old-fashioned
3 handmade

4 short-sighted
5 half-price
6 first class

29.3

1 a; Yes, I have.
2 b; No, I haven't!
3 a; Yes, I have.
4 a; Yes, I have.

Unit 30

30.1

1 believer, believable, unbelievable, unbelieving
2 enjoyable, unenjoyable, enjoyment
3 careful, carefully, careless, carelessness, carer, caring, uncaring

30.2

1 ●•	nation, clinic, public
2 •●•	relation, romantic, discussion
3 ••●•	[population], scientific, pessimistic
4 •••●•	communication, pronunciation, investigation
5 ••••●•	identification
6 •••••●•	telecommunication

30.3
1. introduce – introduction ••●•
2. base – basic ●•
3. economy – economic ••●•
4. describe – description •●•
5. romance – romantic •●•
6. compete – competition ••●•
7. optimist – optimistic ••●•
8. celebrate – celebration ••●•
9. diplomat – diplomatic ••●•
10. operate – operation ••●•
11. explain – explanation ••●•
12. decide – decision •●•

Unit 31

31.1
1. personality ••●••
2. university ••●••
3. publicity •●••
4. majority •●••
5. nationality ••●••
6. reality •●••
7. ability •●••
8. electricity ••●••

31.2

●•	●••	•●••	••●••	••●•
physics history nation	chemistry geography	economy geology photography technology	nationality	[economics] mathematics

31.3 My favourite subjects at school were sciences, especially *chemistry* and *biology*. I've always been good with numbers, so I was good at *mathematics*. I didn't really like the social science subjects like *geography* and *history*. When I went to university I did computer *technology*.

31.4
1. electricity
2. biology
3. reality
4. creativity
5. activity

Unit 32

32.1
1. two
2. for
3. to
4. four
5. to
6. too

32.2 1 Close the door.
2 What happened?
3 They arrived.

32.3

●••●	●●•●	●•●	●•●•
What do you want?	[The bus was late.]	Come and look.	Close the window.
Give me a call.	The water's cold.	Where's the car?	Nice to see you.
What did she say?	It's cold and wet.	What's the time?	Phone and tell me.

32.4 The <u>even</u>ing was <u>cold</u> and <u>dark.</u> ●●••●•●
I was <u>walk</u>ing my <u>dog</u> in the <u>park.</u> ●●●••●●•●
He <u>chased</u> a <u>cat</u> ●●•●
And <u>fan</u>cy <u>that</u>! ●●•●
It <u>sud</u>denly <u>star</u>ted to <u>bark.</u> ●●••●••●

Unit 33

33.1 1 He liked her face.
2 He asked her her name.
3 She gave him her number.
4 He bought her a gift.
5 She showed him her cat.

33.2 1 We thanked them.
They thanked us.
We showed them our house.
They showed us their house.
2 She met me.
I met her.
She met my friend.
She met her friend.
I met her friend.
I met my friend.
3 He bought you a drink.
You bought him a drink.
He told you his name.
You told him your name.
He asked you a question.
You asked him a question.

33.3 1 it; them
2 you; their
3 he; her
4 she; them
5 she; her
6 his
7 your
8 We; our

33.4 1 He's buying presents for them. ●●•●●•••
2 They're opening their presents. ●●•••●•
3 They'll thank him for the presents. ●●•••●•
4 He'll thank her for the money. ●●•••●•

Unit 34

34.1 **1** ●●●●

The garden's green
The sheets are new
The restaurant's fine
The place is nice
The place was cold
The sheets were old
The smell was strong
The doors were low

2 ●●●●

The walls weren't white
The staff weren't nice

3 ●●●●●

The room wasn't light
The bath wasn't long
The bed wasn't right

4 ●●●●●

The blankets are blue
The service is quick
The service was slow
I think there were mice

34.2 Alice: It was wonderful! ●●●●●
Ben: How much was it? ●●●●●
Alice: It wasn't cheap. ●●●●
Ben: Was it worth it? ●●●●
Alice: I think it was. ●●●●
Ben: Were the staff good? ●●●●
Alice: Yes, they were. ●●●
       They were great! ●●●

34.3

1 are			**6** are	
2 was			**7** was	
3 was			**8** is	
4 were			**9** are	
5 are			**10** were	

34.4

1 are			**6** was	
2 were			**7** was	
3 is			**8** are	
4 are			**9** was	
5 was			**10** are	

Unit 35

35.1
1 Where *do they* live?
2 What *did she* say?
3 Where *will they* work?
4 What *did you* see?
5 Where *have they* gone?
6 Who *did we* meet?
7 Where *will he* sit?
8 When *will it* end?
9 Where *have you* been?
10 Who *has she* asked?

35.2
1 Where do you live? ●••●
2 Where do you work? ●••●
3 Are you married? ••●•
4 What does he teach? ●••●
5 Where does he teach? ●••●
6 Where did you meet him? ●••●•
7 When did you get married? ●•••●•

35.3
1 Who've (have) you told?
2 What did he say?
3 When do you start?
4 Where's he gone?
5 How do you do?

Unit 36

36.1

•●•●	•●•●•	•●••●	•●••●•
[a bowl of soup] a pot of tea	a jar of honey a bag of apples	a bottle of juice a carton of milk	a packet of biscuits a kilo of carrrots

36.2
1 and
2 an
3 for
4 of
5 and
6 to
7 a
8 some
9 for
10 of

36.3
1 *it's* time *for* lunch
2 *some* egg *and* chips
3 *the* bag *of* nuts
4 *to* drink *and* eat
5 *to* cook *some* rice
6 *as* fast *as* that
7 *a* meal *for* two
8 *the* box *of* food
9 *some* fish *or* meat

36.4 1 We had a nice cup of tea.
2 I don't want to go out tonight.
3 I need a drink of water.
4 We cooked a chicken.
5 He can't cook a (or *her*) meal.
6 Have an ice cream!
7 Come in and sit down.

Section C

Unit 37

37.1 2 A, B
3 A, B
4 B, A

37.2 // = full stop; // = comma
1 There was nothing inside // it was empty
2 We walked carefully downstairs // it was dark
3 I watched him // silently // he opened the drawer
4 The rain didn't stop the next day // it just carried on
5 The weather was hot // at the weekend // it was 40 degrees
6 I saw her clearly // she was hungry
7 It was cold // last night // the roads were icy

37.3

	A	B
name	ANNA MARIA	ANN AMARIA
street	Windsor Palace Road	Windsor, Palace Road
phone	935 8226	93 58 226
postcode	W116 9FT	W11 69FT

	A	B
name	JON AILTON	JO NAILTON
street	Padgate High Street	Padgate, High Street
phone	710 82 62 65	71 082 6265
postcode	PA15 3HT	PA1 53HT

Unit 38

38.1 Sheila went to the doctor to complain about pains in her hand // the doctor suggested that she should have an operation // Sheila said // If I have the operation // will I be able to type with all my fingers // yes // of course // replied the doctor // great // said Sheila // I've never been able to do that before

38.2 2 A   3 A   4 B   5 A   6 B   7 A   8 B   9 B   10 A

38.3 1 // You should visit the waterfall // 'cause it // is // absolutely // amazing //
2 // I // really // cannot // understand // why people watch this programme //
3 // There's just // no // way // I'm ever // going out with him again //
4 // The view was amazing // I mean words // simply // cannot // describe it //

Unit 39

39.1 **Gill:** // Paul // Have you seen a document in here? // I left it on the table this morning//
Paul: // Why? // Was it something important? //
Gill: // Yes // It's was a contract // If I've lost it // it will be a disaster //
Paul: // Oh // Do you remember where you left it? //
Gill: // Right here // On this table //
Paul: // Oh // I cleared some papers from here at lunch time // I didn't think they were
important //
Gill: // What did you do with them? //
Paul: // I thought they were rubbish //
Gill: //So what did you do with them? //
Paul: // I // I put them in the shredder //
Gill: // I don't believe it! // You've shredded the contract! // And it was the only copy! //
Paul: // Look // I'm sure we can find the pieces // and then we can put it back together //
Gill: //Oh // no //

39.2 **1** // I just called to say thank you //
2 // Do you know what time it is? //
3 // I saw her at the coffee machine //
4 // It was very kind of you //
5 // My computer's so slow //
6 // Could you check the spelling for me? //
7 // I think John's in Frankfurt or somewhere //
8 // Good afternoon Mr Smith //

39.3 **2 a** // I never forget //
b // I never forget //
3 a // I haven't got a car //
b // I haven't got a car //
4 a // I don't like them //
b // I don't like them //
5 a // I'm not married //
b // I'm not married //

Unit 40

40.1 **A:** I won't pass.
B: You will pass.
A: You'll pass.
B: I don't know.
A: You won't fail.
B: I might fail.
A: I will fail.
B: The exam's not hard.
A: It's very hard.
B: But not too hard.
A: Too hard for me.
B: But you're very clever!
A: You're the clever one.
B: Yes, I suppose you're right.

40.2 **2** normal
3 normal
4 emphasised
5 emphasised
6 emphasised
7 normal
8 emphasised

40.3 **2 B:** No, <u>I</u> finished first.
B: No, you <u>didn't</u> finish first.
B: No, you finished <u>last</u>.
3 B: No, <u>you're</u> stupid.
B: I'm <u>not</u> stupid
B: No, I'm <u>clever</u>.

40.4 **1 a** You can watch the match on TV. I haven't <u>got</u> a TV!
b Why didn't you watch the match? I haven't got a <u>TV</u>!
2 a The maths exam wasn't difficult. It <u>was</u> difficult!
b What did you think of the exam? It was <u>difficult</u>!
3 a They always play well, don't they? No, they never <u>win</u>!
b They usually win, don't they? No, they <u>never</u> win!
4 a You need to practise more. <u>You</u> need to practise more!
b I practise quite a lot. You need to practise <u>more</u>!
5 a I don't do any sports. So what <u>do</u> you do then?
b I think everybody should play a sport. So what do <u>you</u> do then?

Unit 41

41.1 **1** It's cold … <u>very</u> cold
2 It's a bag … a <u>plast</u>ic bag
3 My name's Bond … <u>James</u> Bond
4 It's in Asia … <u>cent</u>ral Asia
5 He's a composer … a <u>French</u> composer

41.2 **A:** It's very <u>quiet</u>.
B: <u>Too</u> quiet.
A: I think something's <u>wrong</u>.
B: <u>Very</u> wrong.
A: I don't <u>like</u> it.
B: I don't like it at <u>all</u>.
A: Let's get <u>out</u> of here.
B: Let's get out <u>fast</u>!

41.3 **1 a** <u>Near</u> Milan, yes.
b Near Mi<u>lan</u>, yes.
2 a I'm a graphic <u>designer.</u>
b I'm a <u>graphic</u> designer.
3 a <u>Yes</u>, a very nice <u>flat.</u>
b <u>Yes</u>, a <u>very</u> nice flat.
4 a <u>Well</u>, I'm learning <u>French.</u>
b <u>Well</u>, I'm <u>learn</u>ing French.
5 a <u>Yes</u>, I <u>lived</u> there for a year.
b <u>Yes</u>, I lived there for a <u>year</u>.

6 a <u>Yes</u>, two <u>broth</u>ers.
  b <u>Yes</u>, <u>two</u> brothers.
7 a I like <u>jazz</u> and <u>class</u>ical.
  b I like jazz <u>and</u> classical.

Unit 42

42.1 **2** serve   **6** serve
      3 serve   **7** return
      4 return   **8** return
      5 return

42.2 **A:** // Where do you <u>live</u>? //
      B: // I live with my <u>par</u>ents // And <u>you</u>? // Where do <u>you</u> live? //
      A: // I <u>don't</u> live with my parents //
      B: // So where <u>do</u> you live? //
      A: // In student accommo<u>da</u>tion //
      B: // Why did you leave <u>home</u>? //
      A: // Last Sep<u>tem</u>ber//
      B: // <u>No</u> // <u>Why</u> did you leave home? //
      A: // <u>Oh</u> // I just wanted to be inde<u>pen</u>dent //

42.3 **2** Where are you <u>stay</u>ing?
      3 When <u>was</u> she born?
      4 Why did <u>they</u> leave?
      5 What shall we <u>do</u>?
      6 How does <u>he</u> feel?
      7 <u>Where</u> will I sleep?
      8 What <u>have</u> you done?

42.4 **2** Where are <u>you</u> staying?
      3 but <u>when</u> was she born?
      4 so why did they <u>leave</u>?
      5 What shall <u>we</u> do?
      6 How does he <u>feel</u>?
      7 where will <u>I</u> sleep?
      8 so what <u>have</u> you done?

Unit 43

43.1 **A:** // Is this your <u>first</u> trip to Spain? //
      B: // <u>Well</u> // I've been to the <u>is</u>lands a few times //
      A: // So you don't know <u>Mad</u>rid then //
      B: // <u>No</u> // Do <u>you</u> know Madrid? //
      A: // <u>No</u> // It's <u>my</u> first time // as <u>well</u> //
      B: // So what are you going to <u>do</u> in the city? //
      A: // <u>Well</u> // if it's <u>wet</u> // I'll probably do some <u>art</u> galleries //
      B: // And if it's <u>not</u> wet? //
      A: // I'll go to the <u>beach</u> //
      B: // There <u>isn't</u> a beach //
      A: // <u>Ah</u>! // Can I borrow your <u>guide</u> book a moment?//

43.2   **1** A – B
      2 A – B
      3 B – A
      4 A – B

Unit 44

44.1   **1** b   **2** b   **3** b   **4** a

44.2   **1** No, the <u>bath</u>room
      2 No, he's <u>re</u>tired
      3 No, a book<u>shelf</u>
      4 No, I said im<u>poss</u>ible
      5 No, <u>down</u>stairs

Unit 45

45.1   **A:** // <u>Quick</u>! ↘ //
      B: // <u>What</u>? ↗ //
      A: // <u>Train</u>! ↘ //
      B: // <u>Train</u>? ↗ //
      A: // <u>Train</u>! ↘ //
      B: // <u>Why</u>? ↘ //
      A: // <u>Leav</u>ing! ↘ //
      B: // Al<u>read</u>y? ↗ //
      A: // <u>Gone</u>! ↘ //
      B: // <u>Gone</u>? ↗ //
      A: // <u>Gone</u> ↘ //
      B: // What <u>now</u>? ↘ //
      A: // <u>Bus</u>? ↗ //
      B: // <u>Bus</u>. ↘ //

45.2   **A:** // Are you <u>new</u> here? ↗ //
      B: // <u>Yes</u> ↘ // And <u>you</u>? ↗ //
      A: // <u>No</u> ↘ // I've been here two <u>years</u> ↘ //
      B: // Do you <u>like</u> it? ↗ //
      A: // <u>No</u> ↘ // I <u>don't</u> ↘ //
      B: // Why <u>not</u>? ↘ //
      A: // The boss is <u>aw</u>ful! ↘ //
      B: // <u>Who</u>? ↘ // Do you mean Mr <u>Coll</u>ins? ↗ //
      A: // <u>Yes</u> ↘ // Mr <u>Coll</u>ins ↘ // He's <u>aw</u>ful ↘ //
      B: // You don't <u>real</u>ly think that ↘ // <u>do</u> you? ↗ //
      A: // <u>Yes</u> ↘ // I <u>do</u> ↘ //
      B: // … //
      A: // <u>What</u>? ↘ // Did I say something <u>fun</u>ny? ↗ //
      B: // It's Mr <u>Coll</u>ins! ↘ //
      A: // <u>Where</u>? ↘ //
      B: // Be<u>hind</u> you! ↘ //

Section D

Unit 46

46.1 She uses // Ehm•••// four times.

46.2 Possibly not the best, no. (*laughs*) They tend to be quite high in sugar and salt which
∧   ∧   ∧
can obviously have implications for people so, so yeah certainly balance that with a lot
∧
of good sort of healthy vegetables and fruit really, is ideal, if you can.

46.3 **2 A:** What do you eat?
  B: Beans, rice, fruit and vegetables •••
3 A: Don't you miss eating meat?
  B: It's not something I think about .
4 A: I suppose it's a healthy diet, really.
  B: That's what I think •••
5 A: Why don't you stop drinking coffee?
  B: I don't really want to .
6 A: When do you bake bread?
  B: On Sundays •••

46.4 **2** Debbie: *you know*
3 Kimberly: *kind of*
4 Greg: *like*

46.5 **2** B   **3** B   **4** A   **5** B   **6** A   **7** B

Unit 47

47.1 **1** the   **6** a
2 your   **7** it
3 and   **8** in
4 was   **9** were
5 to

47.2 **2** stuff that you could do and
3 she has to talk to you
4 no I'm going to get it all wrong
5 but it was fine in the end

47.3 **2** and things like that
3 and there was like a list
4 it just made me really nervous

Unit 48

48.2
1 was about
2 went out in
3 shoot a
4 without any
5 drops on
6 was a bit upset

48.4
3 her‿everything
4 she‿asks
5 sure‿about
6 he‿isn't
7 after‿a
8 do‿I

48.5
1 <u>the</u> other guy
2 <u>to</u> ask
3 <u>the</u> end
4 <u>to</u> explain
5 <u>the</u> airport (*university* begins with consonant sound /j/)
6 <u>to</u> invite

Unit 49

49.1
Laura: We <u>could</u> ('coub') make some cakes with the margarine. Some <u>fruit</u> ('frook') cake?
Andy: Yeah. I dunno though. Dunno if I fancy <u>fruit</u> ('frook') cake.
Laura: Or we <u>could</u> ('coub') make a salad with the <u>green</u> ('greem') peppers and the salad cream.
Andy: Yeah, I suppose so.
Laura: Or we <u>could</u> ('coub') make a potato salad, if that would be more interesting?
Andy: Yeah. Or we could just do a <u>jacket</u> ('jackip') potato.
Laura: We haven't got any cheese though.
Andy: That's true. But you <u>could</u> ('coub') put the beans on the po ... eh on the potato.

49.2
1 We drank coffee and <u>ape</u> biscuits. *ate*
2 I went to a <u>grape</u> party last weekend. *great*
3 I had a <u>bag</u> cold so I went to bed. *bad*
4 Jim's got a <u>sung</u> called Tom. *son*
5 Were you <u>talk</u> cookery at school? *taught*
6 I got <u>ache</u> questions correct out of ten. *eight*

49.3
1 eight = '<u>ache</u>' / 'ape'
2 eight = 'ache' / '<u>ape</u>'
3 salad = '<u>salag</u>' / 'salab'
4 salad = 'salag' / '<u>salab</u>'
5 bad = 'bag' / '<u>bab</u>'
6 bad = '<u>bag</u>' / 'bab'
7 one = 'wung' / '<u>wum</u>'
8 one = '<u>wung</u>' / 'wum'
9 ten = '<u>teng</u>' / 'tem'
10 ten = 'teng' / '<u>tem</u>'

49.4 1 F, C   2 F, C   3 C, F   4 C, F   5 C, F   6 F, C   7 C, F   8 F, C   9 F, C   10 C, F

Unit 50

50.1 Three examples of *actually*.

50.2 Do you really know ninety people?
Do you actually know all your Facebook friends?
Have you actually met them all?

50.3 Student's own answer.

50.4 **1** through it all the time and think
2 I don't even speak to you
3 they can see anything
4 if you don't know five hundred of them

Unit 51

51.1 1 ↗ 2 ↘ 3 ↗ 4 ↘ 5 ↗ 6 ↘

51.2 1 ↗ 2 ↗ 3 ↘ 4 ↘ 5 ↗ 6 ↗ 7 ↗

51.3 **1** // The tours start at twelve ↗ // one thirty ↗ // three o'clock ↗ // and five thirty ↘ //
2 // I arrive at work ↗ // sign in ↗ // put on my uniform ↗ // and have a coffee ↘ //
3 // You can swim ↗ // go walking ↗ // visit the sights ↗ // or just relax ↘ //
4 // You can choose small ↗ // medium ↗ // or large ↘ // with milk ↗ // or without milk ↘ //

Unit 52

52.1 1 ↘ 2 ↗ 3 ↘ 4 ↗ 5 ↘ 6 ↗ 7 ↘ 8 ↘ 9 ↘ 10 ↗

52.2 1 ↗ 2 ↗ 3 ↘ 4 ↗ 5 ↗ 6 ↗ 7 ↘ 8 ↗

52.3 **1** ↘
2 ↗ *(The speaker is asking herself if this information is correct.)*
3 ↘
4 ↗ *(The speaker is asking herself if the other people have heard of this author.)*
5 ↘
6 ↗ *(The speaker is asking herself if this information is correct.)*
7 ↗ *(The speaker is asking if the other person likes this idea.)*
8 ↗ *(The speaker is asking herself if this information is correct.)*
9 ↘
10 ↗ *(The speaker is asking herself if this information is correct.)*
11 ↘

Unit 53

53.1 1 ↘ 2 ↗ 3 ↗ 4 ↘ 5 ↗ 6 ↗ 7 ↘ 8 ↗ 9 ↗ 10 ↗

53.2 [1] // Could you put those photos on my pen drive? ↗ //
 8 // Oh ↘ // Right ↘ //
 [5] // OK ↗ // And does the icon come up on the screen? ↗ //
 7 // OK ↗ // So just move the file of photos over the icon ↗ // And that's it ↘ //
 2 // Sure ↘ // How do I do that? ↘ //
 [4] // Uh huh ↗ // OK ↗ //
 3 // Well ↘ // if you plug it into the computer ↗ //
 6 // Yeah ↗ // Uh huh ↗ //

53.3 1 ↗ 2 ↘ 3 ↗ 4 ↘ 5 ↗ 6 ↘ 7 ↗ 8 ↗ 9 ↗ 10 ↗

Unit 54

54.1 1 ↗ 2 ↗ 3 ↘ 4 ↗ 5 ↗ 6 ↘ 7 ↘ 8 ↗

54.2 1 I saw the <u>first</u> programme in the series

2 I <u>quite</u> like Woody Allen films

3 I've never actually <u>seen</u> *Big Brother*

4 I don't usually <u>like</u> thrillers

5 I think <u>some</u>times they can be quite interesting

6 I think I've read <u>most</u> of her books

54.3 1 isn't he?
2 isn't it?
3 isn't it?
4 wasn't it?
5 didn't it?
6 don't you?
7 do you?
8 isn't it?
9 isn't it?

54.4 1 How's your headache? It isn't getting worse, is it? ↗
2 Those flowers are lovely, aren't they? ↘
3 You haven't seen my glasses anywhere, have you? ↗
4 Torsen's a great player, isn't he? ↘
5 I'm not sure. He was from Brazil, wasn't he? ↗
6 I can't quite remember. You need 40 points to win, don't you? ↗
7 Tennis is so boring, isn't it? ↘
8 She isn't a very good swimmer, is she? ↘
9 I'm not sure. It starts at nine, doesn't it? ↗
10 It wasn't a very interesting game, was it? ↘

Unit 55

55.1 // and it's absolutely stunning // to go up there // as you rise //
// as it as it rises it gets a bit chillier // obviously // but it's just fabulous //
// it's very expensive // for what it is // it costs about eh thirty // thirty-six pounds //
something like tha⊠ // thirty-four // thirty-five // thirty six pounds // for a return trip //
// you can obviously do it with the cruise companies // I should say that //
// and then they'll treat you to lunch // and everything // as well //
// but if you want to do it on your own // you can // but it was stunning //
// and eh // there's a massive waterfall // 'bout three quarters of the way up //
// and it's ⊠ it's quite reminiscent // obviously much much smaller //
// but quite reminiscent // actually // of eh⊠ of Niagara //

55.3 1 N   2 E   3 N   4 E   5 E   6 N

55.4 1 a N, b E
2 a E, b N
3 a N, b E
4 a E, b N
5 a E, b N

Unit 56

56.1 **Mark:** Listen, Claire. I'm having a party on Thursday. Would you like to come?
Claire: I'm sorry, Mark, I can't. My brother's visiting on Thursday …
Mark: Bring your brother along – the more the merrier!
Claire: Oh, OK, great! What's the party for?
Mark: It's my birthday. I'll be thirty-four.
Claire: Thirty four! Poor you – one foot in the grave already!
Mark: You're a nurse, Claire – I expected a bit more sympathy!
Claire: Sorry, Mark, just joking. I'm thirty-something myself. Where's the party?

56.2 Claire has an R accent (Scottish)
Mark has a Silent R accent (Southern English)

56.3

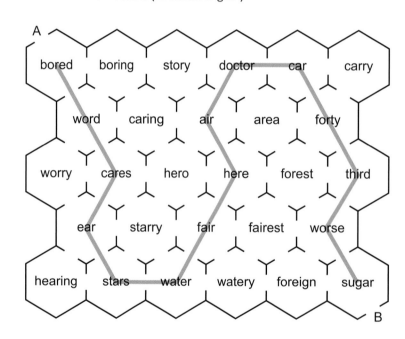

56.4

1 /ɜː/	2 /eə/	3 /ɪə/
[word] third worse	[cares] fair air	[ear] here
4 /ɑː/	**5 /ɔː/**	**6 /ə/ (word-final)**
[stars] car	[bored] forty	[water] doctor sugar

Unit 57

57.1 1 I <u>set</u> on the sofa and <u>head</u> a cup of coffee. *sat, had*
2 The film was so <u>said</u> that everybody cried. *sad*
3 I saw an old <u>men</u> carrying a heavy <u>beg</u>. *man, bag*
4 My mum and <u>dead</u> decided to <u>merry</u> in 1970. *dad, marry*
5 I wanted a nice <u>ten</u> but I got a <u>bed</u> sunburn instead. *tan, bad*

57.2 1 SE   2 NE   3 SE   4 NE   5 NE   6 SE   7 NE   8 SE

57.3 1 **a** SE, **b** Am
2 **a** Am, **b** SE
3 **a** SE, **b** Am
4 **a** SE, **b** Am

57.5 1 walk
2 slowly
3 go
4 o'clock
5 don't
6 shopping
7 not
8 bought
9 shorts

Unit 58

58.1 1 both
2 father
3 than
4 mother
5 three
6 thirty
7 three
8 fourth
9 three
10 brothers

58.2 1 photos letters bottle <u>hotel</u>
2 <u>doctor</u> waiter babysitter daughter
3 better <u>faster</u> lighter hotter
4 hated <u>wasted</u> waited voted

58.3 1 Don't worry – it doesn't <u>madder</u>. *matter*
2 I need reading glasses because I'm short-<u>sided</u>. *sighted*
3 Come on – what are you <u>wading</u> for? *waiting*
4 My grandfather's hair gets <u>wider</u> every year. *whiter*
5 I don't like being <u>seeded</u> by the door in a restaurant. *seated*
6 I <u>ate</u> getting my <u>air</u> cut. *hate, hair*
7 You should <u>old</u> it with both <u>ands</u>. *hold, hands*
8 My <u>airbrush</u> is in my <u>andbag</u>. *hairbrush, handbag*
9 Newtown's in a valley between <u>eye</u> <u>ills</u>. *high, hills*
10 Don't worry – <u>is</u> dog's <u>armless</u>. *his, harmless*

58.4 In this picture we can see a <u>waiter</u> <u>holding</u> a <u>bottle</u> of <u>water</u>. You can see both <u>his</u> <u>hands</u> but you can't see <u>his</u> face. You can also see a woman with long <u>hair</u> <u>sitting</u> at a table – you can just see the back of <u>her</u> <u>head</u>.

58.5 1 = | SE |
2 = | Am |

Unit 59

59.1 Gianluca plays the guitar; Duffy can play the guitar a little and she used to play the bongos.

59.2 **1** Kenya   **2** To watch animals   **3** Snakes

59.3 **1** Laura is from Spain and Kasia is from Poland.
2 Laura is working in a company; Kasia is working at the University of Cambridge.

Laura: Hi, nice to meet you.
Kasia: Hi meet you.
Laura: And eh my name is Laura, I'm from Spain and eh from Madrid actually, and how about you? Where do you come from?
Kasia: Hi I'm my name's is Kasia I'm from I'm coming from Poland.
Laura: Ah hah
Kasia: What are you doing in England?
Laura: Well, I'm working as a secretary in a company. And how about you? What do you do here?
Kasia: I'm here in eh CMS Cleaning Service, I'm working in a company CMS Cleaning Service. I'm supervisor.
Laura: Ah huh.
Kasia: Now I'm working in 'Universitat' Cambridge.
Laura: OK, so it must be hard work.
Kasia: No!

59.4 Student's own answers

59.5 Student's own answers

Unit 60

60.1 **1** doesn't use
2 pronounces
3 /wɜːr/
4 puts
5 /bæˈnænæ/
6 uses

60.2 **1** S   **2** C   **3** S   **4** C

60.3 **1** C   **2** S   **3** C   **4** S   **5** C   **6** S   **7** S

Section E

E1 Introduction to phonemic symbols

E1.1 1 *For writing:* pencil paper <u>pen</u> notebook
2 *In the office:* <u>desk</u> fax computer telephone
3 *Body parts:* neck head hand <u>leg</u>
4 *Farm animals:* <u>hen</u> lamb sheep cow
5 *Colours:* green blue <u>red</u> black
6 *Verbs:* <u>get</u> take give go
7 *Numbers:* seven <u>ten</u> three five

E1.2
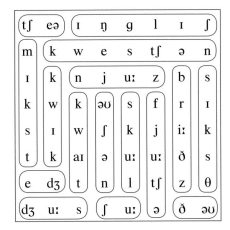

E1.3 1 **Long vowel crossword**

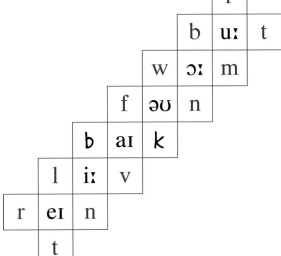

2 Short vowel crossword

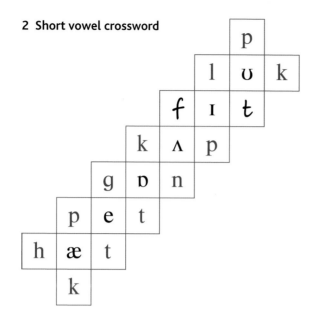

3 Vowels before R crossword

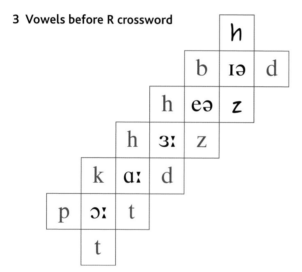

E1.4   1 jumping
2 washing
3 using
4 bathing

5 singing
6 thinking
7 playing

E1.5

	ɔɪ	ɔː	ɪə	eə	aɪ	iː
w		wore		wear	why	we
f		four	fear	fair		
d		door	deer	dare	die	
p		pour	pier	pair	pie	pea
t	toy		tear		tie	tea
b	boy	bore		bear	buy	be
h			here	hair	high	he
ʃ				share	shy	she

E1.6

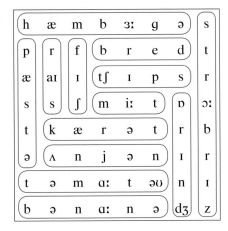

hamburger	bread	chips	meat
carrot	onion	tomato	banana
pasta	rice	fish	orange
strawberries			

E1.7

```
k   d  ɒ  k  t  ə   n
ʊ   d  r  aɪ v  ə   ɜː
k   p  eɪ n  t  ə   s
m   ə  k  æ  n  ɪ   k
f   e  n  dʒ ɪ  n   ɪə
ɑː  v  r  aɪ t  ə   g
m   e  s  ɪ  ŋ  ə   ɑː
ə   t  w  eɪ t  ə   d
```

doctor	driver	painter	mechanic
engineer	writer	singer	waiter
cook	nurse	farmer	vet
guard			

E1.8

1

r	aɪ	m
aɪ	■	aɪ
t	aɪ	t

2

t	ɔː	k
ɔː	■	ɔː
l	ɔː	z

3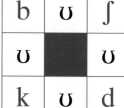

w	ɒ	t
ɒ	■	ɒ
ʃ	ɒ	p

4

k	ʌ	m
ʌ	■	ʌ
t	ʌ	tʃ

5

b	æ	k
æ	■	æ
t	æ	p

6

b	ʊ	ʃ
ʊ	■	ʊ
k	ʊ	d

7

p	eɪ	n
eɪ	■	eɪ
dʒ	eɪ	l

8

j	e	t
e	■	e
s	e	l

9

r	əʊ	t
əʊ	■	əʊ
l	əʊ	n

E2 Pronunciation test

A1
1 want
2 care
3 soup
4 most
5 blood
6 rude
7 bread

A2
1 lamb
2 receipt
3 listen
4 hour
5 half
6 calm
7 here

A3
1 came
2 cake
3 late
4 rose/rows
5 wait/weight
6 size / sighs
7 hi / high
8 bear / bare
9 burn

A4
1 pen
2 cut
3 feel
4 west
5 coat
6 fair
7 women
8 office's
9 vet
10 price
11 suit
12 code
13 pine
14 back
15 hair
16 wash
17 singing
18 collect

A5
1 glass
2 truth
3 smell
4 need
5 wanted
6 thirteen
7 is
8 were
9 and
10 does
11 That's a mile.
12 support
13 pasta
14 guests

A6
1 washes
2 wanted
3 afternoon
4 asked
5 fortieth
6 builds
7 supermarket
8 over

B1
1 potato
2 mistake
3 Japanese
4 Saturday
5 finish
6 education
7 photography

B2

●••●	•●•●	●•●	●•●•
[Where do you live?] What would you like?	I'm cold and tired. I'd like to help.	Go and see. Close the door.	Pleased to meet you. Call and thank him.

B3
1 tomorrow
2 fifteen
3 Close the door.
4 Don't worry!
5 today
6 famous
7 first class
8 economy
9 No, it isn't.

C1 1 a 2 b 3 a 4 a 5 b 6 b 7 a

C2 1 b 2 b 3 a 4 a 5 a 6 b 7 a 8 a

C3 1 Now?
2 Tonight?
3 Five o'clock?
4 Here?
5 Coffee.
6 Milk and sugar?
7 You're tired.

D1 1 <u>you know</u>
2 you know
3 I mean
4 <u>I mean</u>
5 like
6 <u>like</u>

D2 **1** is **2** isn't **3** is **4** does **5** isn't **6** isn't **7** isn't **8** isn't **9** is **10** is

D3 **1** Am **2** SE **3** Am **4** Am **5** Am **6** SE **7** SE **8** Am **9** SE **10** SE **11** Am
12 Am **13** SE **14** Am **15** SE **16** SE

E4 Sound pairs

Sound pair 1

1 S	**2** S	**3** D	**4** S	**5** S	**6** S	**7** S
8 bad	**9** dead	**10** sat	**11** merry		**12** men	

Sound pair 2

1 S	**2** S	**3** D	**4** S	**5** D	**6** S	**7** D
8 fun	**9** cap	**10** rang	**11** cut		**12** He's sung	

Sound pair 3

1 S	**2** D	**3** S	**4** D	**5** D	**6** S	**7** D
8 cat	**9** match	**10** harder	**11** parks		**12** hat	

Sound pair 4

1 D	**2** S	**3** S	**4** S	**5** D	**6** D	**7** D
8 gate	**9** pepper	**10** west	**11** fail		**12** pain	

Sound pair 5

1 S	**2** D	**3** D	**4** S	**5** D	**6** S	**7** D
8 their	**9** stairs	**10** hey	**11** a pear		**12** nowhere	

Sound pair 6

1 S	**2** D	**3** S	**4** S	**5** D	**6** S	**7** S
8 far	**9** bare	**10** cars	**11** fair		**12** stars	

Sound pair 7

1 D	**2** S	**3** D	**4** S	**5** S	**6** D	**7** S
8 form	**9** park	**10** stores	**11** part		**12** four	

Sound pair 8

1 S	**2** D	**3** S	**4** D	**5** D	**6** S	**7** S
8 where	**9** dare	**10** cheers	**11** hear		**12** air	

Sound pair 9

1 S	**2** D	**3** S	**4** S	**5** D	**6** D	**7** S
8 heart	**9** much	**10** dark	**11** cart		**12** come	

Sound pair 10
1 S 2 D 3 D 4 S 5 S 6 S 7 S
8 cheap 9 fit 10 live 11 feel 12 to sit

Sound pair 11
1 D 2 S 3 S 4 D 5 S 6 D 7 S
8 we're 9 knee 10 pier 11 feed 12 here

Sound pair 12
1 S 2 D 3 S 4 S 5 S 6 D 7 S
8 turn 9 learned 10 Jenny 11 bird 12 west

Sound pair 13
1 D 2 S 3 S 4 D 5 S 6 D 7 S
8 mess 9 bill 10 will 11 letter 12 left

Sound pair 14
1 S 2 S 3 S 4 D 5 D 6 D 7 D
8 note 9 rob 10 goat 11 won't 12 cost

Sound pair 15
1 D 2 S 3 D 4 S 5 S 6 D 7 S
8 not 9 luck 10 shut 11 collar 12 they're gone

Sound pair 16
1 S 2 S 3 S 4 D 5 D 6 D 7 D
8 soup 9 rule 10 boot 11 pole 12 grow

Sound pair 17
1 D 2 S 3 D 4 S 5 S 6 S 7 D
8 saw 9 low 10 call 11 bowl 12 walk

Sound pair 18
1 D 2 S 3 D 4 S 5 S 6 D 7 S
8 know 9 blouse 10 allowed 11 a shower 12 phoned

Sound pair 19
1 S 2 S 3 D 4 D 5 S 6 S 7 D
8 Luke 9 fool 10 pool 11 shoe dye 12 butcher saw

Sound pair 20
1 S 2 D 3 D 4 S 5 books 6 luck

Sound pair 21
1 D 2 S 3 S 4 S 5 D 6 D 7 D
8 but 9 hurt 10 earned a 11 suffer 12 shut

Sound pair 22
1 S 2 D 3 S 4 S 5 D 6 S 7 D
8 bet 9 steady 10 won 11 again 12 butter

Sound pair 23
1 S 2 S 3 D 4 D 5 D 6 S 7 S
8 short 9 odder 10 spot 11 water ski 12 port

Sound pair 24
1 S 2 D 3 D 4 D 5 D 6 S 7 S
8 beard 9 we're 10 fur 11 her 12 bird

Sound pair 25

1 D   **2** D   **3** S   **4** S   **5** S   **6** S   **7** D
8 where   **9** stir   **10** bared   **11** hair   **12** fur

Sound pair 26

1 S   **2** S   **3** S   **4** D   **5** D   **6** S   **7** D
8 bored   **9** sir   **10** short   **11** first   **12** walked

Sound pair 27

1 D   **2** S   **3** S   **4** D   **5** D   **6** S   **7** D
8 far   **9** heart   **10** further   **11** hard   **12** firm

Sound pair 28

1 S   **2** S   **3** D   **4** D   **5** D   **6** S   **7** D
8 bill   **9** push   **10** packs   **11** robe   **12** bear

Sound pair 29

1 S   **2** S   **3** S   **4** D   **5** D   **6** D   **7** S
8 vet   **9** They've ached   **10** some of each   **11** Say 'boil'.   **12** I've rushed it.

Sound pair 30

1 S   **2** D   **3** D   **4** S   **5** S   **6** S   **7** S
8 fool   **9** pine   **10** past   **11** a nicer pear   **12** face

Sound pair 31

1 S   **2** D   **3** S   **4** S   **5** D   **6** S   **7** D
8 eyes   **9** sip   **10** raise   **11** niece   **12** peace

Sound pair 32

1 S   **2** D   **3** D   **4** D   **5** S   **6** S   **7** S
8 sign   **9** mash   **10** save   **11** shoot   **12** seat

Sound pairs 33

1 D   **2** S   **3** D   **4** S   **5** S   **6** D   **7** D
8 thing   **9** breeze   **10** thought   **11** mouse   **12** closed

Sound pair 34

1 S   **2** S   **3** D   **4** D   **5** D   **6** S   **7** D
8 said   **9** town   **10** coat   **11** wide   **12** writing

Sound pairs 35

1 S   **2** D   **3** D   **4** S   **5** D   **6** D   **7** D
8 tree   **9** they   **10** thanks   **11** taught   **12** breathe

Sound pairs 36

1 S   **2** S   **3** D   **4** D   **5** D   **6** S   **7** D
8 torch   **9** aid   **10** beat   **11** coach   **12** hedge

Sound pair 37

1 D   **2** S   **3** D   **4** S   **5** D   **6** D   **7** S
8 that's over   **9** lived   **10** few   **11** wife's   **12** of air

Sound pair 38

1 D   **2** D   **3** S   **4** D   **5** S   **6** S   **7** D
8 made aware   **9** verse   **10** a vet   **11** vest   **12** half a weight

Sound pairs 39

1 S   **2** D   **3** D   **4** S   **5** D   **6** S   **7** S
8 thirst   **9** free   **10** thought   **11** What some of us   **12** either

Sound pair 40
1 S 2 D 3 S 4 D 5 D 6 D 7 D
8 gap's 9 back 10 ghost 11 card 12 gold

Sound pair 41
1 S 2 S 3 D 4 D 5 S 6 D 7 S
8 eight 9 heart 10 hair 11 earring 12 heating

Sound pair 42
1 D 2 D 3 S 4 D 5 S 6 S 7 D
8 jet 9 until July 10 yoke 11 yours 12 juice

Sound pairs 43
1 S 2 D 3 S 4 D 5 D 6 S 7 S
8 holder's 9 fold 10 sheet 11 hair 12 fired

Sound pair 44
1 D 2 S 3 S 4 D 5 S 6 D 7 S
8 shoes 9 chair 10 cash 11 chips 12 watch

Sound pair 45
1 D 2 D 3 S 4 S 5 S 6 S 7 D
8 Joe's 9 cheap 10 riches 11 H 12 tune

Sound pairs 46
1 D 2 S 3 S 4 D 5 S 6 D 7 D
8 arch 9 aids 10 each 11 Watch; ! 12 rage

Sound pairs 47
1 S 2 S 3 D 4 S 5 D 6 D 7 S
8 chips 9 drunk 10 train 11 trees 12 jaw

Sound pair 48
1 D 2 S 3 D 4 S 5 S 6 S 7 D
8 hanged 9 win 10 robbing banks 11 ran 12 sinking

Sound pairs 49
1 S 2 S 3 D 4 D 5 D 6 D 7 S
8 turn 9 mice 10 son warned 11 mine 12 swing

Sound pair 50
1 D 2 S 3 S 4 D 5 S 6 S 7 D
8 prayed 9 wrong 10 glow 11 fries 12 collect